PLANNING HOME CARE WITH THE ELDERLY

PLANNING HOME CARE WITH THE ELDERLY

Patient, Family, and Professional Views of An Alternative to Institutionalization

ALAN PETER SAGER, PH.D.

Assistant Professor of Urban and Health Planning
and
Research Director, Levinson Policy Institute

The Florence Heller Graduate School for
Advanced Studies in Social Welfare
Brandeis University

BALLINGER PUBLISHING COMPANY
Cambridge, Massachusetts
A Subsidiary of Harper & Row, Publishers, Inc.

International Standard Book Number: 0-88410-725-6

Library of Congress Catalog Card Number: 82-16311

Printed in the United States of America

Library of Congress Cataloging in Publication Data

Sager, Alan Peter.
  Planning home care for the elderly.

  Bibliography: p.
  Includes index.
    1. Aged—Institutional care—United States—Costs. 2. Aged—Home
care—United States—Costs. I. Title.
[DNLM: 1. Health services for the aged. 2. Health planning. 3. Home
care services. 4. Long term care.
WT 30 S129p]
RA564.8.S23 1982   363.6'3   82-16311
ISBN 0-88410-725-6

This book is dedicated to my wife, who helped make it possible, to my parents and grandparents, and to Dr. Robert Morris, whose work in long-term care has inspired and encouraged me and many others.

CONTENTS

PART III   FINDINGS AND WHAT THEY SUGGEST

LIST OF FIGURES

LIST OF TABLES

FOREWORD

For many years, now, biologists have had the ability to examine a living cell through a variety of microscopic lenses, as well as through the use of a variety of stains that highlighted various characteristics of the cell. An observer using different powered microscopes would notice different features of the cell. The combination of the power of various lenses and the perspective offered by various stains produce an accumulation of in-depth knowledge about the structure and functioning of the cell. In the social sciences, however, neither the variety nor the precision of tools duplicate that of biology. This is particularly evident in the area of research in long term care. The tools have been time series, cross-sectional analysis, somewhat ideosyncratic demonstration programs, and a few longitudinal studies. In this book, Alan Sager offers us another set of tools at which might be called the micro-level of analysis of home care services. Using a sample of 50 cases, along with the device of hypothetical care plans, Sager has illuminated important aspects of the care planning process and the decision-making of families and professionals. This micro-approach supplements the macro-level studies that have characterized long term care.

Some of his findings reinforce those of other studies. For example, he is not able to identify patient characteristics that clearly predict the cost of a nursing home destination as against the cost of a home care destination. The relationship to patient functional disability and costs is not a straightline phenomenon. There is a very identifiable group for whom home care is less expensive than institutional care.

Sager further throws light on the extent to which various professionals agree among themselves on the desired care plan for the frail elderly. There is as much agreement across professionals as there is disagreement within. Family decisions on home care do not stray far from those recommended by the professionals, and frequently incorporate a more narrow and less costly array of services. To Sager this raises the question as to who should be the appropriate allocator of home care services, and he strives to answer that in the concluding chapter of the book.

Sager makes a strong case for increasing the decision-making of families in the home care process. He notes the importance of money, either in the form of adequate Social Security, vouchers, or some other transfer program to allow families to exercise their choices around home care. He suggests a gatekeeper role for the professionals but, once inside the gate, allowing families extensive territory within which to roam.

One of Sager's major findings is that it may cost less to refer to home care those who are destined to go to rehabilitation centers, chronic hospitals, or other expensive settings. In other words, if the setting is more expensive, home care looks less expensive. This suggests two comments. The first is whether or not the package that would be delivered for that particular individual at home would be the same as the package that would be delivered in the rehabilitation center. While some of the same services might be brought into the home, I cannot imagine that the patient would receive the same amount of professional care time, team planning, and facilities had they gone to the rehabilitation center. The other comment, however, relates to the fact that home care looks cheaper when the cost of nursing homes is high. Perhaps the cost of nursing homes is not high enough, because nursing homes do not operate in as responsive a manner as does the home setting. In other words, what would be the cost of a nursing home if an older person can decide when and what time she will go to bed or get up, if she could decide on choice of menu, had the freedom to roam as she would in her own home, or have the privacy of the home setting? To build these characteristics into existing nursing homes would certainly raise their price, and thus make home care a less costly alternative for even more older people.

Throughout the book, Sager's clear commitment to older people and his value orientation to having them enjoy their life in a safe, pleasant environment is obvious. The book provides a rich source, both of data which may be reviewed by other researchers and thoughtful and careful analysis. One may raise some questions about particular aspects of the methodology, the analysis, or the conclusions. The reader will find, however, that he/she probably cannot raise a question that Sager has not already raised in his own mind and to which he has supplied a thoughtful and well-reasoned answer. One looks forward to more micro studies such as this which open up new areas for thought and analysis.

James J. Callahan, Jr.,
Levinson Policy Institute
November 1982

ACKNOWLEDGMENTS

Over two hundred individuals made this book possible. At six participating hospitals, fifty patients and their families were kind enough to agree, at a difficult time in their lives, to participate in this study.

At the hospitals, the contributions of many individuals deserve mention: at the Memorial Hospital, Worcester: Gloria Symonds, R.N., James P. Grady, M.S.W., Peter Levine, M.D., and David A. Barrett; at Mercy Hospital, Springfield: Cemach Goldsmith, A.C.S.W., Sr. Kathleen Popko, S.P., Ph.D., and Sr. M. Catherine Laboure, S.P.; at Norwood Hospital: Sally Greenwood, R.N., Dawn Metcalf, M.S.W., and David Buchmueller; at Mt. Auburn Hospital, Cambridge: Sue Holman, R.N., Judith Freiman, M.S.W., Lawrence M. Witte, and the members of the Clinical Investigations Committee; at New England Memorial Hospital, Stoneham: Gladys Gilmour, R.N., Harold Knox, M.S.W., and James Boyle; at the Peter Bent Brigham Hospital, Boston: Phyllis Goodhue, R.N., and Arlene Lowenstein, R.N.

Also, at each institution, nurses, social workers, and physicians prepared assessment forms, conducted interviews, and prepared care plans. Particular thanks go to the hard-working hospital coordinators. Hospital administrators and boards of trustees granted permission for and gave support to the study's conduct.

Sr. Kathleen Popko, S.P., Ph.D.; Carl Granger, M.D.; Richard Besdine, M.D.; Rosalie Wolf, Ph.D.; and Gail McGuire, R.N. lent their competent help and advice to designing study forms and procedures. Workers at participating hospitals helped perfect them.

Fifteen consultants to the study wrote dozens of lengthy care plans; many visited patients; all graciously endured the demands of schedules and deadlines. They are Richard Besdine, M.D.; Joan Craven, R.N.; Judith Freiman, M.S.W.; Mary Gesek, R.N.; Susan Haas, M.S.W.; Doris Henry, R.N.; Elizabeth Kenney, R.N., M.S.W.; Eileen Kirk, R.N.; Arlene Lowenstein, R.N.; Fran Lytz, B.A.; Kenneth Nobel, M.D.; Joanne O'Brien, R.N.; David O'Toole, M.D.; Jeremy Ruskin, M.D.; and George Siber, M.D. Their contributions have been invaluable.

Lotte Gottschlich's comments on the manuscript have helped clarify my intentions. At the Levinson Policy Institute, Barbara Isaacson and Mary Walazek typed and retyped forms, guidelines, and reports. Barbara Isaacson, Helen Dentler, Marion Rabinowitz, Susan Goodrich, Ina Moses, and Marianne Muscato typed the several drafts of this book. Thanks are due to all.

Barbara Skydell helped select the sample of hospitals, introduced the study at several of them, and helped ensure the smooth functioning of the study process.

The study could not have been conducted without the personal and professional support of Celia Lees-Low, Victor Hoffman, and Sylvia Pendleton. Celia Lees-Low administered the study superbly. She helped design data collection forms, coordinated work in hospitals, and managed the smooth flow of forms from hospitals to consultants to LPI, supervised coding, helped prepare data for analysis, and supervised student assistants.

Victor Hoffman has helped design data analysis plans and performed all programming. He wrote the complex Fortran program which tabulated the study's extremely rich and complex data set and reduced it to analyzable size. He generated all subsequent well-designed computer products for analysis. His advice has been invaluable.

Sylvia Pendleton helped design forms, prepared all code books, helped prepare data for analysis, contributed the wide range of her analytical and data management knowledge and skills to ensure the integrity of the data set. She also competently performed a wide variety of research tasks.

The study was directly inspired by the past work in long-term care by Robert Morris and his colleagues (particularly Frank Caro and Elliott Sclar) at the Levinson Policy Institute. The work of Robert Morris, founding director of the institute, remains the base on which this project was undertaken. His creative and vigorous efforts to articulate the need for noninstitutional long-term care and to suggest ways of meeting that need continue to inspire researchers, policymakers, and administrators in this field.

The detailed comments by Thomas R. Willemain, Bernard J. Frieden, Michael Joroff, and James J. Callahan, Jr. on an earlier draft of this report have been of enormous help.

The U.S. Administration on Aging (Grant No. 90-A-1026-01-02) supported the bulk of this research; visiting consultants' and hospital professionals' care plans, and several sets of overarching analyses were supported by a complementary grant from the National Retired Teachers Association–American Association of Retired Persons' Andrus Foundation. The help of David Dowd and Dr. Al Duncker of AoA, and Mr. Edward Thrasher, project officer, and Dr. Frederick Ferris, Administrator of the Andrus Foundation is gratefully acknowledged. Many of the issues examined in this study were first articulated in the course of earlier work done under the Harry Greenstein Award of the Associated Jewish Charities of Baltimore to the Levinson Policy Institute. It is hoped that this study will help further a central aim of all these organizations—to improve the range of alternatives and the care planning process for older Americans who need long-term care.

1 INTRODUCTION

Today, public efforts to finance and organize a sufficient amount of decent and effective long-term care for the nation's elderly citizens face increasingly serious difficulties. About 1.25 million Americans now live in nursing homes. Almost 90 percent of public long-term care spending is devoted to paying for their care. Yet there is clear dissatisfaction with the humaneness, dignity, or decency of much of this care. The great majority of older people express a clear preference to live out their lives at home.

Nonetheless, federal and state legislators and administrators are afraid to encourage greater public spending for noninstitutional long-term care for fear that costs of expansion would be insupportable. They are concerned that public benefits would replace families and friends ("informal supports") with publicly paid helpers ("formal supports"), leading to little net improvement in the well-being of the elderly living at home. They worry that the use of publicly funded benefits, including homemakers to cook and clean, would be so attractive that use would be difficult to control. Large numbers of older people might come forward to ask for help, and eligibility and level-of-need determination might be difficult. The result could be inequitable, inefficient, or ineffective use of public funds. Because the number of people in need of publicly funded formal noninstitutional care and the average amount of help required are thought by some to be difficult to learn, total program costs of expanded benefits might be unpredictable.

Convincing evidence in support of noninstitutional alternatives has been thought lacking. Even so, the present long-term care system should certainly not be regarded as a stable, barely acceptable, second-best compromise, for it is threatened by profound fiscal and demographic forces.

1

Fiscally, the great bulk of public long-term care funds are made available through the federal–state Medicaid program. Sensitive to the costs of nursing home care (which make up an increasingly visible part of the budgets of many states), states have not reimbursed existing nursing homes adequately in many instances. This does not encourage generous staffing levels, well-prepared food, or other things that would make institutional life more bearable. As costs of nursing home care rise faster than do most states' revenue sources (in large part because long-term care is a service and productivity gains are difficult to win), homes will be reimbursed less and less adequately, and decency of care is bound to decline from current levels.

Inadequate reimbursement of existing homes will reduce desires to build new homes or add beds to existing institutions. But we are witnessing an enormous increase in the populations of very old Americans—those over age seventy-five and especially over age eighty-five—who have been most likely to need and use nursing home care. If the age- and sex-specific rates of nursing home use that prevailed in 1980 were to continue through the end of the century, an increase of 59 percent in the nursing home bed supply would be called for by the year 2000. Even if states were willing to reimburse existing nursing homes adequately, they would still be able to employ certificate-of-need regulatory controls on capital spending to restrict construction of new beds.

For-profit nursing homes that generate newspaper headlines about scandalous conditions are convenient excuses for reducing these state reimbursements, especially during budget crises. Nursing home care will become both less acceptable and more difficult to obtain. Expanded home care benefits offer the promise of caring for increased numbers of older people in the site they prefer—possibly at an acceptable cost.

This book reports the results of a study that aims to learn more about the cost of home care services needed to substitute for some of the institutional care now being provided. It thoroughly examines a group of patients who were being discharged from acute care hospitals to nursing homes, to learn the costs of an equivalent hypothetical home care alternative. Lack of knowledge of the costs of home care for different populations has probably stood in the way of legislation to expand home care eligibility or benefits. It has proven difficult to obtain reliable information on the comparative costs and benefits of home and institutional care through the traditional controlled experiment. The present study therefore adopted the method of hypothetical diversion.

Although the practical difficulties and costs of a controlled experiment are avoided by this method, it becomes necessary to develop acceptable estimates of the costs of the necessary hypothetical home care services. Costs depend on how much of which services are needed and what proportion of them must be provided by paid workers.

The content of a home care plan might well be difficult to agree about; it could be sensitive to the characteristics of the groups or individuals empowered to design the plan. We have therefore sought the views of patients themselves, their families, and eighteen physicians, nurses, and social workers regarding needed in-home services. We sought to learn whether they agreed about the composition of the home care plans and, if not, who was likelier to be right.

Why should we question who should have the right to decide which services are necessary to support older people at home? Why should we not simply continue to permit professionals, who should be qualified by virtue of training and experience, to allocate services? There are several reasons.

First, good care planning is especially important in the present long-term care context. There appears to be a widespread belief among legislators, administrators, and the public at large that the long-term care system—especially its institutional aspects—works poorly. In the absence of proven effectiveness of long-term care services, in view of the difficulty of measuring outcomes, and given perceptions of misappropriation, patient abuse, and inefficiency, it is not surprising that pleas for new funding have been largely unheeded. Such a perceived environment lends itself to complaints that new program initiatives would merely be "throwing money at problems." In this context, improvements in care planning might help build the foundation on which greater funding for noninstitutional long-term care could be placed.

Second, the quality of care planning matters in part because the outcomes of long-term services are so difficult to measure. The very goals of care are often vague. Problems of frailty, disability, or chronic illness are usually difficult to ameliorate. Often, a decline in well-being is inevitable, and services aim principally to slow that decline. Many of the services aim to compensate for functional problems, and the effectiveness of such services—cleaning or cooking, for example—can be difficult to gauge. Without clear evidence relating services to outcomes—without, that is, measures of effectiveness or efficiency—the integrity of care planning becomes vital. This issue extends beyond the bounds of the study reported here to long-term care generally.

Reliability and equity are used in this study as indicators of needed home care services. *Reliability* denotes agreement or consistency. If, for example, a number of individuals agree that certain services are needed, this encourages us to believe that they might be right. If they disagreed, we would not easily know whom to believe, and our faith in the integrity of professionals' judgments would fall as our frustration rose. *Equity* denotes relative appropriateness of care: services would be equitable if long-term care planners assigned more care to those people who seem by reasonable and objectively measured standards to need more care. This is sometimes called vertical equity, but since horizontal equity is not addressed in this study the word equity will be used without qualification.

Third, there appears to be a lack of agreement among professionals about the purposes of long-term care. Some of a professional's advocated purposes might differ from those that patients or families could reasonably be expected to select under some circumstances. Long-term care, and home care in particular, falls at the intersection of several cross-cutting categories. Professionals in both medical care and social service have seemingly valid grounds for claiming influence over care plans of patients in need of long-term care. These professionals are trained variously as physicians, who are internists, phychiatrists, surgeons, and others; nurses; social workers; and physical and occupational therapists. Further, the roles and training of these professionals intermix. Both nurses and social workers, for example, are found in the ranks of both hospital discharge planners and home care planners. Finally, there is frequently a disjunction between knowledge and power in home care planning. Physicians are often legally empowered as care planners, even though other professionals may have greater interest in and understanding of patient needs.

One example of the type of problem raised by competing professional outlooks in home care concerns the appropriate roles of medical care, social care, and physical restoration of function. Several home care plans written to emphasize different goals might be expected to cost markedly different sums and to achieve markedly different results.

Fourth, a considerable literature has arisen that raises doubts about the reliability of professional judgments even when goals are agreed upon. This literature spans several areas of medicine and extends into other professional fields, such as criminal justice, and into such semiprofessional areas as the future of the stock market. Weak professional agreement points to ineffective or inefficient decisionmaking and consequent poor resource allocation.

Fifth, it may be argued both that permitting greater choice to patients can be good in itself, and that, because the success of a plan of in-home care frequently depends on the active cooperation of the family, the family should be asked in advance whether the planned care meets their needs. Long-term care, by virtue of the nontechnical nature of the great bulk of the service hours and costs involved, is a realm well suited to the exercise of a considerable measure of consumer sovereignty. Both family members and patients can be viewed as the consumers of care.

In this study, as in the real world, the costs of home care depend on the types, amounts, and providers of care selected. These, in turn, depend to a considerable degree on who allocates home care services. This investigation lays a foundation for comparing the costs of home and institutional care by learning the views of patients, family members, and various professionals and then attempting to assess the legitimacy of control over allocation of in-home services by members of the three groups. Reliability and equity are analyzed as the two pointers to legitimacy.

CONTEXT OF
THE STUDY

2 THE EVOLVING LONG-TERM CARE CRISIS

Some crises arise unexpectedly and quickly, as when a volcano erupts in a quiet corn field. Most crises in public life, of the type reported in newspapers, are not so surprising. Even when sparked by a sudden event, such as the assassination in Sarajevo in 1914 or the development of an effective oil cartel in the early 1970s, they follow from long-accumulating problems, grievances, or misunderstandings. Crises such as that building in long-term care have grown more gently. Their evolution becomes visible from time to time, as a scandal in nursing home care attracts the interest of a prosecuting attorney or a reporter or as a severe economic crisis leads to reduced public reimbursement to providers, who in turn become very upset.

A society's responsibility to anticipate a crisis and to cope with it successfully—or at least vigorously and intelligently—is probably directly proportionate to that crisis' predictability and potential harm. On both grounds, long-term care merits greater attention than it has been receiving.

This chapter traces three of the reasons for anticipating a genuine crisis in providing satisfactory long-term care to this nation's frail, disabled, or chronically ill older citizens. These are: the high and rapidly growing costs of long-term care; the increased need for care that can be expected in coming decades; and the overwhelmingly institutional nature of publicly funded services.

It is reasonable to expect a crisis in long-term care that will have several visible symptoms:

1. A profound apparent shortage of nursing home beds, evidenced by growing difficulty in placing hospital patients, and by the protests of families unable any longer to care for severely disabled relatives at home.

7

2. Increasingly frequent complaints from both for-profit and voluntary nursing homes of their inability to provide care at rates states are willing to allow under their Medicaid programs.

3. Widespread dissatisfaction with the decency or compassion of nursing home care.

4. Wage increases for long-term care workers that lag behind costs of living.

5. Public unwillingness to fund adequately a useful range of noninstitutional long-term care services, owing to fears of explosive growth in use and to expectations that home care will be an additive benefit, serving new clients, rather than a substitutive benefit, caring for people in need of service who would otherwise have entered institutions.

These phenomena do not appear radically different from those observed in recent years. Indeed they are not different. It is only their intensity that will increase over coming decades. This is an important reason why failure to establish a long-term care system that is adequate (enough care is available), affordable, decent and compassionate (clients are treated humanely and with dignity), and effective (care actually helps clients) is unforgivable.

In this book, "long-term care" refers to both in-home and institutional services. It also includes special services such as adult day care, foster care, or respite care. According to LaVor, long-term care consists of activities:

> designed to provide diagnostic, therapeutic, rehabilitative, and maintenance services for individuals who have chronic physical or mental impairments, in a variety of community and institutional settings, with the goal of promoting the optimum level of physical, social, and psychological functioning.[1]

Since the late 1960s there has been a growing concern in the United States with the problems of rising spending—particularly public spending—on health care in general.[2] During the 1970s, long-term care became a major area of worry within the health care field itself.[3] This chapter will begin by documenting the extent and nature of the growth in long-term care spending in this country. It will then explore the various reasons for recent growth and why it can be expected to continue. The final section will explain why publicly funded long-term care has been principally institutional. Although spending increases and the institutional emphasis are considered separately, this is not meant to imply that the two are believed to be unrelated. Because of the weakness of evidence on the comparative cost of in-home and institutional care, judgment on any possible relation should be withheld.

THE EXTENT AND NATURE OF INCREASED LONG-TERM SPENDING

From 1970 to 1977, total public nursing home and home care spending on the elderly increased by about 313 percent, from $1.4 to $5.9 billion.[4] This seemingly rapid rate of increase may be only partly real and partly perceived. The preponderance of this spending—about 90 percent—is devoted to nursing home care, and nursing home care has achieved a high degree of visibility in this country. From time to time, powerful journalistic accounts of horrible living conditions are published. These are frequently combined with charges of misappropriations of huge sums. There are other reasons for the visibility of long-term care spending. A relatively high proportion of long-term care funds are channeled through the Medicaid program, which is the subject not only of federal debate, but of state and frequently local legislative discussion as well. Constant calls for increased choice in setting for long-term care—for greater availability of noninstitutional care—keep vivid the perceptions of high spending on nursing homes—spending that appears to vacuum up long-term care funds that might otherwise have been spent with greater flexibility and discretion. Finally, in recent years, talk of a gray or graying federal budget—one that allocates "too great" a share to the elderly—has raised fears that perceptions of excessive long-term care spending may preclude more generous funding in the future.

It may be useful to examine these perceptions critically. First, it should be noted that they are, to varying degrees, well grounded. Tables 2-1, 2-2, and 2-3 set out data that might be interpreted to support the view that recent increases in long-term care spending have been unreasonable.

Table 2-1, for example, sets out both total and public nursing home spending for various years between 1940 and 1980. From 1960 to 1980 alone, total nursing home spending rose by over 4,700 percent, and public spending increased by over 10,000 percent. But these data are both limited and unreliable. Nursing home spending data are limited because they exclude for all years expenditures for long-term mental hospital care, chronic hospital care, and home care for the elderly. Thus, the best available longitudinal data in the field of long-term care spending exclude important elements of that care. This is particularly noteworthy because the share of these other elements has been changing over time. The nursing home spending data reported in Table 2-1, while the best available, are themselves unreliable for the earlier years in that they exclude the costs of care for an unknown but probably significant number of older Americans residing in boarding homes and similar facilities in the 1940s and 1950s. (Most of these precursors of modern "rest homes" and other institutions seem to have been excluded in earlier bed counts, while nursing homes, their more regulated and formally organized successors, seem increasingly to have been included.)

Table 2–1. Nursing Home Spending in the United States.[a]

	FY 1940 ($ million)	FY 1950 ($ million)	FY 1960 ($ million)	FY 1966 ($ million)	FY 1977 ($ million)	FY 1980 ($ million)
Total spending	$28	$178	$480	$1,407	$12,618	$23,000
Public spending	0	11	127	602	7,184	13,200
Public percentage of total	0%	6.2%	26.5%	42.8%	56.9%	57.0%

Sources:

1940–1966: Office of Research and Statistics, Social Security Administration, *Compendium of National Health Expenditures Data* (Washington, D.C.: Government Printing Office, 1973): Table 5.

1977: Robert M. Gibson and Charles R. Fisher, "National Health Expenditures, Fiscal Year 1977," *Social Security Bulletin* 41, no. 7 (July 1978): Table 5.

1980: *Health Care Financing Trends* 2, no. 5 (March 1982): Table A–1. Public share is extrapolated from CY 1980 experience.

a. In recent years, approximately 90 percent of nursing home residents have been aged sixty-five and above, the group usually considered "elderly." Virtually all the remainder are aged fifty-five to sixty-four. See U.S. Bureau of Census, *Statistical Abstract of the U.S., 1977* (Washington, D.C.: Government Printing Office, 1977): Table 166.

Thus, while the increase in public nursing home spending indicated in Table 2-1 is accurate, it does not reflect possible offsetting reductions in public spending on behalf of older people relocated from other institutions to nursing homes. The growth of formal federal reimbursement programs has led to vastly improved record keeping over time. The fragmented records of spending by thousands of jurisdictions on many forms of long-term care have given way to consolidated reports for the Medicare, Medicaid, and Title XX-community service block grant programs. For this reason, some of the more useful longitudinal data concern beds—on which data are more reliable than on spending. Such a longitudinal comparison is presented shortly. The rate of increase in total spending is similarly inflated by the exclusion in earlier years of many nursing homes' predecessors.[5]

Critics of nursing home spending frequently contrast spending increases in various sectors. Table 2-2 presents one such picture. While interesting in itself, and a useful weapon in the hands of those who would criticize long-term care spending, this contrast is incomplete. It also fails to allow for the increase in the nursing home population brought about by such forces as the deinstitutionalization of large numbers of former mental hospital residents. Still, this table does indicate the very rapid rate of increase of residents of places called nursing homes.

Keeping in mind the weaknesses in longitudinal data about nursing homes, it is instructive to consider nursing home spending for one year. Nursing home care is especially expensive to the states and to the federal government. In no other major health sector do governments bear so high a proportion of the cost of care. Table 2-3 indicates total spending by sector in calendar year 1980.

Table 2-3 also indicates the high state and local contribution (almost entirely state) to nursing home spending. This is worthy of contrast to the hospital sector, the other area of high public effort. Further, the states' share of the state-local contribution to nursing home spending is markedly higher than is their share of hospital spending. This is because of high local spending on city–county acute care hospitals, and the absence of a comparable local function in long-term care today. For these reasons, increases in nursing home spending are particularly visible to the states. This helps make states especially sensitive to increased costs of nursing home care, particularly in the Medicaid program, in which nursing home spending looms very large. In 1980, the state share of total Medicaid spending of $25.3 billion was $11.4 billion (45.1%). Of the $11.4 billion state Medicaid total, $4.7 billion (41.2%) went to finance nursing home care.[6]

While nursing home spending increases over the past decades appear impressive, data problems noted earlier point to the need to ground longitudinal comparisons more firmly. Total long-term care bed changes, and changes in the bed-to-population ratios constitute yardsticks more reliable than nursing home spending. Data in Table 2-4 indeed indicate a considerable increase in the total number of long-term care beds available to the elderly from 1939 to 1975. Dur-

Table 2-2. Proportionate Total Spending Increases: Various Sectors.

	FY 1960 ($ million)	FY 1977 ($ million)	Percent Increase 1960–1977	FY 1980 ($ million)	Percent Increase 1960–1980
Nursing homes	$ 480[a]	$ 12,618[b]	2,529%	$ 19,976	4,062%
Hospital care	8,499[a]	65,627[b]	672	96,036	1,030
Total health care	25,856[a]	162,627[b]	529	237,450	818
Total health care	24,700	131,100	431	166,200	573
Education[c]	50,700	118,500	134	157,000	210
National defense[c]	10,300	71,300	592	100,615	877
OASI[d]	90,300	358,900	297	526,300	483
Total federal spending[c]	61,000	321,400[c]	427	432,300	609
Total state and local spending					

Note:

FY 1980 = last quarter of CY 1979 and first three quarters of CY 1980.

a. Figure from Office of Research and Statistics, Social Security Administration, *Compendium of National Health Expenditures Data*, Table 5 (Washington, D.C.: Government Printing Office, 1973).

b. Figures from Robert M. Gibson and Charles R. Fisher, "National Health Expenditures, Fiscal Year 1977," *Social Security Bulletin* 4, no. 7 (July 1978): Table 5; Robert M. Gibson, "National Health Expenditures, 1979," *Health Care Financing Review* 2, no. 1 (Summer 1980): Table 2-A; Robert M. Gibson and Daniel R. Waldo, "National Health Expenditures, 1980," *Health Care Financing Review* 3, no. 1 (September 1981): Table 2-A.

c. Figures from U.S. Bureau of Census, *Statistical Abstract of the U.S. 1977*, Tables 201 and 217; *Statistical Abstract of the U.S., 1981*, Tables 456, 468, 564, 580 (Washington, D.C.: Government Printing Office, 1982).

d. Figures from *Social Security Bulletin* 45, no. 3 (March 1982): 28.

Table 2-3. Total and Public Spending by Health Sector, Calendar Year 1977.

Sector	Total Spending ($ billion)	Federal Percentage	State-Local Percentage	Total Public Percentage
Hospital care	$ 99.6	41.5%	13.0%	54.4%
Physicians' services	46.6	20.2	6.2	26.4
Dentists' services	15.9	1.9	1.9	3.8
Drugs	19.2	4.2	4.1	8.3
Nursing home care	20.7	30.9	25.6	57.0
TOTAL	$247.2	28.7%	13.5%	42.2%

Source:
Robert M. Gibson and Daniel R. Waldo, "National Health Expenditures, 1980," *Health Care Financing Review* 3, no. 1 (September 1981): Table 2-A.

ing this time, total beds rose by 452 percent and beds per 1,000 aged sixty-five and above increased by 116 percent; beds per 1,000 aged seventy-five and above increased by 68 percent. The marked reduction in the rates of increase in all measures during the years 1961 to 1975 suggests that needs are beginning to be met or that controls on spending or admissions are constraining bed growth.

These data clearly modify the picture of long-term care spending and utilization that was formed by viewing only the explosive increase in nursing home spending. Assuming little change in occupancy rates or in average cost per long-term care bed occasioned by the changed proportions of mental hospital, chronic hospital, and nursing home beds in the long-term care bed totals, it can be asserted that overall spending on institutional care has indeed increased markedly since 1939. In recent years, however, this increase has been relatively undramatic.

Another implication of this information should be noted. The deceleration of the rate of increase in long-term beds per thousand elderly, combined with the steady growth in the long-term care bed supply observed since 1939 would seem to indicate that the provision of institutional long-term care is more than a recent artifact that is purely a response to federal legislation of the past fifteen years. Rather, the nature of the growth of the long-term care bed supply points to a deep-seated pattern, one which might well prove difficult to control or reverse—especially in view of the increased need for publicly supported long-term care that can be expected, in combination with the demonstrated policy of paying principally for institutional care.

While the rise in nursing home spending overstates the true increase in the size of the institutional long-term care sector, examination of the number of long-term care beds available to the elderly does document a steady increase. The growth of the nursing home as the site of care for the disabled elderly, com-

Table 2–4. Estimated Number of Long-term Care Beds Available to the Elderly, 1939-1961-1975.

Institution	(thousands of beds)			Percentage Change 1939–1975	Percentage Change 1961–1975
	1939	1961	1975		
Nursing homes[a]	25[d]	534[f]	1,330[a]	+5,220%	+149%
Long-term hospitals[b]	61[e]	71[e]	51[e]	− 16%	− 28%
Mental hospitals[c]	182[e]	212[e]	99[e]	− 46%	− 53%
TOTAL	268	817	1,480	+ 452%	+ 81%
Beds/1000 ≥ age 65	30.6	47.8	66.1	+ 116%	+ 38%
Beds/1000 ≥ age 75	103.4	140.4	173.6	+ 68%	+ 34%

a. Ninety percent of nursing home beds are included; approximately the proportion of residents aged sixty-five and above. See U.S. Bureau of the Census, *Statistical Abstract of the United States, 1977*. (Washington, D.C.: Government Printing Office, 1977), Tables 163 and 166. Nursing homes are places providing some form of nursing, personal care, or domiciliary care; standards vary widely among states.

b. "Long-term general and other special" hospitals.

c. Thirty percent of all mental hospital beds in Massachusetts were occupied by persons aged sixty-five and above in 1973. See a Massachusetts Department of Mental Health study cited in Commonwealth of Massachusetts, *Report of the Long-term Task Force* (Boston: Office of State Health Planning, August 1977). (Mimeo.) Only 30 percent of all beds in mental hospitals are therefore included in all estimates of availability of mental hospital beds for the elderly.

d. Figure from L. Block, Hospital and Other Institutional Facilities and Services, 1939, *Vital Statistics*, Special Reports 13, nos. 1–57 (Washington, D.C.: U.S. Bureau of the Census, 1942).

e. Figures from U.S. Bureau of the Census, *Historical Statistics of the United States, Colonial Times to 1970*, pt. 1 (Washington, D.C.: Government Printing Office, September 1975), sers. B–310, B–312, B–324, B–328.

f. Figure from H.B. Speir, "Characteristics of Nursing Homes and Related Facilities: Report of a 1961 Nationwide Inventory," U.S. Public Health Service Pub. no. 930–F–S (Washington, D.C.: Government Printing Office, 1963).

bined with the financing of that care under Medicaid, has probably increased the visibility of institutional long-term care expenditures. Care of thousands of residents of mental hospitals, financed by the states, and of thousands of county infirmary and poor farm residents, financed by localities, became the responsibility of nursing homes. Under the Medicaid budget, the costs of this care are visible to both the federal government and the states.

EXPLAINING INCREASED USE OF LONG-TERM CARE

There are three types of explanations for increased need for organized long-term care services. They are sociodemographic, economic, and epidemiologic. In concert with increased public funding for long-term care, the three indicate why actual use of services has risen in recent decades.

The three factors may be thought of as acting both independently and synergistically. Certain forces in each area act to increase the overall need for long-term care, no matter how provided. Some of these forces act specifically to increase the demand for formally organized (paid) services or to reduce the supply of informal (unpaid) services provided by family, friend, or neighbor. Family behavior is important because small changes in patterns of family effort can powerfully affect need for formal, paid supports.

No attempt will be made to assess comprehensively the relative importance of the various sources of higher use of formally organized, publicly funded long-term care. Rather, the general size and direction of these sources will be set out. Further, no serious attempt will be made to resolve the question of whether the family's willingness to care for its older dependent members has declined. Family members—spouses and adult children in particular—have been castigated by some analysts and some advocates for the elderly as selfish and unfeeling when they place their relatives in nursing homes. Critics of families who do so point to the increase in the proportion and absolute number of the elderly residing in long-term care institutions, the greater proportion who die as residents of institutions, the well-publicized abuses of rights and dignity of institutional residents, and the general preference of the elderly for home care[7] as arguments against institutionalization.

Others have responded by asserting that the level of effort exerted by families to care for their dependent members has changed very little, and that family members continue to provide the great majority of the services required by the dependent elderly. Moroney's study of the family in Britain concludes that by most available measures, "there is no clear evidence that the state is assuming the primary responsibility for the care of the elderly."[8] Morris, Benedict, and Maddox are among those who argue that the most reliable U.S. national data indicate that almost 80 percent of the older Americans who need long-term care are aided wholly or partly by related household members.[9] Analysis by Shanas of data from a 1975 national study further supports the contention that members of the household and nonresident children of noninstitutionalized, bedfast elderly Americans provide the great bulk of services needed.[10] A new study at the Levinson Policy Institute has found that a group of 100 disabled older citizens of Massachusetts who were receiving fully fifteen to twenty hours per week of paid in-home care still had 72 percent of their total hours of home care met by unpaid informal supports, principally family members living with the disabled person.[11] The thrust of these arguments is that the importance of the three-generation family in caring for the elderly—and the extent and impact of its decline—may well have been exaggerated in almost mythical fashion.

Families do more than provide most of the care to those of their disabled members who reside at home; families also care for at least as many older Americans as do institutions. While the average disabled older person residing at home is more independent, and therefore requires less help than the average disabled older person residing in an institution, the needs of the former group are still very considerable. Maddox notes that one-third of older Americans who receive care at home "require constant care over a long period of time." Surprisingly high proportions have been receiving help from family members for over one year.[12]

By some measures, such as the large numbers of residents in nursing homes, some families may be viewed as abandoning their responsibilities to their dependent elderly members. By other measures, such as the large numbers of disabled citizens living at home through their relatives' assistance, families seem to be doing quite a good job. What is most important to public policy in long-term care, however, is not whether families are "discharging their responsibilities," but rather the size and direction of gradual and marginal shifts in the level of family effort. Even after decades of growth in the use of institutional care, only a small proportion of those aged sixty-five and above reside in institutions. Families do provide most of the services needed by those who require help. *Consequently, a small reduction in the level of family effort means a significantly larger percentage increase in the number of older Americans who require formal support in either the home or an institution.* Understanding the variables that affect the level of family effort over time should inform public attempts to buttress families. In the context of the present study, such understanding should also help explain differences in ability across families at the present time to provide help to relatives at home. Changes in ability, in turn, affect the need for different types of paid, formally organized home care services.

Of the three forces affecting the need and supply of informal support, epidemiologic changes have worked to increase the need for long-term care generally. Sociodemographic and economic changes appear to have increased this need through their impacts on the availability and ability of family members to provide informal support for the elderly. An apparently reduced supply of informal help, in relation to the number of elderly Americans needing long-term support, helps explain the increased need for formal, paid help. This formal help could be provided either in homes or in institutions. The final section of this chapter seeks to explain why the institutional site has been more common.

Epidemiologic Changes

Three epidemiologic forces affecting the need for long-term care can be identified: (1) Americans are living longer; (2) the causes of death are changing; and (3) the gap between male and female longevity is widening. That these forces work on a larger population base strongly influences the number of persons in need and, consequently, the potential cost of public programs.

Life expectancy at birth has increased considerably during this century— forty-nine years in 1900; sixty-three years in 1940; seventy-one years in 1970; and seventy-two and a half years in 1975.[13] The proportion of the U.S. population aged sixty-five and above has risen with life expectancy.

The rise in the proportion of the population aged seventy-five and above is even greater and even more significant in explaining the increased demand for long-term care. As the data in Table 2–5 indicate, the proportion of the population institutionalized rises steadily with age. The Federal Council on Aging refers to those seventy-five and older collectively as the "frail elderly," indicating that a "critical mass occurs within this age range which is worthy of national attention."[14]

If the age- and sex-specific rates of nursing home use that currently prevail were to continue until the year 2000, an increase of about 59 percent in nursing home beds would be required. While no such increase is likely under current or foreseeable fiscal or political circumstances, the size of this increase is worth noting as a profound indicator of the growth of the population in need that this nation faces in coming decades.

Table 2–5. Utilization of Nursing Homes, 1977.

Age	Percentage of Population[a] (216,332,000)	Percentage of Nursing Home Residents[b]	Percentage of Age Group in Nursing Home
Under 65 years	81.1%	14.7%	0.098%
⩾ 65	10.9	85.3	4.7
65–74	6.7	15.7	1.4
75–84	3.2	36.6	6.9
⩾ 85	1.0	33.0	20.5

a. Figures from Administration on Aging, Office of Human Development Services, *Statistical Notes* from the National Clearinghouse on Aging, no. 2 (August 1978), p. 3.

b. Figures from National Center for Health Statistics, *Advance Data from Vital and Health Statistics*, no. 29, 17 May, 1978, Table 1.

Age is correlated with both nursing home and home care use. Table 2-6 presents home care use under Medicare by age. The pattern of the use of home care services increases with age in a manner different from that of institutional care. Home care use by the oldest group, that aged eighty-five and above, is proportionately less than institutional care use. This reflects both the present difficulty of organizing home care services for the very disabled, who are likely to be older, and the lack of sufficient funding for the considerable amounts of home care services needed by the very disabled.

Given that age correlates so strongly with use of long-term services, it is important to note the projected rise in the numbers and proportions of people over age seventy-five—the very groups most likely to use long-term care. These data are set out in Table 2-7. A further consequence of the growth of the very elderly population is the increasing likelihood that the children of parents in need of care would themselves be relatively old and therefore often too frail to provide care.

Americans are now living longer, partly because they are dying of causes different from those most prevalent in the past. Many of the illnesses that killed quickly in earlier years were infectious. Their importance, both absolutely and relatively, has been reduced. Influenza and pneumonia, the leading causes of death in 1900, have been replaced by heart disease and cancer. Both of the latter are degenerative diseases associated with the aging process.[15] "Degeneration" suggests not only deterioration of tissue and organ, but also reduction in functional capacity and independence. In addition, as more Americans live to be very old, the nonfatal illnesses and infirmities of old age—arthritis, weakness, and the like—affect greater numbers of people. Problems associated with both fatal and nonfatal diseases can lead to increased need for long-term care services. Public health and medical care advances and improved real incomes have done more than change the causes of death; they have permitted large numbers of older citizens in developed countries to survive even though greatly disabled, therefore requiring much care from others, often for a very long time.[16]

This is an important point, one often lost sight of. For example, Wegman has written:

It is a truism to the point of being a cliché that the major way to cut health care costs is to prevent disease from occurring in the first place: so-called primary prevention, whether addressed to the individual or to the environment.[17]

Prevention of some diseases may save certain costs for a time, especially in the acute medical care sector, but many of these savings are only postponements of spending for acute care or transfers of spending to long-term care. The costs of treating illnesses may be put off for a time, until people become ill from something that we do not yet know how to prevent. Many of the cheap-to-treat illnesses have been prevented. It may be argued that increasing proportions of us

Table 2-6. Utilization of Home Health Services under Medicare, Calendar Year 1975.

Age	Visits[a] (000)	Percentage of Total Visits	Visits per 1000[a,b] Medicare Population per Each Age Group (000)	Percentage of Enrolled[a,b] Medicare Population by Age Group Served by Home Care	Percentage Served by Nursing Homes Divided by Percentage Receiving Medicare-funded Home Care
Under 65	797	7.4%	368	1.4%	
65 and above	10,007	92.6	445	2.1	
65–74	3,891	36.0	290	1.4	1.00
75–84	4,432	41.0	628	2.9	2.38
85 and above	1,684	15.6	846	3.9	5.26
TOTAL	10,805	100.0%			

a. Figures from Health Care Financing Administration, DHEW, *Research and Statistics Note*, no. 2 (June 1978).
b. Figures from *Social Security Bulletin, Annual Statistical Supplement, 1975*, Tables 138, 139.

Table 2-7. U.S. Elderly Population: 1870–2000 (in thousands).

Year	Total Population	Population Aged 65 and Above	Percent	Population Aged 75 and Above	Percent	Population Aged 85 and Above	Percent
1870[a]	38,558	1,154	3.0%	325[b]	0.84%	55[b]	0.14%
1900	75,995	3,080	4.1	899[c]	1.2	122[c]	0.16
1930	122,775	6,634	5.4	1,945[c]	1.6	272[c]	0.22
1940	131,669	9,019	6.8	2,664[c]	2.0	370[c]	0.28
1950	150,697	12,270	8.1	3,904[c]	2.6	590[c]	0.39
1960	179,323	16,560	9.2	5,621[c]	3.1	940[c]	0.52
1970	203,211	20,066	10.0	7,598[c]	3.7	1,432[c]	0.70
1975	213,540[d]	22,405[d]	10.5	8,527[c]	4.0	1,877[c]	0.88
1980	222,159	24,927	11.2	9,434	4.2	2,294	1.0
1990	243,513	29,824	12.2	12,021	4.9	2,881	1.2
2000	260,378	31,822	12.2	14,368	5.5	3,756	1.4

a. U.S. Bureau of the Census, *Historical Statistics of the United States, Colonial Times to 1970* (Washington, D.C.: Government Printing Office, 1975) Series A-119, -133; U.S. Bureau of the Census, *Projections of the Population of the United States: 1977 to 2050,* Current Population Reports, ser. P-25, no. 704 (Washington, D.C.: Government Printing Office, July 1977): Table 8.

b. *Statistical Atlas of the United States Based on the Results of the Ninth Census 1870 with Contributions from Many Eminent Men of Science and Several Departments of the Government.* Compiled under Authority of Congress by Francis A. Walker, M.A., Superintendent of the 9th Census, Professor of Political Economy and History, Sheffield Scientific School of Yale College, Julius Bien, Lith. 1874, Table 1.

c. U.S. Bureau of the Census, *Demographic Aspects of Aging and the Older Population in the United States,* Current Population Reports, Special Studies, ser. P-23, no. 59 (Washington, D.C.: Government Printing Office, Jan. 1978): Table 2-1.

d. U.S. Bureau of the Census, *Statistical Abstract of the United States: 1977* (Washington, D.C.: Government Printing Office, 1977): Table 3.

now become sick and ultimately die from illnesses that linger and are expensive to treat.

A striking secular change in the relative longevity of men and women has occurred since the beginning of this century, as shown in Table 2-8. The considerable, and growing, gap between male and female longevity is captured by the sex ratio of the elder population and results in differences between the living arrangements of elderly men and women.

Table 2-9 indicates the relative size of the elderly U.S. male and female populations today. Overall, there are about 149 women for every 100 men aged sixty-five and above. In the age groups most likely to require long-term care, there are 186 women for every 100 men.

This has had a measurable effect both on the need for long-term care and on the share of that need that can be met by informal supports. In 1975, only about 18 percent of men aged seventy-five and above were living alone; over 40 percent of women that age were living alone. Table 2-10 indicates the marked increase over the past quarter-century in the percentages of older men and, especially, older women who live alone. Sixty-three percent of all men aged seventy-five and over lived with a spouse. These factors are reflected in different rates of institutionalization: 7.4 percent of men aged seventy-five and above lived in nursing homes or other institutions, while fully 10.0 percent of all women did so.[18] There is some evidence that one reason why women have been disproportionately obliged to enter institutions (few do so from choice)[19] is the absence of a spouse to care for them at home when the need for help becomes pressing.[20] Table 2-10 presents striking data on the proportions of older men and women who live alone. In 1977, the proportion of women over age sixty-five living alone was over two and one-half times that of men. The long-term trend, based on historic patterns, is toward increasing proportions of older women living alone.

Table 2-8. Changes in Male and Female Longevity, 1900-1975.

	Life Expectancy at Birth (years)		
Period	Male	Female	Gap (years)
1900-1902	47.9	50.7	2.8
1949-1951	65.5	71.0	5.5
1969-1971	67.0	74.6	7.6
1975	68.7	76.5	7.8

Source:
National Center for Health Statistics, "Some Trends and Comparisons of United States Life-table Data: 1900-1971," U.S. Decennial Life Tables for 1969-71, vol. 1, no. 4 (Washington, D.C.: Government Printing Office, May 1975), Table 1; U.S. Bureau of the Census, *Statistical Abstract of the United States, 1977* (Washington, D.C.: Government Printing Office, 1977): Table 94.

Table 2-9. Aged Men and Women in the United States, 1978.

| | Aged Population (thousands) | | |
| | | | |
Age	Men	Women	Women per 100 Men
65-69	3,786	4,773	126
70-74	2,680	3,676	137
75-79	1,627	2,531	156
80-84	791	1,763	223
85 and above	671	1,463	218
65 and above	9,555	14,206	149
75 and above	3,089	5,757	186

Source:
U.S. Bureau of the Census, *Projections of the Population of the United States: 1977–2050,* Current Population Report, ser. P-25, no. 704 (Washington, D. C.: Government Printing Office, July 1977).

Thus, the epidemiologic considerations of longer life spans (with women outliving men) and more debilitating disease have increased need for long-term help by older Americans as a group. The supply of this long-term care by family members or other informal supports depends on the availability, ability, and willingness of these informal supports to help the elderly. Availability means that informal supports are present and have the time to help. Ability signals the physical strength, skills, and energy necessary to provide needed help. Willingness indicates that a choice to help is made. It is clear that all three elements are required before informal support can be provided. In recent years, the availability and ability of family members has been affected by both economic and sociodemographic changes in American society.

Industrialization

Four consequences of industrialization—geographic mobility, rising real incomes, urbanization, and careers for women—have reduced the availability of family members to aid one another.

Industrialization has meant a decline in the role of the family as a unit of production and probably also a decline in shared residence. The generations had more often lived together when farm or shop was the site of joint production. Geographic mobility in the United States in recent years has been considerable. From 1970 to 1975 alone, over 41 percent of the U.S. population over age five moved to a different residence; over 17 percent moved to a different county or a different state.[21] It is not known how many older Americans who need help fail to receive it because family members live too far away to provide it. Further, it

Table 2-10. Population Aged Sixty-five and Above Living Alone, 1950–1977 (thousands).

Year	Total	Living Alone	Percentage Living Alone	Male	Living Alone	Percentage Living Alone	Female	Living Alone	Percentage Living Alone
1950g	12,397a	1,559b	12.6%	5,856a	518b	8.8%	6,541a	1,041b	15.9%
1960g	16,560c	2,898d	17.5	7,503c	853d	11.4	9,056c	2,045d	22.6
1970	19,972c	5,071e	25.4	8,367c	1,174e	14.1	11,605c	3,897e	33.6
1977	23,431f	6,482e	27.7	9,545f	1,343e	14.1	13,885f	5,139e	37.0

a. U.S. Bureau of the Census, Statistical Abstract of the United States, 1975 (Washington, D.C.: Government Printing Office, 1975), Table 3.

b. U.S. Bureau of the Census, U.S. Census of Population : 1960, vol. 1, Characteristics of the Population, pt. 1, U.S. Summary (Washington, D.C.: Government Printing Office, 1964), Table 185.

c. U.S. Bureau of the Census, Statistical Abstract of the United States, 1977 (Washington, D.C.: Government Printing Office, 1977), Table 23.

d. U.S. Bureau of the Census, Persons by Family Characteristics, Subject Reports, Final Report PC (2)–4B. U.S. Census of Population: 1960 (Washington, D.C.: Government Printing Office, 1964), Table 3.

e. U.S. Bureau of the Census, "Household and Families by Type: March 1977 (Advance Report)," Current Population Reports, ser. P–20, no. 313 (Washington, D.C.: Government Printing Office, September 1977), Table 3.

f. U.S. Bureau of the Census, Projections of the Population of the United States: 1977–2050, Current Population Reports, ser. P–25, no. 704 (Washington, D.C.: 1977), Table 8.

g. Figures for 1960 and 1950: estimates of those living alone are based on data for primary unrelated individuals presented in notes d and f. By definition (note d, p. 9 and U.S. Census of Population: 1950, vol. 4, General Characteristics of Families (Washington, D.C.: Government Printing Office, 1955), pp. 2A–7 and 2A–10)), a primary individual is a household head living alone or with nonrelative only. Figures for 1960 indicate that 88.6 percent of all primary individuals live in a household of one person, while 91.8 percent of male primary individuals age sixty-five and above and 90.5 percent of female primary individuals age sixty-five and above live in a household of one person. Based on a statement in the 1950 census that "five out of every six primary individuals were living alone in 1950, ratios were calculated of the 1960 percentages (91.8/88.6 and 90.5/88.6), these ratios adjusted to account for a change between 1950 and 1960 in the percentage of sixty-five and above males (−0.9%) and sixty-five and above females (+5.5%) constituting the primary individual category, and the final ratios applied to the 1950 living-alone percentage (83.3%) to estimate the percentage of each sex group living alone in 1950. These percentages were then applied to the total primary individual figures for that age/sex group for 1950 and the resulting numbers used to estimate percentages of that total age/sex group living alone.

is not known whether families are less or more available today than 200, 100, 50, or 10 years ago. What does seem clear is that adult children and other potential caregivers of the elderly often live hundreds or thousands of miles away.

Rising real incomes of both the elderly and the nonelderly permitted increasing proportions of Americans to live apart from their parents or children. If separate dwelling units are established far from one another, usually at a time of good health for members of both households, availability of help for aged members of the family who subsequently require aid is reduced.

The growth of large American cities and suburbs has entailed more than the construction of buildings. It has also created the spatial and social setting for patterns that are in some respects inimical to family support of elders. Spatially, in the years since World War II, residential land-use patterns in large older cities have often obliged young families seeking homes of their own to move many miles from the homes of their parents. This has been particularly true when incomes or lifestyles of the two generations have differed. To help families live together, more mixed-income, mixed-class neighborhoods would be desirable. Then, distant residential relocation would no longer need to be the price of income or lifestyle differences across generations. Racial and ethnic succession in cities has been accompanied by the disproportionate departure of the young and mobile and the continued residence of elders. Large-scale public projects in many cities—urban renewal, public housing, highway construction—have displaced thousands, often into tight housing markets that made collective relocation of large families very difficult.[22] The effect of these events has probably been to reduce the availability of family support for older citizens.

Socially, the city has been the setting for changes accompanying urbanization and industrialization. Even when parents were not physically left behind by their children, parental authority was often set aside. For this there are many reasons: uprooting of traditional culture by the stress of international migration or the journey from farm to city; loss by the parents of land ownership as a source of control; and perceived obsolescence of traditional values and skills carried by parents.[23] Loss of parental authority has by no means meant a collapse of intergenerational support. It has, however, reduced parents' ability to compel provision of aid by children. Other things being equal, it cannot be decided whether children are willing to do more or less for parents today than in past years.

Industrialization and urbanization have made it possible for increasing proportions of women to take jobs outside the home. This has reduced their traditional availability as providers of care to older relatives who could not be left alone. (Women may work on the farm and work at keeping house in cities, but they are not counted as members of the "labor force" unless they are paid.) In 1940, 17 percent of all married women worked outside the home; by 1976, this figure had risen to 46 percent.[24]

Taken together, the economic forces just discussed seem to have reduced the availability of families to care for their aged members. Several sociodemographic changes that have had similar consequences are also worthy of mention.

Sociodemographic Changes

Three forces that have affected availability, ability, and willingness of family members to care for their aged relatives are: (1) the decline in the number of children per family; (2) the aging of potential providers of care; and (3) the increase in the rates of divorce and remarriage.

The number of children per aged patient is one of the most important variables influencing whether a dependent older person comes to live with a child and thereby avoids or postpones institutionalization.[25] Since the number of children born in each family has been declining, fewer children are available—even potentially—to care for aged parents. The decline has not been continuous. Neugarten notes that there will be almost 50 percent more children for each surviving sixty-five-year-old woman in the year 2000 than there are today.[26] This suggests an opportunity for a breathing space in coming years, as the greater number of children available will help reduce the rate of increase in likely need for publicly funded long-term care that would be expected from the increase in the number of very old Americans. If so, the time offered should be used wisely to build a long-term care system we will be willing to sustain for future generations. At the other extreme, the danger of blandly relying on children to provide care should be avoided. The ratio will worsen again after the year 2020 as the children of the post-World War II baby boom are replaced as potential caregivers by the children born in recent years. This will mean that women now of childbearing age (and their husbands) will be able to draw on fewer children to provide help than did preceding generations. Support for this contention is provided by the decline in the total fertility rate—one crudely standardized measure of the ratio of children born to women of childbearing age. It has dropped steadily from a post-World War II high of 3,690 births per 1,000 women in 1955-1959 to only 1,799 per 1,000 women in 1975,[27] though it has risen again more recently.

The age of adult children is also an important factor. When very old parents come to need care, an appreciable number of children will be unable to provide that help because they may themselves be ill or frail. The same difficulty may prevent elderly spouses from helping each other.

The ability of family members to aid dependent older relatives is impaired not only by the frailty of the potential family provider, but also by the technical difficulty of rendering needed help. Advances in medicine and related fields have made more complex the tasks of providing home care for some dependent older persons. The proportion of home care services that can be provided by family members in the absence of training or other skilled support from outside the home has probably been reduced. Such training and support may well merit increased investment in the future.

Availability of family members to provide help—and perhaps their willingness to help—has very likely been impaired by the rising rates of divorce and remarriage. A small proportion of the elderly are themselves divorced or separated; in these cases, the spouse is therefore unavailable to help. More often, older parents may divorce or remarry; their children may do the same. In either case, bonds of affection and obligation can become diffused. Children and stepchildren may be left uncertain about whom to care for.

Slater has argued that Americans have valued independence to an inappropriate degree. It is possible that self-reliance has been carried to excess by younger and by working-aged Americans; it is much more than possible that a great acceptance of interdependence would both accustom citizens to accept help from others and provide disabled persons with a community of friends, relatives, and neighbors better disposed to provide that help.[28]

In considering epidemiologic, economic, and sociodemographic influences on the demand for long-term care and on the supply of informal support, important interactions between the sources of increased demand and reduced supply should be noted. For example, higher real incomes have done much to improve longevity; at the same time, they have enabled the generations to live apart and be unavailable to each other. Further, at least until very recently, different sex roles in the labor market may have helped increase the gap between male and female longevity. This is true of deaths caused by cancer although probably less so of deaths caused by cardiovascular diseases. Another example is the decline in the number of children per family due in part to the reduced importance of the family as a unit of production and the perceived availability of Social Security's Old Age and Survivors Insurance (OASI) cash to replace care by children. Public attempts to enhance informal supports' availability, ability, or willingness to help the aged by manipulating individual variables should take changes such as these into account.

The major force leading to increased need for, and pressure for spending on, long-term care is the growing number of very old Americans. The estimate of an increase of 59 percent in the age- and sex-adjusted rate of nursing home need between the years 1980 and 2000 is frightening. Anticipated reductions in families' availability, ability, and perhaps willingness to help frail, disabled, or chronically ill older citizens point to a greater than 59 percent increase in need for publicly supported services.

Some public officials react to this growing crisis by blaming families for not doing more. A few try to devise ways of obliging families to pay for expensive nursing home care. This is inappropriate, ineffective, and unfair. More constructive steps would be to learn ways of spending existing and incremental long-term care funds more productively. To do so requires a clear understanding of the rea-

sons for the historic preference to make publicly supported long-term care services available principally in institutions. From such understanding may grow
suggestions for devising a universally accessible (and affordable) system of long-
term care—one that supports and encourages families with needed services and
incentives instead of blaming them with empty words.

PUBLIC RESPONSES TO INCREASED
NEED FOR LONG-TERM CARE:
INSTITUTIONAL PREFERENCES

Since the second half of the nineteenth century, a combination of social changes
of the types just discussed and public responses to these changes has induced or
forced a growing proportion of older citizens to live out their lives in nursing
homes, hospitals, and other institutions.

This trend has contributed to the evolving crisis in long-term care in two
ways. First, most older people themselves and their families are badly dissatisfied with public programs that oblige institutionalization as the price of obtaining public support. Second, the costs even of current levels of institutional care—
often inadequate in number of beds and indecent in dignity and compassion—
are so great that the vast growth in need for publicly supported long-term care
that can be anticipated during coming decades will not possibly be accommodated by significant increases in the number of nursing home beds.

A better balance between publicly supported institutional and noninstitutional care would be desirable because it probably offers the best chance of con-
structing a system that is adequate in that it serves all those in need who seek
help, decent in that it offers dignified and compassionate care, and affordable in
that we are willing as a society to pay the bill for adequacy and decency. Various
proposed reforms in long-term care are taken up in Chapter 3. First, it will be
useful to consider the sources of our present emphasis on institutional long-term
care. This requires brief examination of the histories of hospitals and their successors, nursing homes, as providers of long-term care.

Evolution of the Hospital

During the Middle Ages, hospitals were founded as places for pilgrims and other
travelers to rest, especially when ill.[29] Early hospitals provided care, not cure.
Few cures were available. Patients either succumbed to their problem or recov-
ered; rest and food were the major therapeutic interventions. Hospitals also
housed victims of infectious diseases considered dangerous to the community.
Both types of patients were impoverished. Patients able to afford to pay for
care generally hired physicians to attend on them at home.

In the United States, many early hospitals gradually evolved out of local
almshouses. As the latter grew and specialized, they were considered appro-

priate for those of their residents who were not only impoverished or insane, but had recognizable physical problems as well. The number of hospitals increased slowly. By 1873, there were only 178. Their numbers increased to 4,359 in 1909 and to 6,291 in 1940. Their beds rose from 421,000 in 1909 to 1,226,000 in 1940.[30]

Five important factors that contributed to the growth of hospitals have been identified as: (1) advances in medical science (especially during wars, which resulted in rapid progress in surgical specialities, the focus of nineteenth and early twentieth century hospital care); (2) modern nursing; (3) education for doctors and other personnel; (4) religious and philanthropic impulses; and (5) increased per capita income (permitting allocation of resources to hospital care without imperiling other areas of consumption).[31] Corwin pointed to two additional pressures leading to hospital expansion: increasing urbanization, which induced a recognition that health was not solely a personal matter, but in part a public concern as well; and a desire to conserve physicians' time by gathering patients conveniently together.[32] Belknap and Steinle endorse the argument that hospitals grew because medical advances converted them into sites where special tools of diagnosis and treatment—x-ray, antiseptic surgery, and modern nursing, for example—could be conveniently organized. They also emphasize the importance of economic and social factors supporting the founding and expansion of hospitals: the growth of industrial production in the United States after the Civil War; the consequent accumulation of large surpluses in the hands of a wealthy few; and the widely received doctrine that philanthopy was as necessary to high status as was wealth.[33]

As hospital care became more effective, it came to be desired by greater numbers of people. While some hospitals began accepting some paying patients as early as 1850,[34] it was not until the turn of the century that all classes of the U.S. population came to seek hospital care. Until 1908, for example, doctors at the Massachusetts General Hospital could not charge patients fees; New York Hospital, Johns Hopkins, and the Pennsylvania Hospital did not organize special facilities for private, paying patients until the first decade of this century.[35]

As effective, active, and aggressive therapies were developed, patients who did not need them became increasingly peripherial to hospitals. In many respects, early hospitals had resembled today's nursing homes. They cared for poorer patients suffering from chronic problems for which effective cures were not available. Interestingly, nursing homes now have staff-to-patient ratios similar to those prevailing at many community hospitals as recently as the 1930s and 1940s.

As hospitals assumed new roles as providers of acute care, the low-income chronic care patients that they had formerly served have gradually been displaced. Hospitals' and physicians' interests in such patients declined; new sites of care had to be found. Had this not been done, the needs of long-term patients could have deflected hospitals from their new missions by occupying beds and resources thought needed for acute care.

Origins of the Modern Nursing Home

The present pattern of providing institutional long-term care for the elderly in the United States did not emerge spontaneously in response to the Medicaid legislation of 1965. Enactment of Medicaid did lead to a significant increase in public funding for nursing home care, and the regulations promulgated in Washington to carry out the law did a great deal to standardize design and services in what had been an inchoate and diverse group of facilities. Skilled nursing facilities (SNF), intermediate care facilities (ICF), and rest homes/domiciliary care facilities have succeeded the homes for the aged, boarding homes, convalescent homes, and poor farms of several decades ago. Many of the characteristic assets and liabilities of today's system of long-term care, however, represent continuations of patterns long established. Today's problems can be regarded partly as products of inadvertence and of half-successful efforts to cope with earlier difficulties.

Since the turn of the century, hospitals have become progressively employed as sites of short-term interventions. Today, care for patients who are medically unstable but for whom effective interventions are lacking is provided largely in skilled nursing facilities. Services to less unstable patients, who might nonetheless require a great deal of help owing to frailty or disability, are given in intermediate care facilities. Services in these two settings are reimbursed under Medicaid. Another type of long-term care institution is the rest home, which provides room, board, and very small amounts of supervision. (Facilities are licensed under different names in different states. New York's ICFs are called "health-related facilities"; and rest homes are "domiciliaries.") Frail or isolated older citizens might also live in boarding homes, older single room occupancy buildings, and older hotels—all of which provide some level of service. Care outside SNFs and ICFs can be paid for partly or wholly under the Supplemental Security Income (SSI) program. This is a successor to the Old Age Assistance (OAA) program. Income received under Social Security's Old Age and Survivors Insurance (OASI) can be applied to care in any setting.

Long-term care for patients too frail or unstable to be served in SNFs is sometimes provided in chronic disease hospitals. Patients recovering from accidents or acute illnesses often spend time in specialized rehabilitation hospitals before returning home or seeking permanent placement in a nursing home. Within the hospital sector, a long-term care facility is one whose average length of stay exceeds thirty days. Rehabilitation and chronic disease hospitals will not generally be considered here.

In the United States, early nursing homes were a heterogeneous lot. They had a variety of names and institutional origins and housed diverse populations. In many cases, they were not easy to distinguish from other types of facilities.[36] The earliest institution commonly housing the poor in the United States was the almshouse, which had its origins in the 1601 English Poor Law and was the product of two events. The first was the suppression by Henry VIII of Roman Catholic institutions for the care of the frail poor; the second was the perceived need to manage the large numbers of dispossessed subjects driven to towns and cities by "enclosures" of common land for private use of a few, or attracted there by the prospect of employment. The almshouse was transplanted to the American colonies in the seventeenth century. Housing an undifferentiated population of persons considered paupers, criminals, retarded, and disabled, it often provided little in the way of decent care to the elderly. By contrast, while the earliest hospitals—Pennsylvania, Philadelphia General, New York, and Bellevue—all evolved from infirmaries of almshouses, they can be seen as expressions of more charitable impulses toward the frail and chronically ill. Possibly because early hospitals were designed to house solely those who could not work, the standard of living that they offered the elderly was usually higher than that of the almshouse.

During the last quarter of the nineteenth century, hospitals became recognizable as increasingly different from the almshouses for the impoverished, disabled, or incurable elderly. Acute care hospitals provided active treatment and recuperation for all classes, usually under voluntary nonprofit auspices. Publicly owned county infirmaries—poor farms—continued as institutions of last resort for the elderly.

During the 1920s, a new long-term care facility became visible. This was the convalescent home, offering post-surgery and other recuperative care to those unable to return directly home from the hospital and able to pay for their room, board, and nursing care. The convalescent home, usually privately owned and operated to earn a profit, can be seen as the most direct ancestor of the typical SNF. Another institution, the nonprofit "home for the aged," developed at about the same time as the convalescent home. Its residents typically remained in the facility for stays lengthier than those of convalescent home patients.

It can be seen that hospitals shed first the function of caring for the frail elderly, and second that of housing convalescents. Specialized long-term care facilities arose to perform these tasks on behalf of the different social groups: almshouses for the poor and short-term convalescent homes or long-term homes for the aged for those who could pay. (Note that the almshouse itself was engaged in a similar shedding as the "insane" were placed in asylums and "criminals" were placed in penitentiaries.) It is not known what proportion of the population these institutions served or how well they cared for their residents. It does seem likely that most frail older persons lived out their years cared for at home by their families, and that others—fewer in number—suffered unnecessarily and died prematurely because they lacked help to live in their homes but could not or would not enter an institution.

The quality of institutional care was uncertain. Some almshouses, though publicly owned, were managed under contract by individuals whose incomes depended on keeping costs low or on selling the services of residents. Locally financed from property taxes, almshouses discouraged optional admissions.

Utilization and taxes were controlled in part by making it clear to the elderly that these unattractive institutions were only a last resort for those who failed, who had not worked hard enough, who had not saved enough, or who were "morally defective." In those cities where almshouses came to be run by local political machines as genuine social welfare services, the quality of life for the elderly may have been somewhat better than the average. In contrast to almshouses, convalescent homes cared for a paying population and probably felt some competitive pressures to satisfy their residents.

With the passage of Titles I and II of the Social Security Act in 1935 came national programs of Old Age Assistance (or OAA, building on earlier state legislation) and also of federal Old Age and Survivors Insurance (OASI).[37] Over time, these programs raised the incomes of most elderly Americans and placed cash in the hands of many who had been destitute.

The availability of these funds affected decisions by both the elderly and their families. Those elderly citizens who had desired to live apart from their children now had the wherewithal to do so. Those spouses or adult children who had been unable or unwilling to continue to care for their husbands, wives, or parents at home, but had not been prepared to make the decision—widely perceived as shameful—to place them in the poor house, now saw OAA and OASI as the means with which to pay for institutional care.

During the 1940s and 1950s, these alternatives slowly grew. Boarding homes, homes for the aged, nursing homes, rest homes, and other facilities were founded in increasing numbers. Reliable national data on the number of facilities of different types and on the services provided are lacking because of inconsistent nomenclature and fragmented regulation. It does seem, however, that they were generally small and offered relatively few services beyond room and board. Many crudely resembled the foster care programs rediscovered in recent years—for example, an elderly couple or widow might take in two to five boarders. Skilled nursing or rehabilitative services were generally lacking.

Figure 2-1 portrays, in general terms, the evolution of functions and organizations in the institutional long-term care field from the last half of the nineteenth century to the present. While only a crude representation, it serves several useful purposes: First, it indicates the diverse origins of today's long-term care facilities, which range from the intensive help provided in rehabilitation hospitals to the low level of support offered in rest homes. These facilities have evolved as successors to several types of earlier institutions. They acquired some of the functions successively sloughed off by acute and mental hospitals; they reorganized the heterogeneous functions of antecedent facilities into more-or-less systematic levels of care.

Second, Figure 2-1 indicates that there exists today a logical framework for viewing the functions of long-term care facilities. Perhaps until the passage of Medicaid, nonhospital institutions were distinguished more by their source of revenue than by the types and intensity of services they provided their patients.

Figure 2-1. Institutional Antecedents of Today's Long-term Care Facilities.

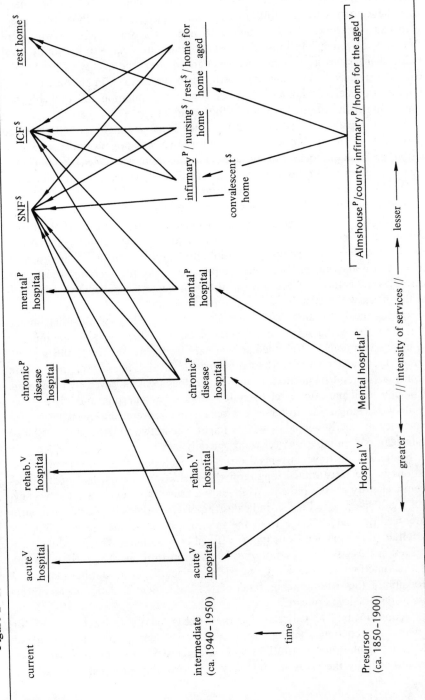

Code: dominant control: V = Voluntary, non-profit; P = Public; $ = Proprietary.

(Despite the regulations accompanying federal financing, which have systematized federally reimbursed services, many of the inconsistencies of the older system survive. For example, life safety codes may prevent some county infirmaries from obtaining certification as intermediate care facilities even though they provide that level of care. Similarly, voluntary nonprofit SNFs and ICFs still tend to house middle-income patients.)

The organizational growth and evolution of long-term care institutions is a product of more than greater availability of funds to pay for services or the efforts of acute care and mental hospitals to shed their chronically ill patients. It also has been influenced by subtle yet powerful legislative preferences for institutions as sites of publicly funded long-term care.

Explaining the Institutional Preference in Federal Long-Term Care Funding

The profound public emphasis on institutional care is clear. While, as Table 2-11 indicates, there was a slight increase in the proportion of public long-term care spending devoted to home care from 1970 to 1977, it is still less than 12 percent of the total. It should be noted that this small rise took place during a time of intense pressure for greater public funding for home care.

Further, much of the increase in publicly funded home care spending is not really devoted to long-term care. A large share of Medicare support for home care (as for nursing home care) is restricted in practice to relatively short-term post-hospital convalescence. It is possible that the share of public long-term care funds actually devoted to home care has not increased in recent years.

Since 1977, Medicare home care spending has continued to rise fairly steadily. Medicaid-funded home care remains largely a one-state program. Title XX social services block grant funds have been further collapsed into a larger community services block grant, and have suffered a significant cut in total funds. Clearly, the near-term prospects for enhanced public funding for noninstitutional long-term care are not good. A reduced federal community services block grant will mean reduced home care spending on the elderly in many states. Constrained Medicaid spending will further reduce states' desires to do more than care for the more visible patients for whom they are already responsible – those residing in nursing homes.

The growing importance of institutional care for the elderly is reflected in the increasing proportion of the population dying in hospitals and nursing homes, principally the former. In 1955, about two-thirds of all deaths were in institutions; by 1967, this proportion had risen to almost three-fourths. There is every reason to believe that these data capture only a recent segment of a trend that began in the nineteenth century.[38]

Table 2-11. Distribution of Public Long-term Care Spending on the Elderly.

	(Fiscal Years, Except as Noted)	
	1970 ($ thousands)	*1977 ($ thousands)*
Total Public Long-term Care Spending	$1,424,339	$5,887,433
Nursing Home Spending		
Medicare	$ 249,911[b]	$ 288,597[c]
Medicaid[a]	1,058,557[d]	4,902,890[e]
Subtotal—nursing home spending	1,308,468	5,191,487
Nursing home percent of Total	91.9%	88.2%
Home Care Spending		
Medicare Part A	$ 46,539[b]	$ 217,718[c]
Medicare Part B	28,307[f]	90,360[g]
Medicaid	9,010[d]	141,514[h]
Title XX–Social Security Act	32,015[i]	229,446[j]
Title III–Older Americans Act	NA	16,908[k]
Subtotal—home care spending	115,871	695,946
Home care percent of Total	8.1%	11.8%

a. Excludes ICF-MR.

b. U.S. Social Security Administration, *Social Security Bulletin* 33, no. 12 (December 1970), Table M-18 and vol. 34, no. 6 (June 1971), Table M-18.

c. U.S. Social Security Administration, *Social Security Bulletin* 41 no. 7 (July 1978), Table M-18.

d. Calculated for CY 1970 from data in: DHEW, Social and Rehabilitation Service, National Center for Social Statistics, *Numbers of Recipients and Amounts of Payments Under Medicaid and Other Medical Programs Financed from Other Public Assistance Funds—1970.* DHEW Pub. no. (SRS) 73-03153, NCSS Report B-4 (CY 70), Tables 20, 21, and 22. October 1972; DHEW, Social and Rehabilitation Service, National Center for Social Statistics, *Findings of the 1970 AB Study*, and *Findings of the 1970 APTD Study, Part 1*, Demographic and Program Statistics, Table 1. 1972.

e. DHEW, Health Care Financing Administration, Medicaid Statistics, June 1977, Research Report B-1 (6/77), December 1977, Table Q1. Estimated payments from SNFs and ICFs (excluding mentally retarded) by summing Quarters October–December 1976, January–March 1977, and twice April–June 1977, subtracting 10 percent to allow for nursing population under age sixty-five.

f. U.S. Social Security Administration, *Social Security Bulletin* 33, no. 6 (June 1970), Table M-20 and vol. 34, no. 4 (April 1971), Table M-20.

g. U.S. Social Security Administration, *Social Security Bulletin* 41, no. 7 (July 1978), Table M-20.

h. DHEW, Health Care Financing Administration Medicaid Statistics June 1977, Research Report B-1 (6/77), December 1977, Table Q1. Estimated payments for home health services for FY 1977 by summing Quarters October–December 1976, January–March 1977, and twice April–June 1977, subtracting 20 percent to allow for services to those under age sixty-five.

Notes to Table 2-11 *(continued)*

i. Figures estimated by:

1. Calculating percent of all Homemaker and Chore service recipients in OAA, APTD, and AB categories (U.S. DHEW), Social and Rehabilitation Service, National Center for Social Statistics, *Findings of the 1970 OAA Study*, pt. 1, Table 37, *Findings of the 1970 APTD Study*, pt. 1, Tables 1 and 37, and *Findings of the 1970 AB Study*, Tables 1 and 37. 1972;

2. Applying these percents to the total social service dollar figure expended for Homemaker and Chore services for adult titles, (OAA, APTD, AB) for FY 1971 (U.S. DHEW, Social and Rehabilitation Service, *Cost Analysis of Social Services, Fiscal Year 1972; An Update of the Cost Analysis of Social Services for FY 1971* (Washington, D.C.: Touche Ross and Co., February 1973). Exhibit 4;

3. Calculating percent of APTD and AB recipients age 65+ (OAA = 100% age 65+);

4. Applying these percents to the respective dollar figures derived in 2;

5. Summing the final dollar figures derived in 4.

j. Figures estimated by:

1. Calculating average percent of home-based service dollar figure allocated to age 60+ according to a four-state survey (Bill Benton, Tracey Field, and Rhona Millar, "State and Area Agency on Aging Intervention in Title XX," Working Paper 0990-24 (Washington, D.C.: The Urban Institute, December 1977), figs. 7, 9, 10, 13, 15.);

2. Reducing average percents by five to eliminate an amount estimated to be allocated to persons sixty to sixty-four years old;

3. Applying net percent to total estimated expenditures for home-based services for FY 1977. Fileen Wolff, Barbara E. Bird, Patricia L. Sullivan, *Technical Notes; Summaries and Characteristics of States' Title XX Social Services Plans for Fiscal Year 1977*, (Washington, D.C.: DHEW, Office of the Secretary, 1977), p. 89.

k. U.S. Senate, Special Committee on Aging, *Developments in Aging: 1977*, pt. 1, Report no. 95-771 (Washington, D.C.: Government Printing Office, 1978), p. 120.

What is new in the years since World War II is the striking increase in the use of long-term care facilities by the elderly in the years before death. The number of nursing homes alone increased from 1,200 in 1939 to 16,701 in 1963, to 21,834 in 1973. At the same time, the number of residents increased from below 25,000 in 1939 to 491,000 in 1963 to 1,198,000 in 1973.[39] By 1973, almost 5 percent of Americans aged sixty-five and above were residing in nursing homes.

The proportion of the elderly receiving nursing home care during their last years was even greater. Lerner found that the percentage of all deaths occurring in nursing homes, homes for the aged, and similar facilities increased dramatically from 1.6 percent of all deaths in 1949 to somewhat under 6.0 percent in 1958.[40] More recent work by Kastenbaum and Candy[41] shows that there has been a rapid increase in nursing home use during the last years of life. They criticized then-current use of population data indicating that, at any one time, only 4 percent of those aged sixty-five and over were in nursing homes or other long-term care facilities. They argued that application of these cross-sectional data seriously underestimated any older person's true chances of using such long-term care. By studying obituary notices, they estimated that 13.3 percent of all deaths occur in nursing homes; by studying death certificates, they found that 20.3 percent of deaths occur in nursing homes and 23.7 percent in nursing homes or other extended care facilities. These proportions were themselves thought to be underestimates in that they did not include those residents of extended care facilities whose conditions became unstable, leading to transfer to a hospital and to death in that facility.

Both OAA and OASI funds could be spent on institutional care, and each could be regarded as public spending, taxed and disbursed out of proportion to funded contributions. It was only in 1940 that spending on nursing home care was identified by federal statistics. This sum, $33 million, was thought to have been spent entirely by private consumers. Local public spending and philanthropic contributions were not included.[42]

The first federal program of direct vendor payments to nursing homes was authorized by the social security amendments of 1950. By 1965, the final pre-Medicaid year, public payments to nursing homes equalled $502 million (or 37.8% of the total). Federal–state medical vendor payments were made under a 50 percent federal match (Old Age Assistance) or under a 50 to 80 percent federal match (Kerr–Mills Medical Assistance to the Aged).[43] In 1965, 60 percent of all patients in nursing homes received partial or full support under one of these two welfare programs.[44] Table 2-1 summarizes the growth of public spending for nursing home care. By fiscal year 1980, total spending had risen to $23 billion; the public share was 57.0 percent.

A series of legislative changes helped underwrite this increase in funding. Medicare directly covered for the first time long-term institutional care without a means test. This was—and is—available only for short post-hospital recuperative stays, and amounts to only a small share of public payments for nursing home care today (see Table 2-11), but it may prove an important precedent. The 1960 Kerr–Mills Medical Assistance to the Aged and the 1965 Medicaid programs departed from the OAA medical vendor payment schemes for skilled nursing facility care by increasing the federal share of nursing home spending in many states and by removing the cap on the maximum daily rate in which the federal government would share. Medicaid itself should not be held responsible for the acceleration of the rate of public spending on nursing home care. Public spending increased 152 percent from 1961 to 1965 under the combined OAA and Kerr–Mills authorizations; it increased by an additional 167 percent from 1966 to 1970 under Medicaid.[45] Finally, the Social Security Amendments of 1972 expanded coverage under the Medicaid program beyond skilled nursing facility care to include intermediate care facilities.

Three major programs currently fund home care services for the elderly: Medicare; Medicaid; and Title XX (community social service block grants). Medicare will pay for post-hospital care under Part A and other skilled care under

Part B supplemental services. Services under both parts are limited to home-bound patients requiring short-term, intermittent assistance from a registered nurse or physical or speech therapist. Some assistance by a home health aide may be reimbursed, but this is limited to medically related services. The home health aide may perform incidental housekeeping tasks, such as cooking or clean-ing, only if this does not substantially increase the time spent in the home. Gen-eral homemaker services are not covered. In sum, Medicare pays almost exclu-sively for skilled, short-term home care.[46]

The state–federal Medicaid program is free of the legal and regulatory stric-tures of Medicare. Even in Medicaid, however, a striking symptom of federal policy's institutional preference is manifested. This is done through the "deem-ing" rule, under which the income of a relative is deemed available to a disabled person if the two are living together but not if the disabled person resides in an institution. Since Medicaid benefits are means tested, a person may be eligible for Medicaid-supported nursing home care but not for home care. Since 1970, home health care has been a mandated benefit (one that states are legally obliged to finance), and states are in practice free to write and administer Medicaid plans to reimburse a wide range of services to those eligible for the program. Patients need neither be homebound nor in need of skilled services. Covered benefits may extend beyond those permitted by Medicare to include homemaking and chore services. Nonetheless, viewed nationally, the Medicaid home health pro-gram must be considered a profound disappointment. It is not even a national program. In fiscal year 1979, for example, of total Medicaid spending on home care of $264 million, $203 million (76.9%) was spent in New York State.[47] Of this, the bulk was spent in New York City. The United States, then, can be thought of as having not a national Medicaid home health program, but rather a one-city program. Other jurisdictions forego the opportunity of mobilizing fed-eral matching funds (at least they did so prior to the 1981 limits on federal participation in Medicaid). Most states are out of compliance with the federal mandate to provide home care services to eligible Medicaid beneficiaries. They have not been willing to spend enough of their own money to create adequate programs. A few states have pursued the Title XX path to funding home care.

Title XX of the Social Security Act (community social services block grant) is the third major source of public funding for home care. Home-based services for the elderly consume a large proportion of the money allocated under many states' Title XX plans. Home care helps support attainment of most of the fed-erally legislated goals of Title XX: aiding families in becoming or remaining self-sufficient and self-supporting; protecting older citizens who are unable to care for themselves; and helping individuals avoid institutionalization.[48]

One useful way to begin explaining the marked legislative emphasis on insti-tutional long-term care is by examining nursing home and home care spending under Medicaid. This program pays for more long-term care than any other.

By contrast, Medicare's focus is clearly on acute care. Medicaid is a "means tested" program. If an older person initially has the income or assets to support normal life at home but subsequently comes to require supporting home care services from another individual, even if the state has a Medicaid home care program, Medicaid will not pay the bill unless the person in need of service "spends down" (a euphemism for impoverishment) to levels of Medicaid eligibility. This may easily mean depleting assets or income necessary for ordinary maintenance at home. Or, more likely, home care services simply are not available under Medicaid. The older person's alternative then is to enter a nursing home, spend down assets (or illegally dispose of them), and then rely on Medicaid to pay for long-term institutional care, usually in combination with OASI income. In one sense, then, the incentive to enter a long-term care facility follows from the difficulty of coordinating personal and public resources to sustain oneself at home. In a larger sense, it should be asked: Why is it so hard to obtain the services of a Medicaid home care provider and relatively so easy to enter a nursing home?

Medicaid's long-term care program seems to have been designed to support institutional care. Despite Congress's mandating provision of home care in 1970, there seems to be a desire manifested in the administration of the Medicaid program—either in the states, the federal government, or both—to constrain home care spending. Circumstances in both the home care and nursing home industries supported this purpose. Home care has been fragmented and delivered by nonprofit and governmental providers. Nursing home care has come to be dominated by proprietary providers who have entered the field in response to opportunities for profit. Not only providers, but services as well, have been more easily mobilized in the institutional arena. In the hope of spurring new construction to ensure bed availability, some states allowed generous profits to be made on nursing home real estate transactions in the years following enactment of Medicaid.

When Medicaid was legislated, there were relatively few organized providers of home care. Most were voluntary, nonprofit groups like visiting nurse associations or public units like branches of county health departments. No evidence of the existence of either mid- or large-size proprietary home care providers can be found. Many individuals, such as private duty nurses and companions, provided home care as independent contractors; small agencies to furnish such workers could be found in many cities. In the years since the passage of Medicaid, some organized providers of in-home services have become large enough to attain national visibility. Homemakers–Upjohn is one example. Until recently, proprietary home care agencies could be reimbursed by Medicare or Medicaid only if licensed by the state in which they operate. By 1975, only sixteen states had done so.[49] Pressures from proprietary providers, desires to "deregulate," and hopes to expand home care availability have led to repeal of the state licensing requirement.

Not only were home care providers badly organized as a lobbying force and lacking in the ability to identify and serve (and perhaps mobilize) populations in need of care, but home care suffered the further weakness of being difficult to organize on behalf of individual patients in need. In part, this follows from some of the same reasons why home care providers were difficult to bring together as a lobbying force. Home care providers typically were (and are) small organizations, each providing only some home care services for some of the people in need who resided in a fairly small geographic area. Disabled older people living at home frequently require a complex set of goods, income support, and services delivered by many types of trained and untrained individual providers and by public agencies. In only a very small number of communities in this country are all needed services available today; when available, they are still difficult to organize. Several promising administrative devices have been explored in recent years to attempt to overcome fragmentation.[50] A related difficulty faced by home care in past years cannot be ignored. As physicians became increasingly reluctant to visit patients at home, the setting of medical care for the chronically ill elderly shifted increasingly to the acute care hospital, chronic care hospital, and the nursing home. Recent developments in the use of nurse practitioners and physician assistants may do much to decentralize long-term care once again.[51]

Below the logistical difficulty of coordinating home care services, and the funding under Medicaid of established institutional care lie more fundamental explanations for the preference in this country for allocating public funds to institutional long-term care.

A first explanation follows from a desire to control utilization and spending. Home care, preferred by the elderly may be an attractive benefit. Many older— and not so old—persons might desire the regular help of a homemaker (whose tasks resemble those of a servant), especially if publicly paid. It can be hard to decide appropriate levels of help for a given person and to adjust those levels from month to month as patient needs change. Further, it is feared that help currently provided by family members and other informal supports would be displaced. Some family members might tire of the job of providing care and thus fall back on a public service. Others might resent their own continued efforts when their neighbors receive publicly provided substitutes. Allocation of public services in a fashion that would encourage families to continue providing care without appearing to be arbitrary or capricious could be a difficult task. Total utilization could consequently be hard to control.

By contrast, long-term care that emphasizes institutional services appears to offer a number of advantages to public payors. Total utilization can be restricted to equal the number of beds built or licensed. The type of care is itself relatively unattractive, feared, and stigmatizing.[52] It is unattractive to many older Americans in part because it entails a loss of control over such daily activities as when to eat or wake up. This loss can be particularly resented because it often comes at a time of loss of control in other spheres due to reduced income, mobility, and other factors. In addition, many nursing homes are unpleasant; some are monstrous. Entry into the nursing home is feared by some older citizens because it is perceived, often with justification, as the last step before the grave. Entry is stigmatizing to those who see the nursing home as the successor to the alms-house—the site of residence of the improvident or unworthy.

Payment for medical services in long-term care facilities has another origin. Funding for chronically ill or convalescing patients extruded from acute care hospitals follows in part from medical insurance principles of paying for those services thought to have a low and unpredictable chance of being needed but which are costly when required. It has been realized increasingly that little in the health care field adheres to these principles. Utilization often is predictable or manipulable by providers or patients; consequently, frequency of use may rise above levels predicted by skilled actuaries. Nursing home care is no exception. Another reason for funding institutional skilled and intermediate care is that they were thought to be cheaper substitutes for institutional care in hospitals and skilled nursing homes, respectively. Home care has been promoted by some as a less costly substitute for nursing home care; questions about the savings realized by past substitutions have made legislators and administrators wary of promises of new cost reductions.

The emphasis on institutional care in public programs also follows from their medical thrust. Skilled and intermediate care facilities reimbursed under Medicare and Medicaid are designed for patients with substantial medical problems. Home care funding under Medicare is similarly a short-term, medically related benefit. Only Medicaid is permitted to pay for a wide range of home care services. Its low rates of spending, noted above, testify to the states' probable views that socially oriented services in the home are less important to fund than medically related services in institutions.

The medical emphasis of nursing homes initially appeared to be a welcome alternative to the nonmedical, disorganized, and often inadequate patterns of boarding home and adult foster care that had been common until the 1950s and perhaps until the early 1960s.[53] (And which, to an unfortunate extent, persist today. Witness both the large numbers of older persons killed annually in hotel and boarding home fires, and the poor quality of life in many nonmedical boarding homes.) Nursing supervision may have promoted more responsible care of very dependent older persons.

It seems that the present pattern of long-term nursing home care for this nation's elderly was firmly reinforced by the passage of the Medicaid legislation in 1965. At that time, little concrete evidence of the argued evils of nursing home care for the elderly had become visible to legislators. Little of the pressure for deinstitutionalization that has arisen in related sectors—care of the retarded, juvenile delinquents, and adult criminals as well as other incarcerated groups—seems to have been applied to the problems of the elderly during the hurried deliberations on the Medicaid legislation.

A useful parallel to the need to provide noninstitutional care for the disabled elderly had appeared in the exodus from mental hospitals. Indeed, the

Community Mental Health Center Act of 1962 did appear to signal increased federal interest in noninstitutional care of a group whose needs closely paralleled those of the frail elderly. For a number of reasons, this parallel was not visible to Congress in 1965. New medications had been largely responsible for permitting deinstitutionalization of many mental hospital residents, and no similar opportunity was present in the case of the elderly. Further, it may have been clear to some in Congress that nursing homes would need increased funding to care for many of those whose discharge from mental hospitals only meant reinstitutionalization in nursing homes. Had the horrors of other institutions and the perils of deinstitutionalization from mental hospitals been documented and made visible to legislators, they might have affected the Medicaid legislation itself. But, as Vladeck states:

> The history of public policy toward nursing homes is largely a by-product of broader social welfare legislation, but in a tangential fashion. Recounting that history is like describing the opening of the American West from the perspective of the mules; they were certainly there, and the epochal events were certainly critical to the mules, but hardly anyone was paying very much attention to them at the time.[54]

Another explanation for the emphasis on institutional funding may follow from a desire to serve those most in need in what is perceived to be the more efficient site. Patients most in need of long-term care may be viewed as those requiring the most help. Some evidence exists that these are the persons likeliest to be cheaper to care for in institutions.[55] This follows from the efficiency of organizing such services in a common site and perhaps from the lower standard of living that many institutions provide.

Given the extent of dissatisfaction with nursing homes in this country today, and the seeming attractiveness of home care as an alternative, why have the advocates of home care fared so poorly? Advocates have not been able to bring to bear on Congress a concentrated lobbying force. The frail or medically unstable disabled older person can only with difficulty act as an effective self-advocate. Further, although perhaps 25 percent of older Americans will live in a nursing home before they die, and most say they fear or dislike the prospect, older persons who do not yet need long-term care do not seem to have been able or willing to invest a great deal of their political assets in improved long-term care. As Binstock[56] and Hudson[57] have argued, the elderly and their allies have been unable to secure enactment of legislation to reduce the severe imbalance in quality of life that exists between those older Americans who are well-off and healthy, and those who are very old, poor, dependent, ill, and alone. They have been far more successful in gaining higher social security payments. This behavior may perhaps be explained in part by self-interest and in part by denial of the prospect of (much feared) dependence. Finally, those who care for the disabled elderly may themselves be old, frail, and ill. This contrasts with the position of parents and others who vigorously advocate better programs for the developmentally disabled.

A second set of obstacles to increased home care funding lies in the dissatisfaction with long-term care generally. Early evidence in support of these suspicions has already appeared.[58] In recent years in Washington (and perhaps for some time to come), it has been difficult to secure an objective assessment of home care's merits and liabilities. It is likely that a similar state of affairs is current in such other areas as welfare reform and improved public housing.

Third, the fear that problems that have been associated with nursing home care will spill over to home care should be viewed within a larger legislative context. This begins with the interest in devising a national health insurance program (for acute care only) and the comparative disinterest in long-term care. It continues with suspicions that the elderly already receive more than their fair share of federal funds.[59] And it concludes within the perceived national mood of tax and spending limits. Seemingly, it is feared that the costs of new home care benefits would be unpredictable and uncontrollable.

NOTES TO CHAPTER 2

1. Judith LaVor, "Long-term Care: A Challenge to Service Systems," rev. ed., (Washington, D.C.: Office of the Assistant Secretary for Planning and Evaluation, DHEW, April 1977). (Photo-offset), app. A.

2. Three examples are: Council on Wage and Price Stability, *The Complex Puzzle of Rising Health Care Costs* (Washington: Executive Office of the President, December 1976); David Mechanic, "Approaches to Controlling the Costs of Medical Care; Short-range and Long-range Alternatives," *New England Journal of Medicine* 298, no. 5 (2 February 1978): 249–54; Comptroller General of the United States, "History of the Rising Costs of the Medicare and Medicaid Programs and Attempts to Control These Costs: 1966–1975" (Washington, D.C.: General Accounting Office, 11 February 1976).

3. Health Policy Group, Commonwealth of Massachusetts, "Health Care Expenditures in Massachusetts: 1978 Update," a White Paper (Boston: Office of State Health Planning, Massachusetts Department of Public Health, 9 June 1978). (Multilith); Department of Health, Education and Welfare, "Control Medicaid Cost Increases for Expensive Institutional Long-term Care," *Memorandum for July 14, 1978 Briefing, Major Initiative: Long-term Care/Community Services*, app. 6; Marcia B. Cohen, "Long-term Care and Cost Control: A Critical Analysis, *Health and Social Work* 4, no. 1, (February 1979): 61–88.

4. For sources, see notes to Table 2–11.

5. Comprehensive reviews of the costs of long-term care discourse frequently on data problems. See, for example, Congressional Budget Office, *Long-term Care: Actuarial Cost Estimates* (Washington, D.C.: Government Printing Office, August 1977); Commonwealth of Massachusetts, *Report of*

the Long-term Task Force (Boston: Office of State Health Planning, August 1977). (Mimeo.)

6.　Robert M. Gibson and Daniel R. Waldo, "National Health Expenditures, 1980," *Health Care Financing Review* 3, no. 1 (September 1981): Table 6A.

7.　See, for example, Claire Townsend, *Old Age: The Last Segregation* (New York: Grossman, 1971), pp. 133–35; also, Donald P. Kent, "Aging – Fact or Fancy," *The Gerontologist* 5, no. 2 (June 1955): 51–56.

8.　Robert Moroney, *The Family and the State: Considerations for Social Policy* (London: Longman, 1976), p. 56.

9.　Robert Morris, "Family Responsibility: Implications of Recent Demographic and Service Trends for a Natural Helping System," (Waltham, Mass.: Levinson Policy Institute, Brandeis University, Working Paper, November 1977); George L. Maddox, "Families as Context and Resource in Chronic Illness," in Sylvia Sherwood, ed., *Long-term Care: A Handbook for Researchers, Planners, and Providers* (Holliswood, N.Y.: Spectrum, 1975), pp. 317–48; Robert Benedict, "The Family and Long-term Care Alternatives" (Address to the 1978 Groves Conference on Marriage and the Family, Washington, D.C., April 28, 1978); National Center for Health Statistics, "Home Care for Persons Fifty-five and Over, United States, July 1966–June 1968," *Vital and Health Statistics*, ser. 10, no. 73 (July 1972), p. 8. See also the discussion by Elaine M. Brody, "The Aging and the Family," *Annals* of the American Academy of Political and Social Sciences, *Planning for the Elderly* 438 (July 1978): 13–26.

10.　Ethel Shanas, "The Family as a Social Support System in Old Age," (Paper presented at the 30th Annual Meeting of the Gerontological Society, San Francisco, November 1977).

11.　Alan Sager, et al., *Living at Home: The Role of Public and Informal Supports in Sustaining Disabled Older Americans* (Waltham, Mass.: Levinson Policy Institute, Brandeis University, May 1982).

12.　George L. Maddox, "Community and Home Care: United States and United Kingdom," in A.N. Exton–Smith and J. Grimley Evans, eds., *Care of the Elderly: Meeting the Challenge of Dependency* (New York: Grune and Stratton, 1977), pp. 147–60.

13.　National Center for Health Statistics, "Some Trends and Comparisons of United States Life-table Data: 1900–1971," U.S. Decennial Life Tables for 1969–71, vol. 1, no. 4 (Washington, D.C.: Government Printing Office, May 1975), Table 1; U.S. Bureau of the Census, *Statistical Abstract of the United States, 1977* (Washington, D.C.: Government Printing Office, 1977), Table 94.

14.　*Federal Council on the Aging, Annual Report to the President – 1976*, Washington, D.C.: Government Printing Office, 1977), pp. 23–31.

15.　Monroe Lerner, "When, Why and Where People Die," in Orville G. Brim, Jr., et al., eds., *The Dying Patient* (New York: Russell Sage Foundation, 1970), pp. 14–16.

16.　For a striking account, see Bernard Isaacs, Maureen Livingstone, and Yvonne Neville, *Survival of the Unfittest: A Study of Geriatric Patients in*

Glasgow (London: Routledge and Kegan Paul, 1972). See also, Elihu M. Gerson and Anselm L. Straus, "Time for Living: Problems in Chronic Illness Care," *Social Policy* 6, no. 3 (November–December 1975): 12–18.

17. Myron E. Wegman, "Health Departments: Then and Now," editorial, *American Journal of Public Health* 67, no. 10 (October 1977): 913–14.

18. U.S. Bureau of the Census, "Demographic Aspects of Aging and the Older Populations in the United States," *Current Population Statistics*, ser. P–23, no. 59 (Washington, D.C.: Government Printing Office, May 1976), Table 6–2.

19. William G. Bell, et al., *Community Care for the Elderly: An Alternative to Institutionalization* (Tallahassee, Florida: Program in Social Policy and the Aging, Florida State University, June 1971).

20. National Center for Health Statistics, "Marital Status and Living Arrangements Before Admission to Nursing and Personal Care Homes, United States, May–June 1964," *Vital and Health Statistics*, ser. 12, no. 12 (Washington, D.C.: Government Printing Office, May 1969), Table 2.

21. U.S. Bureau of the Census, *Statistical Abstract*, Table 46.

22. Herbert Gans, *The Urban Villagers* (New York: The Free Press, 1962) contains an account of the difficulties of large-scale relocation.

23. For discussion of this pattern, see Harold L. Wolensky and Charles N. Lebeaux, *Industrial Society and Social Welfare* (New York: Free Press, 1965), especially, pp. 77–79; also Maurice R. Stein, *The Eclipse of Community* (Princeton, N.J.: Princeton University Press, 1960), ch. 1.

24. U.S. Bureau of the Census, *Historical Statistics of the United States from Colonial Times to 1970*, ser. D–60 (Washington, D.C.: Government Printing Office, 1975). U.S. Bureau of the Census, *Statistical Abstract*, Table 632.

25. Marvin B. Sussman, "Family Life of Old People," in Robert Binstock and Ethel Shanas, eds., *Handbook of Aging and the Social Sciences* (New York: Van Nostrand, 1976), pp. 218–43, citing A. Chevan and J.H. Korson, "Living Arrangements of Widows in the United States and Israel," *Demography* 12: 505–18.

26. Bernice L. Neugarten, "Commentary," in A.N. Exton–Smith and J. Grimley, pp. 102–104.

27. U.S. Bureau of the Census, *Statistical Abstract*, Table 76. See also Judith Treas, "Family Support Systems for the Aged: Some Social and Demographic Considerations," *The Gerontologist* 17, no. 6 (December 1977): 486–91.

28. Philip Slater, *The Pursuit of Loneliness* (Boston: Beacon, 1970).

29. See, "25 Years for Health," *Cleveland Press*, May 16, 1941; Ivan Belknap and John G. Steinle, *The Community and Its Hospitals* (Syracuse, N.Y.: Syracuse University Press, 1963), pp. 9–10; and Michael M. Davis, *Clinics, Hospitals, and Health Centers* (New York: Harpers, 1929), p. 17.

30. E.H.L. Corwin, *The American Hospital* (New York: Commonwealth Fund, 1946), pp. 1, 7, citing a study by J.M. Toner, "Statistics of Regular Medical Associations and Hospitals of the United States: Section II," *Transactions of the American Medical Association*, 24 (1873): 314–33; U.S. Bureau of the Census, *Historical Statistics of the United States, Colonial*

Times to 1970, Part 1 sers. B–345 and B–346 (Washington, D.C.: Government Printing Office, September 1975).

31. Commission on Hospital Care, *Hospital Care in the United States*, (New York: Commonwealth Fund, 1947), pp. 43–51.
32. Corwin, pp. 9, 11.
33. Belknap and Steinle, p. 13.
34. George Rosen, "The Hospital: Historical Sociology of a Community Institution," in Eliot Friedson, ed., *The Hospital in Modern Society* (New York: Free Press, 1963), pp. 29–30.
35. Belknap and Steinle, pp. 9–10.
36. The following discussion draws heavily on Samuel Levey and Bernard A. Stotsky, "Nursing Homes in Massachusetts" (Massachusetts Research Institute, Inc., 1968), (Mimeo.) pp. 1–5; and on Robert M. Moroney and Norman R. Kurtz, "The Evolution of Long-Term Care Institutions," in Sherwood, especially pp. 81–89.
37. See Edwin Witte, *The Development of the Social Security Act* (Madison, Wis.: University of Wisconsin Press, 1963).
38. Monroe Lerner, "When, Why, and Where People Die," in Brim, Table 4.
39. U.S. Bureau of Census, *Statistical Abstract*, Table 163. L. Block, "Hospital and Other Institutional Facilities and Services, 1939," *Vital Statistics, Special Reports* 13, nos. 1–57 (Washington, D.C.: U.S. Bureau of the Census, 1942). The 1939 estimates of 1200 nursing homes and 25,000 residents may be low. Wrote Bigelow and Lombard, "In 1933, 'there were 435 nursing homes known to exist in the Commonwealth of Massachusetts, and the existence of others is suspected.'" (G.H. Bigelow and H.L. Lombard, *Cancer and Other Chronic Diseases in Massachusetts* (Boston: Houghton Mifflin, 1933), p. 69, cited in Levey and Stotsky, p. 5.) It seems clear that varying definitions of "nursing homes" were used. Alternatively, Massachusetts may simply have been well advanced in the provision of long-term care in "nursing homes."
40. Lerner, pp. 22–23.
41. Robert Kastenbaum and Sandra E. Candy, "The 4% Fallacy: A Methodological and Empirical Critique of Extended Care Facility Population Statistics," *International Journal of Aging and Human Development* 4, no. 1 (1973): 15–21. See also Harold J. Wershow, "The Four Percent Fallacy: Some Further Evidence and Policy Implications," *The Gerontologist* 16, no. 1, pt. 1 (1976): 52–55.
42. Office of Research and Statistics, Social Security Administration, *Compendium of National Health Expenditures Data* (Washington, D.C.: Government Printing Office, 1973), Table 6.
43. Robert J. Myers, *Medicare* (Homewood, Ill.: Irwin, 1970), pp. 40–41.
44. National Center for Health Statistics, "Chronic Illness Among Residents of Nursing and Personal Care Homes, United States, May–June 1964," *PHS Pub. no. 1000*, ser. 12, no. 7 (Washington, D.C.: Government Printing Office, 1967), cited in Moroney and Kurtz.
45. Office of Research and Statistics, Social Security Administration, *Compendium of National Health Expenditures Data* (Washington, D.C.: Government Printing Office, 1973), Table 6.

46. For careful summaries of these issues, see Comptroller General of the United States, "Report to the Congress: Home Health Care Benefits Under Medicare and Medicaid," Report B-164031 (3) (Washington, D.C.: General Accounting Office, July 9, 1974), pp. 16-18; also LaVor, p. 49.

47. National Center for Social Statistics, "Medicaid Statistics, Fiscal Year 1979," NCSS Report B-1 (Washington, D.C.: NCSS), Table 5.

48. Candace Mueller and Eileen Wolff, "Home Based Services," Title XX CASP Plans, Technical Note no. 10 (Washington, D.C.: Office of Assistant Secretary for Planning and Evaluation, DHEW, February 20, 1976). (Multilith.)

49. For a discussion of this issue, see Department of Health, Education, and Welfare, "Home Health Care: Report on the Regional Public Hearings" (Washington, D.C.: DHEW, October 29, 1975). (Multilith), especially pp. 40-42.

50. Dennis F. Beatrice, "Case Management: A Policy Option for Long-term Care," and James J. Callahan, Jr., "Single Agency Option for Long-term Care," in James J. Callahan, Jr. and Stanley S. Wallack, eds., *Reforming the Long-term Care System* (Lexington, Mass.: D.C. Heath, 1981), chs. 6 and 7.

51. Robert J. Master, et al., "A Continuum of Care for the Inner City: An Assessment of Its Benefits for Boston's Elderly and High-risk Populations," *New England Journal of Medicine* 302, no. 26 (June 26, 1980): 1434-40.

52. William G. Bell, *Community Care for the Elderly: An Alternative to Institutionalization* (Tallahassee, Fla.: Program in Social Policy and the Aging, Florida State University, June 1971).

53. See, for example, Pearl R. Roberts, "Human Warehouses: A Boarding Home Study," *American Journal of Public Health* 64, no. 3 (March 1974): 277-82.

54. Bruce C. Vladeck, *Unloving Care* (New York: Basic, 1980), p. 31.

55. General Accounting Office, "Home Health—The Need for a National Policy to Better Provide for the Elderly" (a Report to the Congress, HRD-78-19, December 30, 1977).

56. R.H. Binstock, "Interest Group Liberalism and the Politics of Aging," *The Gerontologist* 12, no. 3 (Autumn 1972): 265-80.

57. Robert B. Hudson, "The 'Graying' of the Federal Budget and Its Consequences for Old-age Policy," *The Gerontologist* 18, no. 5, Part 1 (October 1978): pp. 428-40.

58. U.S. Senate, Committee on Government Operations, Subcommittee on Federal Spending Practices, Efficiency, and Open Government, "Problems Associated with Home Health Agencies and Medicare Program in the State of Florida" (Washington, D.C.: Government Printing Office, August 1976); U.S. House of Representatives, Select Committee on Aging, "New York Home Care Abuse," Pub. no. 95-145 (Washington, D.C.: Government Printing Office, 1978).

59. See Hudson.

3 REFORM
Pressures and Barriers

From the standpoint of public payors, the major long-term care problem today is probably the high level and rate of increase in public spending. For the elderly and their families, the major problem is probably the profound institutional emphasis of that spending, along with dissatisfaction with the decency of care provided and the amount of care available. The ideal long-term care system would control the rate of increase in spending while expanding eligibility and allowing something approaching freedom of choice between in-home and nursing home care.

That system will be difficult to achieve. Many fear that improved noninstitutional benefits will seldom substitute for existing nursing home services, but rather would be incremental. This may be entirely appropriate, since many persons are not being adequately served today, but it would cost money.

At the other extreme, there are several candidates for worst long-term care system. One would be federal de-funding for long-term benefits. Another would be a gradual reduction in age- and sex-adjusted real per capita long-term care spending. Yet another would be to entrench the existing institution-based scheme by building more beds to accommodate the growing numbers of frail citizens without funding care in these beds at humane levels.

Long-term care reformers have aimed to expand eligibility, range of services covered, and spending on home care. They have sought financing and organizational reforms that will help make home care more efficient and capable of serving even those considerably disabled citizens who today are often obliged to enter institutions. Opponents to reform have worried about the cost of improving noninstitutional benefits.

THE RANGE OF REFORMS

The advocates of increased home care funding have not been silent, nor have they been without allies in the U.S. Congress. In the 94th Congress of the mid-1970s, for example, over eighty bills were filed to expand home care benefits or eligibility.[1] This total includes only legislation that would specifically fund home care and excludes bills that would make more money for home care available indirectly through such general approaches as raising the ceiling on federal spending under the Title XX social services block grant. While the volume of proposed legislation has fluctuated from year to year, congressional interest in promoting noninstitutional long-term care appears to have remained high. These reforms would, to varying degrees, implement the fine noninstitutional intentions and goals already legally and publicly declared in Medicaid, Title XX, and the Older Americans Act.[2]

Several types of incremental reforms have been embodied in proposed legislation. Most would make possible public payment for noninstitutional, nonmedical, nontechnical long-term services of the sorts not widely available today. Complementary improvements to more flexibly finance and organize a broadened range of home care benefits have been suggested in some instances.

One straightforward incremental approach has been to improve Medicare's in-home benefit and make this a true long-term program. Medicare's near-universal entitlement and lack of means test make this a strategy congenial to many. Minor successes have been achieved here, with the recent removal of the 100-visit limit under both Parts A and B of Medicare, and the elimination of the prior hospitalization requirement for use of Part A. These changes should mean that older citizens who have not been hospitalized will find it slightly easier to use Medicare-funded home care benefits. Using Part A, they no longer have to pay the deductibles or coinsurance that are required for Part B benefits.

The impact of this reform appears to have been minor, because the skilled nursing and homeboundedness requirements for Medicare in-home benefits have been retained and home health aides are still prohibited from providing other than incidental personal care. Consequently, Medicare's home care benefit remains very largely a short-term convalescent one. One change that might have modified Medicare was the addition of occupational therapy to skilled nursing (and speech therapy) as a primary service engendering eligibility for other services. Chronically disabled homebound citizens in need of occupational therapy could then have qualified for long-term home care. Occupational therapy was retained as a qualifying service for only about one year before succumbing to the budget cuts of the Ominous Budget Reconciliation Act (OBRA) of 1981.

One recent proposal introduced in the 97th Congress by Senator Hatch would improve eligibility for Medicare's in-home benefits by making the need for homemaker care a qualifying service if the person in need would be forced to enter an institution without homemaker care. Citizens eligible for Medicare-funded home care only because they needed a homemaker's help would be forced to pay half the cost of that help.[3] One aim embodied in this approach is to expand the range of publicly paid or subsidized noninstitutional services only for those who would otherwise be likely to require publicly supported nursing home care. This has been a popular theme in long-term care reform since at least the mid-1970s. The requirement of the 50 percent copayment reflects a fear that use of the benefit would be difficult to control administratively, so financial disincentives are thought necessary. Any such copayment would be grossly unfair unless it were scaled to income. Those most in need of home care tend to be living alone and in poverty.

Interestingly, the same OBRA that eliminated occupational therapy as a primary qualifying service under Medicare has authorized the secretary of the Department of Health and Human Services (HHS) to waive many of the requirements under Medicaid's home care program. States would be permitted to provide a greater number of in-home benefits on the condition that total long-term care spending not be affected.[4]

Section 2176 waiver authority evolved generally from the reform set out in a bill introduced in the 96th Congress (H.R. 6194) by Representatives Pepper and Waxman. The way in which the waiver authority is being implemented by the Department of HHS is not yet clear. Regulations for administering the waiver appear to require very strong proof by the states that expanded in-home benefits are not leading to an increase in long-term care spending.[5]

Wulsin has criticized the stringency of the regulatory language and claims it may deter states from vigorously employing waivers Congress intended to encourage. He contrasts the detailed regulations to implement Section 2176 with the national administration's generally nonregulatory stance.[6] Apparently, fears of difficult-to-control home care spending engender efforts at tight regulation of public benefits for the elderly even from those who would customarily oppose such efforts. A private industry is not being regulated here.

Surprisingly, and perhaps somewhat schizophrenically, the administration aims to employ Section 2176 waivers to encourage home care for individuals who are now being institutionalized simply because of the "deeming" rule, under which a relative's income is deemed available to a disabled person if the two live together, thereby blocking Medicaid eligibility. Deeming is unattractive politically only when it is costly. In November 1981, for example, the president became aware of the case of a child who was expensively hospitalized because of the deeming requirement. Subsequently, in addition to the Section 2176 waiver authority for regularizing selective relaxation of the deeming rule, the Health Care Financing Administration plans to establish a special national board to review individual cases.[7] This ad hoc approach avoids confronting the central issue of investigating the design and cost of an affordable and generally available public program of noninstitutional care for the disabled.

The Section 2176 approach resembles the "diversion" strategy that has guided the research reported in this book. A wider range of home care benefits are made available, especially to persons who would otherwise have entered nursing homes, in the hope of expanding freedom of choice over setting of care without increasing total spending.

One alternative to financing reform under Medicare has been proposed by Senator Packwood. A bill introduced in the 97th Congress, S. 861, would establish a separate trust fund under a new Title XXI of the Social Security Act. All federal noninstitutional long-term care funds would be placed in this trust fund, and a broader range of services would be financed. This would help overcome fragmentation. Presently, this legislation would call only for a demonstration program for six years in a number of states.

Much of the interest in improving federal noninstitutional long-term care has for some time been channeled in the direction of demonstration projects. These have attempted in various ways to compare the costs and effects of improving home care eligibility, services, or administration. Clear-cut findings have generally been lacking. A new round of demonstrations, the "channeling" projects, is now being attempted. These projects feature case management, an organizational reform under which prospective home care recipients are comprehensively assessed at a single intake agency, a professional care plan is devised, and arrangements are made with noninstitutional providers to implement the plan. Case management can be thought of as an organizational parallel to financing consolidations such as those entertained in the proposed Title XXI legislation. Consolidated long-term care financing would assist a case management agency. One eligibility determination would be followed by centralized capacity to determine and arrange for appropriate care. Much of the fragmentation of the current home care system would be overcome. More broadly, the case management agency could serve as a single entry point for all prospective recipients of publicly funded long-term care, institutional and in-home. An appropriate setting for care could be negotiated and suitable services could be arranged. If properly administered, appropriately controlled, and adequately funded, a case management agency could be held responsible for spending wisely a consolidated budget for a community's long-term care needs.[8] An alternative approach would be to place both the case management and home care service delivery functions in a single agency.[9]

More sweeping still is the proposal to combine both forms of long-term care with acute care. Funds to pay for all would be allotted to a "social/health maintenance organization" (S/HMO), originated by Robert Morris.[10] Capitation funds for each S/HMO enrollee would be drawn from existing third-party payors. The S/HMO would be responsible for determining which services were necessary, providing them, and paying for them. Since health maintenance is most useful to a chronically ill or disabled population, because problems which need to be stabilized are already identified, the S/HMO could "invest" some of its resources in preventing problems from exacerbating. Hopefully, some expensive hospitalizations could be prevented or shortened, and the money saved could be applied to pay for the earlier investment in in-home support care. This sort of sweeping organizational innovation may well be required to help control both acute and long-term care spending on the elderly in ways that do not harm affected citizens.

It is entirely possible that, in the absence of thoughtful reform in long-term care financing and organization (either alone or in concert with acute care reform) our society will face an alternative long-term care future that is as unattractive as it is likely. Funds to care for the growing numbers of older citizens who would be expected to need long-term care in coming decades will probably not be forthcoming. Age- and sex-adjusted per capita long-term care spending can be expected to fall steadily, as fiscal and economic problems persist, as the number in need grows, and as we are dissatisfied with the cost and quality of institutional care but balk at the possible costs of adequate and decent alternatives.

We may retain our institutional focus even though unwilling adequately to fund needed care. Abuses of the rights of nursing home patients and thefts of public funds may offer states an excuse for continuing to underpay the generally for-profit nursing homes. Owners may continue to claim that they cannot provide decent care at current Medicaid reimbursement levels. Unable to bear the costs even of existing beds, states may refuse to allow construction of new nursing home beds. The average institutional resident will become older, sicker, and in greater need. Perceived decency and adequacy of care may decline further. Families will be forced to make greater efforts to care for elderly relatives at home, even without adequate publicly funded in-home supports. Families will suffer strains, and those in need of care will suffer harm that could have been prevented. Rates of hospitalization may increase as a result.

If Congress and the Department of HHS could be more confident about the comparative effectiveness and cost of home and nursing home care, they would find it easier to design and defend a coherent long-term care policy. Long-term care may be an area of national policy in which better information could make a difference. Few oppose decent and adequate care for the elderly out of meanness; many worry over the costs of effective noninstitutional services.

ADVANCING ARGUMENTS FOR PUBLICLY FUNDED HOME CARE

Considering the small amount of money spent on noninstitutional long-term care, it is not surprising to find a large number of vocal advocates of increased public funding for such care.[11] Observing both past trends and the evidence suggesting that the need by the elderly for long-term care is going to grow in coming years, these advocates have put forth several arguments in favor of greater funding for noninstitutional alternatives. While this book investigates home care as an alternative to the nursing home, this writer believes that many of the arguments for home care also support such other alternatives as adult foster care, day care, and a variety of congregate and other intermediate housing arrangements. From this point, the terms "institution" and "nursing home" are used interchangeably unless special distinctions are made. Thus, "nursing homes" also refer to nonmedical rest homes, boarding homes, or homes for the aged, as well as such more intensive centers of care as the rehabilitation or chronic disease hospitals.

Some proponents have asserted that problems of decency, effectiveness, and cost in long-term care can be ameliorated by increased home care funding. They argue that home care can be both better and cheaper for many older people than the nursing home care they would otherwise receive. If this is true, they argue further, legislators should at the very least be indifferent to where long-term care for these people is delivered, and permit older patients to choose the site of their care, assuming that outcomes are not worsened by the process of choosing.

Some definitions will be useful. "Decency" refers to the process of care—whether patients are treated humanely, compassionately, and with dignity. (The word "quality" concerns the technical competence of services; comparative quality of in-home and nursing home care is not discussed here.) "Effectiveness" refers only to outcomes of care—how similar populations cared for at home and in institutions compare in their morbidity and mortality rates, in changes in their level of independent functioning in activities of daily living, in their psychosocial functioning and morale, and in their satisfaction with how adequately and how well compensatory services are performed.

Decency

Nursing homes have frequently been denounced for lacking humaneness of care. Among the reported types of abuse of patients are beatings, torture, intimidation, overdrugging, deprivation of freedom, inadequate or dangerous food, insufficient heat and ventilation, filth and squalor, and lack of fire precautions.[12]

It is impossible to know just how widespread these abuses are, but they appear to be common. Because so little home care is provided in this country, particularly to people as dependent as typical nursing home residents, and because evidence would be very difficult to compile, it is difficult to decide if home care is or would be open to the same sorts of patient abuse.

It can be argued, on one hand, that home care recipients would find it easier than would nursing home residents to change providers if they suffered harm. At home, a phone call will yield a change in provider; in the nursing home case, the patient must be relocated. This is often difficult and sometimes dangerous. On the other hand, abuses may be easier to detect in a nursing home; one family visitor or vigorous state inspector may bring to light a collective problem. Also, an effective nursing home administrator is able to supervise employees with less difficulty than the manager of decentralized home care services. Finally, if a home care recipient's family or a paid helper of an isolated person is committing the abuse, the patient may lack anyone to whom to appeal.[13]

Possibly, abuse of dependent older patients is a generic problem, difficult to solve by manipulating the site of care. Certainly, reports of abuse of children, mental patients, and the frail elderly are common. These citizens have a problem in common: they are weak and depend on others who are sometimes not able, trained, or motivated to provide good care. Usually, formal providers of care to the dependent are poorly trained and poorly paid. They face a difficult, dirty, and often unpleasant job. Those they care for are not always pleasant and are sometimes even abusive. Rewards either for good direct service or good supervision are difficult to provide.

Despite the weak and mixed evidence on the comparative decency of home and institutional care today, home care advocates have made the argument that a more balanced long-term care system, one which made more available the option of home care, would induce providers in both settings to compete in part by monitoring decency carefully.

It may be, however, that those who attempt to buttress claims of the desirability of home care by pointing to decency problems of nursing homes are paying insufficient attention to generic problems in assuring the quality of long-term care. The history of long-term care policy in this country offers several examples of spasmodic change produced by reaction to visible evil, absent careful consideration of the value of alternatives proposed. Advocates of home care should be more mindful of both past events in the evolution of institutional long-term care for the elderly and recent changes in the long-term care of other groups of disabled people. Historically, it should be recalled that mental hospitals and nursing homes were themselves designed and funded in response to identified abuses of the forms of care that preceded them.[14]

Proponents of home care should also bear in mind recent difficulties encountered in the course of deinstitutionalization of mental hospital patients. Noninstitutional care may be promoted by some only as an excuse to close expensive facilities; "community alternatives" are often not established in sufficient numbers. In the mental hospital case, it is by no means clear that the deinstitutionalization movement has yielded any net benefit to those discharged or to those denied admission under new policies.[15]

Despite these obstacles, decent care can and must be achieved in both home and institution. Kane and others describe a caregiving team that both improves the conditions of patients' lives and saves money. [16] A Veterans Administration committee has described a number of measures to enhance patients' rights and dignity. These include a place to be alone; a stable environment; an environment that encourages choice about time to go to sleep, what to wear, and several other areas.[17] Barney has called for increased family and community visiting and other involvement in nursing homes as means of improving decency.[18] Visibility of family and visitors doubtless influences the quality of all forms of service—from public education to hospital, nursing home, and home care. Friedman and others present practical steps toward improvement of in-home services.[19]

Effectiveness

The effects or outcomes of long-term care are at least as difficult to measure as the decency of that care. Issues of major concern in this study—the comparative costs of home and institutional care and who should design plans of care—would be far easier to resolve if outcomes could conveniently be measured. The difficulty of gauging the outcomes of care of comparable populations in the two settings impedes efforts to decide what services are necessary and who should allocate them. Costs of in-home and institutional care are difficult to compare because if outcomes are not easily measured they cannot easily be controlled. This difficulty is further compounded by the practical and ethical problems of controlling for the characteristics of the members of the two samples. This triad of problems makes it difficult to establish benchmarks by which to learn confidently the relative benefits and costs of home and institutional care. As a result, this study has pursued a variety of indirect pointers to the effectiveness of long-term care. Appropriate care planning is particularly important in the absence of good outcome measures.

Proponents of home care sometimes argue that nursing home care is relatively ineffective in that admission to the nursing home is associated with mortality rates that appear very high.[20] Kasl, after a careful review of this literature, has argued that little is known about whether nursing home admission is the cause or correlate of higher mortality rates.[21] He notes that most studies of "unexpected" mortality at nursing home admission fail to control for the age, physical frailty, or medical instability of nursing home entrants. It is possible that a regression to agnosticism is taking place. Outcomes of nursing home care are unclear. They may not be as bad as often feared. On the home care side, reanalysis by Bigot and his associates[22] of findings and data generated by Nielsen and others[23] suggests that early evidence indicating a negative impact of home care on mortality should be discounted because of methodological uncertainties in those early analyses.

This climate of agnosticism has been reinforced by the failure to develop a large set of reliable evidence on the comparative effects of home and institutional care. Mitchell's study of outcomes of long-term care in three Veterans Administration settings is a valuable exception.[24] While patients in this study could not be randomly assigned to treatment sites, nonequivalent control groups and multivariate techniques were used to control for patient characteristics.

Holding other variables constant, home care patients typically enjoyed greater improvement than did patients in two types of nursing homes. Improvement was measured by an index of functional health status.

Another carefully designed study, by Katz and others,[25] considers only the effect of home care. Half of a group of older patients discharged from a short-term rehabilitation hospital received home care services from a visiting nurse association. After two years, a major finding was that "the avoidance of deterioration was . . . the most consistent favorable effect, and that even this result could be achieved only with the younger and less disabled patients." This constitutes a cautious endorsement of home care.

Despite the methodological uncertainties mentioned earlier, the work by Nielsen and her associates also stands as an important effort to learn the effects of home care. Through a randomized trial, those receiving home care enjoyed higher levels of contentment, fewer long-term care admissions, and fewer long-term care patient-days than those who did not.[26]

Why are the effects of long-term care so difficult to measure? Some of the major difficulties in gauging outcome in long-term care can be introduced by contrast with acute care. In acute care, measured events are clearer and it is probably easier to relate interventions to changes in patient status. In acute care, mortality, morbidity, and pain are outcomes to avoid. Identified goods, services, and techniques aim to forestall or prevent these outcomes.

The goals and desired outcomes of long-term care are by no means as clear. Good health and restoration of full functional ability are not possible in many cases. Often, the goal is to slow a decline, but no minimum expectable rate of decline has been established for most conditions. Frequently, chronically ill patients suffer from more than one problem, making a medical, functional, or psychological prognosis difficult.

The relation of caring services to outcomes poses a particularly difficult problem. In both nursing homes and home care, most services are nonmedical. The great preponderance of effort is devoted to compensating or substituting for deficits in functional ability (to perform activities of daily living like bathing, dressing, and the like) and in such instrumental activities as shopping, cooking, and cleaning. Measures of functional ability, discussed in Chapter 4, are used to *predict* the need for such compensating services. But changes recorded by functional ability measures usually cannot be expected to *reflect* the effectiveness of these compensatory services. That is, an older woman's functional independence, for example, does not improve because a home health aide bathes her daily. Rather, she is cleaner.

Thus, measures of outcome of long-term care must attend to personal and household cleanliness, personal mobility and nutritional levels, and the like. Some services may be devoted to preventing, slowing, or reversing medical, functional, or psychosocial deterioration. Reliable and valid measures exist in some of these domains of well-being but must be developed in others.

In the study designed to explore questions raised in this book, Sager and others found that fully 81.3 percent of the hours of actual in-home help received by a sample of about one hundred disabled older citizens of the Commonwealth of Massachusetts were devoted to compensating for functional deficits.[27]

Comprehensive assessment of outcomes in all of these domains is a difficult, costly, and time-consuming job. Instruments to do this job are being developed. When available, these devices will prove to be invaluable benchmarks for assessing the effectiveness of long-term care.[28] For the present, the lack of good measures of the outcomes of long-term care combined with our desire to learn the cost of "comparable" care in homes and institutions obliges that thoughtful consideration be given to the *process* of planning long-term care.

Costs

The total cost of a home care program is the product of the number of people using it and the average cost of care received by those helped. Because at the time the present study was designed it appeared that relatively good estimates were available of the size of the population needing home care but not receiving it, and relatively poor estimates were available of the average cost per person of home care, it was decided to learn more about the latter.[29] Although this study concentrates on cost of care for individuals and pays little attention to system costs, Chapter 7 will consider the effect on system costs of various types of diversion of nursing home residents to home care.

Four methods have been used to compare costs. One customary approach to comparing the costs of home and institutional care has been to introduce a new home care service, measure its costs, and then compare these with the savings thought to be realized by shortening or eliminating institutional stays. The sample serves, in a sense, as its own control. This approach has been applied to home care as a substitute for various types of nursing home and hospital care. Studies that take this approach usually show that the introduction of an in-home benefit leads to a net reduction in cost of care. Such results have complemented the arguments of those who propose increased public home care funding on grounds of quality and effectiveness.

Among the compilations of data that take this approach are those of the home care programs of Blue Cross of Greater Philadelphia and Associated Hospital Services of New York.[30] Both of these programs have been well run, but neither was designed principally to obtain data on comparative long-term care costs. This is common. As LaVor and Callender note, "Most of the available literature on cost effectiveness of home care has resulted from the application of certain criteria to already existing programs that were not designed to be re-search studies."[31]

It appears that this first method presents at least five problems: 1) Seldom is any evidence offered of reduction in nursing home costs or even of reduction in the rate of increase of those costs. Nursing home beds emptied may be quickly filled. If so, is this new use marginal and discretionary, or does it represent a legitimate demand for beds that are in too-short supply? 2) The question of whether the patients receiving home care would really have required the dura-tion of institutional care thought "saved" is often addressed inadequately. The assumption is usually made by a professional on the scene that a given patient would have required n days of institutional care without assessing whether other professionals would have made the same assumption. 3) The home care benefit investigated is usually for short-term recuperation from an acute illness. Seldom is funding included for even short-term custodial care in the home. The costs of these services are therefore usually excluded. 4) Savings from institutional care foregone are taken at the average cost of institutional care. If these patients were less ill than the average resident of the institutions concerned, the real cost of nursing home care for these patients would be below average. It often seems difficult to know whether all the substitute services are needed, or whether other services would have been appropriate. As presented, these studies seldom provide adequate descriptions of their patient samples. This information would help answer some of the questions just raised.

This first approach to learning the cost of a home alternative seeks to learn the savings that accrue from avoiding institutionalization. A second common method, a mirror image of the first, has been to examine the individual and pro-gram costs of removing from nursing homes those "inappropriately institutional-ized." Here, too, the sample serves as its own control. Regrettably, the word "inappropriately" is not always tightly defined. In some reports, it refers to pa-tients who do not require some or all of the services in their facility or at their level of care; in others, it signifies patients who could be cared for more cheaply in other settings. Further, it sometimes means all patients wrongly placed, receiving too much or too little care; at other times, only those receiving too much care. Methods of determining who is wrongly placed vary with these definitions.[32]

Estimates by different methods in different places and at different levels of institutional care reveal a wide variation in the proportion of patients consid-ered wrongly placed. A useful compilation by the Congressional Budget Office identifies estimates that 6 percent to 76 percent of various institutional popula-tions are inappropriately placed.[33]

The present study adopts some of the methods embodied in these two ap-proaches to cost comparisons. It seeks to learn what proportion of certain new nursing home residents are being "inappropriately institutionalized" in that they could be cared for more cheaply at home. Therefore, it must face up to the problems just identified. This task is attempted in Chapter 4.

A third method for comparing the costs of home and institutional care involves a natural experiment, using retrospective selection of matched samples. Here, clients of home care agencies are matched with residents of nursing homes who have similar medical, functional, psychosocial, demographic, and environmental characteristics.

Retrospective matching suffers from practical and conceptual problems. Matching is difficult to accomplish when the patients served in the two settings are generally dissimilar. This seems to have been the experience of a recent project in Minnesota.[34] Reports by the Congressional Budget Office and by Smyer, however, argue that there does exist a group in the community that is similar to a fraction of institutionalized patients.[35]

Greenberg has recently asserted that if it is possible to model the basis on which patients ultimately received care in two settings, it is possible to adjust for the different characteristics of the two groups.[36] When this can be done, it promises to be a useful tool in comparing the costs of long-term care in different settings.

These three approaches to comparing costs have generally been regarded in long-term care as second-best substitutes for controlled experiments. The best way to measure the costs of different services is usually thought to be a prospective randomized clinical trial (RCT). Cochrane has offered several arguments in favor of this approach, which would apply the controlled experiment to health and social services.[37]

When the RCT can be used, it is the most persuasive of any comparative evaluation of cost. In long-term care, however, the RCT has two distinct liabilities. One is that sample size must be considerable to permit measurement of the effects of all the variables being manipulated—sites, types, quantities, and providers of services. This is true also of any facet of acute care if its impact on health status is indeed small.[38] It may be true of long-term care for the same reason. Moreover, in long-term care, effects themselves are relatively difficult to measure or are conceptually imprecise: contrast morale and functional ability with mortality.

The need to control for secular changes in the status of recipients of long-term care probably tends to increase desired sample size. If the number of variables being manipulated under any one cost comparison could be limited, needed sample size would shrink accordingly. Regrettably, the number of variables is difficult to limit. Patient characteristics—medical, functional, demographic, psychosocial, and environmental—all appear to influence needed services. In addition, they interact. Finally, if the number of variables is successfully restricted in the interest of controlling sample size, the generalizability of the findings is likely to be restricted as well.

The second type of liability of the RCT in long-term care lies in the ethical hazard of requesting informed consent for experimental manipulation of care, and in the practical difficulty of securing that consent. The traditional RCT begins with: (1) an accepted treatment for a problem; (2) an alternative; and (3) evidence for suspecting that (2) is better than (1). In some cases, belief in the accepted treatment is so strong that innovators find it hard even to win the right to test their alternative. Witness Fisher's efforts to gain the right to measure the effectiveness of more conservative treatments for breast cancer.[39]

In other instances, such as in many areas of long-term care, the factors mentioned above are lacking. While there seems to be no validated treatment for individual problems, there are accepted modes of practice. Most publicly supported long-term care is delivered in nursing homes. This site appears to be the safest, in conventional medical respects, inasmuch as the traditional devices of medical intervention—trained workers and sophisticated machinery—can, in some circumstances, be brought to bear sooner. In comparing the costs of care in different sites, it would probably be desirable to manipulate inputs—types, quantities, and providers of services—and thereby learn the costs of delivering to similar patients care of equal effectiveness. To upset established patterns with an experiment requires seeking informed consent. Human subjects protection committees now demand that consent forms contain information revealing expected benefits and risks of established and experimental treatments. Such information is difficult to offer in long-term care. For these reasons, the RCT appears never to have been used to compare the costs of home and institutional care.

What is known about comparative costs? In the face of the difficulties of comparing the costs of home and institutional care, it is not surprising that most recent reviews of empirical studies conclude that little is reliably known and that more careful research is indicated. A review by Robinson and others of the comparative costs of home and institutional care concluded that:

> The available data support the thesis that homemaker-home health aide services, when provided alone or as one of an array of in-home services, are usually less costly than any of the out-of-home alternatives.[40]

On the whole, however, as the authors of this review indicate, most of the data summarized derive from studies that do not control patient characteristics or outcome measures. A similar difficulty plagues a review of home care cost studies by Homemakers Upjohn.[41] Both of these efforts call attention to the need to consider separately home care as an alternative to hospital care and to short- or long-term nursing home care. One of the dominant findings in this literature is that home care for many convalescents costs less than hospital care — taking the hospital cost to be the per diem charge. (This may inflate the real cost of convalescent care in hospitals.)

A 1975 General Accounting Office review of twenty studies of home and nursing home costs concluded that nineteen "presented data which supported the proposition that home health care can be less expensive under some circumstances than alternative institutional care."[42] Several problems in making cost comparisons were noted: finding samples of similar patients who receive similar services, relying on charges (which may be arbitrary) as surrogates for cost, and relying on average institutional costs as measures of the costs for particular patients.

Three other reviews have been more critical in their judgments of the methods and findings of comparative and other studies of the costs and effects of home and institutional care for the elderly. The three had some reasons in common; other reasons were individual. Each decided that research and demonstration projects were, in sum, inconclusive.

Craig's analysis of twenty-three studies of home care reported three general barriers to the accumulation of systematic knowledge: (1) individual efforts varied in their objectives; (2) client populations and program environments were not controlled; and (3) benefits and their administration were widely dissimilar.[43]

The firm of Applied Management Sciences (AMS) reviewed several alternatives to nursing home care, including home care and adult day care. Only eight studies were located that investigated the costs, efficiency and/or effectiveness of these alternatives. AMS concluded that "the available evidence is insufficient either to refute or support the assertion that in-home care is cost-efficient and/or effective for all elderly persons."[44] This can hardly have been a surprising finding. Care in any one site could not be thought best, by all or any measures, for "all elderly persons." AMS did identify certain subpopulations for whom in-home care might be preferable.

AMS faulted individual studies of alternatives to institutionalization on several grounds: sampling methods were thought inadequate; samples were too small; patients were followed for too short a time; cost data were not sufficiently detailed; and evaluators were typically themselves numbered among the direct service providers.

Collectively, several major demonstrations were criticized for their failure to adopt common methods. Outcome measures, patient variables, and services offered exhibited considerable differences. Most projects developed their own instruments for gauging outcomes; in only a few cases were standard measures, such as the Katz ADL score, used. AMS further criticized five major demonstration projects then in process because all were located in the northeast and all but one were in urban areas.

Based on its assessment of the inadequacies of past efforts, AMS recommended a $58 million demonstration program to test the utility of four administrative arrangements, four financing mechanisms, and four reimbursement mechanisms in six delivery systems.

A contrary plan was put forth by the Office of Social Services and Human Development in the Office of the Assistant Secretary for Planning and Evaluation, DHEW.[45] An evaluation of twenty-five experimental, noninstitutional long-term care projects for their enhancement of clients' daily functioning and their effectiveness in preventing institutionalization was extremely critical of both research procedures and results. Therefore, it was recommended that "new experimental research should be preceded by development of theory and by non-experimental research."

In the face of these assessments and those of such other authorities in the field of long-term care as LaVor and Callender[46] and Doherty and others,[47] the prospects for soon obtaining data on the comparative costs of home and institutional care for the elderly do not appear bright. Thus, it seems likely that home care advocates will be obliged to continue to argue without the support that valid cost data might provide.

After examining the evidence on the likely costs and effects of improved non-institutional benefits, a recent Health Care Financing Administration White Paper has concluded that:

A significant proportion of patients can be effectively treated at a lower cost in the community. However, as a client's disability level increases, a break-even point exists, past which it is more expensive to maintain a person at home or in the community than in a nursing home.

A broader coverage of in-home and community-based benefits would largely go to a new population rather than substituting for more expensive nursing home care. Hence, such coverage would likely increase public expenditures.

Broadened coverage tends to lower mortality rates and increase life satisfaction among clients receiving the alternative services, but differences in functional ability are not discernible.[48]

This probably constitutes a fair representation of current federal administrative thinking. Some patients now bound for nursing homes could indeed be served more cheaply at home. But it would be difficult to restrict improved home care benefits to those patients. Federal officials seem not to regard non-institutional compensatory care as a value in itself.

The current channeling demonstrations probably testify in part to federal frustrations with conducting RCTs on the costs and effects of home and nursing home care. Channeling is designed as a set of RCTs testing case management (and possibly enriched services) against traditionally more fragmented home care.

Two recent major studies that aimed to compare costs of in-home and institutional services reinforce this conclusion. These are the General Accounting Office's Cleveland studies and the evaluation of the "222" demonstrations.

Careful work by the U.S. General Accounting Office in Cleveland may help prepare for better comparisons of the effects and costs of in-home and institutional care in the future, but this study has not yet developed needed evidence. A general matching of institutional and noninstitutional populations, by controlling for disability using the Duke Older Americans Resources and Services (OARS) instrument, suggests that all but the most disabled elder citizens could be cared for at home less expensively.[49] Because institutionalization becomes a real risk largely within this most disabled group, the Cleveland study does not seem adequately to investigate whether the people really at risk of institutionalization could be cared for more cheaply at home. Some of the problems with this work, such as use of a statewide cost for institutional care, for all levels of intensity, could probably be addressed, leading to more refined estimates of the costs of caring for similar populations in different sites.[50]

Evaluations of the Medicare-funded demonstrations done under the waiver authority of Section 222 of P.L. 92-603 have proven more controversial. These demonstrations had been supposed to attempt random clinical trials of the costs and effects of providing homemaker or adult day care services to individuals who would otherwise have been institutionalized. Weissert and others have evaluated the demonstrations and generally found little evidence that a wider range of noninstitutional benefits would be worthwhile.[51] Both advocates of greater public funding for noninstitutional care and neutral researchers have attacked the methods and analyses used in the demonstrations and in their evaluation. Site selection, randomization criteria, assessment instruments, statistical techniques, and methods of comparing costs and outcomes have been emphatically questioned and criticized.[52]

Choice and Consumer Sovereignty

There are several reasons for permitting choice to patients. First, to permit choice may in itself improve outcome of care. Long-term services are delivered principally to compensate for losses in functional ability. Physically, these losses reduce the freedom of action formerly enjoyed by the person. In this context, to be compelled to accept care in an institution can be demoralizing.

Second, patients may typically be able to select settings and types of services that objectively yield outcomes superior to those of settings and services selected by professionals. Most long-term care services are nontechnical in nature, involving help with personal care, housekeeping, and related functions. Older people may indeed have excellent ideas of what help they require. For technical matters, such as monitoring vital signs or special nursing or therapeutic procedures, advice from expert professionals should be provided and, hopefully, used. Devices for accomplishing joint care planning in a cooperative atmosphere would have to be designed. What would have to be avoided, therefore, is the defining of long-term care as a purely medical problem. For, "when medicalization is based on the problems of living and the determination of the 'quality' of one's life, the limits of social control seem boundless."[53]

To permit patients choice in this area follows common patterns of permitting consumers to spend their disposable incomes as they wish. Consumers are considered competent to do this unless they harm themselves. We need to find ways to identify which older persons could not safely exercise influence or control over the settings and types of services they receive.

This pragmatic argument for permitting patients some measure of freedom to decide their long-term care services helps sustain this study. It is considered in the contexts of difficulties of measuring outcomes, difficulties of comparing the costs of in-home and institutional care, and uncertainties surrounding the reliability of decisionmaking by professionals.

For some, the right of the elderly to choose the site in which they receive long-term care is posed as an ethical issue.[54] Others assert this right as a practical matter: Older people may know best what is in their interest. Alternatively, being permitted to choose, to avoid compulsory institutionalization (or remaining at home) is itself so beneficial as to outweigh the ill effects produced by choice of a site of care believed by professionals to be relatively ineffective. In either case, it is argued, the consequence of choice is preferable to the consequence of compulsion.[55]

In long-term care, a wide range of choices to be permitted to patients has been endorsed. It is insisted that patient choice as to which nursing home to enter, combined with a greater bed supply, would help improve the quality of institutional care.[56] Greater choice would be permitted by those who would grant the elderly some measure of influence on whether they would be cared for at home or in an institution.[57] Others go further and assert that the elderly can and should be permitted to make "necessary decisions regarding such major changes in their lives as being moved to an institution for needed care."[58] Significant judicial support for the right of disabled groups other than the elderly to obtain care in the "least restrictive" setting has been developed. This has been especially true for the mentally retarded.[59] One decision, that of *Sheldon* v. *Tucker*,[60] noted that a "purpose cannot be pursued by means that broadly stifle personal liberties when the end can be more narrowly achieved."[61] This principle is of great importance. It may be extended logically to groups other than the retarded, as in *Linden* v. *King*, which aims to compel provision of adequate home care to Massachusetts citizens now obliged to enter intermediate care facilities.[62]

Calls for choice of site or provider of service are by no means limited to care of the elderly or the mentally retarded. Women who desire to give birth at home, attended by a physician or other caregiver, raise this issue as well.[63] If the effect of freedom of choice on outcome in long-term care were strong and positive, it might be possible to improve both autonomy and safety. This would be particularly true if the decisions of patients were as appropriate—and no more costly—than those of typical professionals.

Greater choice of site of care for the elderly should not be restricted to various kinds of long-term care. Trades between acute and long-term care should be considered as well. Indeed, one possible source of funds for greater choice in long-term care—to permit more care at home—would be to divert funds now spent on acute care, as through the S/HMO. The "death with dignity" movement raises clearly the need to choose between more comfortable living arrangements during one's last years at home and costly acute care in a hospital. As a society, we are probably not able or willing to pay for both. In part, this movement springs from medical advances that permit many of the very ill or disabled to live longer today than in earlier years. These treatments are usually fully reimbursed for the elderly by Medicare or Medicaid. Tubiana argues that "doctors . . . must learn to give up their relentless right-to-live therapies and end the laughable lies that surround the dying."[64] The hospice, as a device for in-patient and in-home delivery of services to the terminally ill, is designed to deliver balanced care and elicit and then respect (to a greater degree than do many conventional providers) the preferences of those who are dying.

The principle of care in the least restrictive environment may also be extended logically for the elderly to make available choice about the *content* of care in a given site. Freedom over both site and content of care would be supported by a general extension to all the disabled of the scheme of cash payments, "the aid and attendance allowance," devised to enable disabled veterans to purchase some of the help they need.[65] A considerable, though somewhat more narrow, range of choice would be permitted by voucher schemes such as those advocated in the field of public education.

Proponents of cash benefits and vouchers make it clear that choice by the disabled is to be permitted. This would allow selection of a more restrictive site of care, if the patient desired. While guarantees would be needed to prevent inappropriate pressure by families or professionals to induce patients to enter institutions, Brody's position "that the service to be provided is the least restrictive alternative"[66] may be too strong if it removes desirable elements of freedom. To protect the elderly who may prefer or who may require institutional care from judges desiring to mandate freedom or administrators and legislators desiring to save money, the right to choose institutional care should probably be guaranteed. Brody's position can perhaps be understood in part as a reaction against historic institutional preferences in public policy.

The right of older patients to have wider latitude to exercise their preferences for the setting of their long-term care has received a fair measure of attention only in recent years. Guttman has noted that: "the study of decision-making in old age, with regard to resource utilization is a relatively new and uncharted territory as far as social gerontology is concerned."[67] Davis[68] and Schulz and Hanusa[69] have begun the job of testing practical methods to increase older dependent citizens' choice and control.

Proclaimed rights of the elderly to select the site in which they will receive long-term care, and the practical work to support such a right, seem to have had little impact. In a Florida study, Bell found that over 80 percent of mentally alert Medicaid recipients of nursing home care and a similar proportion of those at home "would prefer to live out the remaining years of their lives at home and not in an institution."[70] Nonetheless, as Barney[71] has noted and the data on proportionate spending on home and institutional care confirm, the option of choosing home care is usually denied.

There are several reasons for this. One is the fear that to permit greater choice of site of care would lead to a considerable increase in long-term care spending. Many of the services covered under the heading of home care, such as help with cleaning or cooking, may seem quite desirable in themselves, especially in contrast to institutional long-term care.

Beyond this visible pattern in long-term care looms a problem in social services, medical care, and perhaps publicly funded goods and services generally. In the face of the need to ration resources in medical care itself, Mechanic foresees a growth in bureaucratic power. This could scarcely work to yield greater autonomy for patients.[72]

A problem beyond cost may stand in the way of granting the patient control over long-term care site and services. This is that some (the proportion is not known) consumers may really prefer not to choose. Neuhauser refers to the positive effect of the placebo on some acute care patients, benefiting from blind trust in authoritative decisions.[73]

It seems to some that older patients should not be trusted to choose the setting in which they will receive care or the services to be delivered to them, as they might ask for far more than they need, ruining budgets and leading to avoidable overdependence. Conversely, it may be feared that some older patients heroically—but inappropriately—insist that they "can manage fine" with levels of assistance so low that preventable harm is suffered in the form of bedsores, falls, malnutrition, or other damage. These considerations should be borne in mind in evaluating the data presented in Part III of this study.

Responses to these positions might be to permit choice only to those patients who desire it. A process for identifying and protecting others would have to be devised. Further, costs could be constrained by permitting choice only by a population that, in total, could be cared for at the same cost in institutions or in their homes. This theme is embodied in New York States's "nursing home without walls" program, the Ominous Budget Reconciliation Act of 1981's Section 2176 Medicaid home care waiver authority, and, in part, the study reported in this book.

DIVERSION: POLICY AND RESEARCH

More generous public funding of in-home services could benefit several groups of older citizens. It could permit individuals now obliged to enter nursing homes to remain at home. It could finance services for individuals who would not have entered institutions but who would have remained at home under miserable circumstances. In the first instance, home care costs could substitute for institutional spending. In the second, hospital spending might be reduced. For a third group of citizens, now largely helped by family members, it is feared that public benefits might displace unpaid efforts. While many people see this as a wholly bad thing, some family members might be considerably relieved, often from profound physical or emotional sacrifices.

Unfortunately, the evidence on comparative decency, effectiveness, and costs—and the arguments concerning consumer sovereignty—do not suggest easy resolution of the debate over improved public support of home care. To a great degree, advocates of improved home care funding for the elderly on one side, and public administrators and researchers on the other, talk past one another. Administrators and researchers tend to demand or seek evidence that more public home care spending will mean less public spending of other kinds, or at least to be assured that tangible benefits will be won. They look for identification of specific populations that would need and receive new benefits.[74]

Home care advocates argue that we know enough to construct an adequate program and that we have the resources to finance it. They argue further that most current research is unlikely to generate information needed to make better policy.[75] They place greater emphasis on the benefits that older clients are thought likely to receive than do most administrators and researchers, although they seem to feel that these benefits are hard to measure.

A policy of allowing prospective nursing home patients to elect home care if, collectively, no increase in total cost was incurred, is attractive in both fiscal and human terms. Fiscally, no new spending would be required. Humanely, some older people would have an opportunity to choose site of care, and this could become an opening wedge for improved funding of noninstitutional services.

In effect, this approach was designed to allow a marginal increase in freedom of choice of site of long-term care for those about to enter nursing homes, while attempting to hold harmless federal and state fiscal liabilities. (It is acknowledged that such a policy presents several problems. For example, efforts to control costs could fail if large numbers of older Americans suddenly presented themselves as candidates for nursing home care only in the ultimate hope of receiving nontechnical home care services.)

Measurement of costs and effects of hypothetical diversion is one sensible way to form a preliminary estimate of the costs per person of real diversion. As a research plan, diversion offers several opportunities for avoiding or finessing problems encountered in comparing costs and effects of in-home and institutional care through either prospective or retrospective investigations. The present study seeks to compare the costs of the two types of care only hypothetically. The entire study sample is actually cared for only in one site—the nursing home.

Thus, the sample serves as its own control, and the problem of comparability of experimental and control groups is avoided.

This leaves the very substantial problems of estimating what would have been the costs and outcomes of care in the two sites. Outcome is handled by seeking prescriptions for home care packages that are expected to be at least as effective as the institutional services actually provided. The devices for obtaining these prescriptions are described in Chapters 4 and 5.

Cost is handled on the nursing home side by relying on the real-world costs of institutional care, delivered by an established and, in Massachusetts, tightly reimbursed industry. Institutional costs may well be stated conservatively in the present study.

The study deliberately does not take as given the real-world costs of home care. Home care, in most parts of this country today, is not well coordinated. Physician, home health, and social services are fragmented. In many areas, vital services are not available. Daily service around the clock can seldom be obtained. Finally, until outcomes can be measured, we will not know with confidence what services people require to live at home safely. Without this knowledge, comparisons of the cost of in-home and institutional care are extremely difficult to conduct.

Therefore, if the hypothetical costs of home care are to be compared with the real costs of institutional care, it must be decided whose views of types, quantities, and providers of home care—and therefore its cost—should be employed. Who can be trusted to know what package of home care services is "appropriate"? Whose views can be taken to be valid, in that they recommend not so much care that patients become dependent nor so little care that they suffer avoidable harm? Since home care services are not actually provided, the general difficulty in long-term care of measuring outcome is compounded in the present study. Consequently, indicators of the equity of care planning and of the reliability of care planners' views are of prime importance.

In summary, patients, families, or various professionals are the logical candidates for planning home care. Each offers advantages. For patients, influence or control over care planning may be good in itself, in that greater choice about services, at a time of declining autonomy in other realms, may directly improve health, functional ability, or morale. Further, most services are nontechnical, so patients may know themselves and their needs best and perhaps can be trusted to request only those services needed.

Families, alternatively, may be more able to be objective about patients' needs. Especially if they reside with the patient, they will be familiar with his or her needs. In addition, if families are providing help prior to receipt of formal support, it will be most important that they are content with the level of that support, or they may refuse to continue their share of the burden.

There are several arguments in favor of professionals as decisionmakers in home care: they may be trusted to be objective; by virtue of training and experience they can both supply technical information—about rehabilitation potential and techniques, opportunities for training for independence, need for medical monitoring or special nursing procedures, and the like—and make the interpatient comparisons necessary to equity.

Control by members of each group also carries, in theory, possible disadvantages. Because the nontechnical home care services could be attractive in themselves to many patients, they might demand inappropriately high volumes of help. Consequently, costs would be higher than necessary. Well-being could suffer if patients become avoidably dependent and passive. (Some patients might prefer passivity; inappropriately placing values on "objective" behaviors and outcomes in long-term care is all too easy.) Alternatively, patients might err in the other direction and seek less than might really be needed to permit them to live at home safely. Being unduly optimistic, they might suffer harm. Patients might find it difficult to gauge how much care is actually required to accomplish what they desire.

Families, given control, might seek more than the help needed to support their own efforts and thereby slough off onto paid providers jobs that they could reasonably be expected to continue to do.

Finally, professionals might inappropriately assign too high a proportion of home care effort to skilled curative services and too little effort to supportive caring services. They might dispute questions of boundaries of control such as: In which areas of home care are nurses expert? How about physicians, physical or occupational therapists, or social workers? What if they disagree markedly within or across lines of training? Who then should control the allocation of in-home services? Perhaps professionals might in general be too cautious or too prone to take risks. If so, how might it be decided which is the case?

If professionals' views of patients' home care needs were generally consistent or reliable, this would arguably strengthen the case that professionals should control allocation of home care resources. It was suspected, however, that professionals would not agree very well among one another about patients' needs. A considerable literature, principally in other fields but touching on long-term care as well, generated this suspicion.

Planning Care: The Reliability of Professional Views

The extent of agreement among professionals about what patients or other people need—here called reliability or consistency—should be seen as a prerequisite for validity. That is, if professionals do not agree with one another about the needs of an individual patient, they cannot be expected to produce effective or valid plans of care. Reliability is not in itself enough to ensure validity. Professionals may agree with one another, but they may all be wrong. Nonetheless, confidence in professionals is greater if their views are consistent. How much consistency is enough is hard to say, but, other things equal, more is better.

In this study, it was decided to obtain many views about the home care needs of individual patients because the literature on professional decisionmaking did not inspire a great deal of confidence in the general reliability of professionals, and because the special circumstances of long-term care seemed likely to increase the chance of disagreement. The general literature on decisionmaking is important also because it places possible disagreement in perspective. That is, given circumstances likely to engender considerable professional disagreement in the field of long-term care, against an overall background of widespread disagreement in other professional fields, actual discovery of a measure of disagreement in long-term care would not discredit the field as an object for funding.

A note on definitions is important. The process of obtaining professional views of patient need will be referred to as "care planning." The products of this process will be called "care plans," "prescriptions," "professional recommendations," and the like. Thus, deciding what people need will be distinguished from describing their past or current physical, medical, functional, psychosocial or other status. The latter task will be referred to as "assessment." Assessment, to produce a timely and objective (insofar as possible) view of patient status is only a foundation for deciding needed care.

All too frequently, care planning and assessment are confused, or it is thought that they are identical, or that the content of the care plan flows smoothly and inevitably from an understanding of current condition. This view appears, for example, in the generally excellent report on long-term care by a task force of the National Conference on Social Welfare:

> Once a functional capability assessment of a sample base of the population is obtained, the data can be translated into service[s] . . . , costs can be determined, standards established and the technology moved into place to serve the needs. Interventions and therapies are readily related to functional levels.[76]

In opposition to this outlook, there is a widely held opinion that "there is no set of criteria matching levels and combinations of disability with appropriate types of institutional or noninstitutional treatment"[77] and that "we lack methods to . . . relate the assessment of a patient's medical condition to the quality of care and types of LTC services they receive."[78]

The difficulty of making this linkage is by no means restricted to long-term care. It is a problem, of debated dimensions, in acute care as well.[79] That such a debate should occur signals a departure from Weber's view of the professional as a rational cog. The judge, for example:

> in the bureaucratic state with its rational laws is more or less an automaton of paragraphs: the legal documents together with the costs and fees are dropped in at the top with the expectation that the judgment will emerge at the bottom together with more or less sound agreements — an apparatus, that is, whose functioning is by and large calculable and predictable.[80]

Critics of professionals today may on occasion state their case more forcefully than the available evidence warrants. This may be in part a reaction to descriptions, such as that by Weber, of professionals as disinterested truth processors. In part also, it may be a reaction to claims that competent professionals, such as doctors, simply did their best and that objective standards for judging their ability were unavailable. An example of this view is the definition of good medical care put forth by Lee and Jones in 1933 (and asserted often today). It is "the kind of medicine practiced and taught by the recognized leaders of the medical profession at a given time or period."[81]

Hamburg and Spaght, and Cochrane[82] have been among those calling for better outcome measures in acute care; Kane and Kane[83] have done the same in long-term care. Difficulties in measuring outcome[84] have led to renewed interest in grounding medical therapy in process or in consensus among experts.[85] It is likely, however, that critics of health professionals will regard other than outcome measures as clearly second-best.

Critics of professionals' ability—that they have unique access to special knowledge—and of their motives in seeking control over knowledge, resources, or decisions, have been linked by Glazer to critics of professions and institutions themselves.[86] The present purpose is not to assign blame, but rather to understand service needs and costs and how to make good decisions in long-term care.

In home care itself, the care planning process that underpins resource allocation appears to have been the subject of only one detailed study.[87] This investigation found a considerable measure of inequity; clients with similar needs were frequently treated differently, and clients with different levels of disability frequently did not receive services commensurate with their requirements. Moreover, patterns of care varied by county of residence and by procedure for assessment and care planning. Like reliability of planning, equity would point toward validity or effectiveness. Consistent plans could prescribe inappropriate services, and equitable plans could be ineffective or wasteful, but they carry a greater presumption of thoughtful consideration of client need.

In view of these results, and others presented shortly, certain assumptions made by federal institutional long-term care regulators should be carefully examined. (Similar thoughts are not manifest in home care, probably because it has not yet been the object of significant regulation.) These assumptions were visible in two areas: (1) Professional Standards Review Organization (PSRO) monitoring of nursing home care; and (2) the proposed revised conditions of participation for skilled and intermediate care facilities in Medicare and Medicaid, withdrawn early in 1981.

One of the three components of pilot PSRO review of nursing home care was "medical care evaluation." This was the component most closely related to patient care. Nonetheless, medical care evaluation did not review the content of care against validated standards. Rather, it called for the completion of procedures reasonably thought to be necessary (but not sufficient) for good care: physician completion of a plan of care, reasonable relation of medications to diagnoses, and so on. Unlike the PSRO medical audit for acute care, which does attempt to rely on a broad consensus among physicians about what constitutes acceptable care, PSRO review of long-term care lacked a firm scientific base. In part, this followed from PSROs' control by physicians, who almost always are less interested in long-term care than in acute care. Physician domination of PSROs nonetheless limited the latitude of knowledgeable and interested nurses, social workers, and other professionals in helping to prepare standards for long-term care. Further, less certainty in diagnosis or treatment of long-term care problems can typically be expected, in comparison to acute care problems. The nature of chronic problems themselves, the likelihood of multiple diagnoses, and the relative lack of data on outcomes in long-term care may well contribute to this.[88]

Nonetheless, optimistic assumptions about the efficacy of regulation of long-term care appear in the now-withdrawn draft conditions of participation for skilled and intermediate care facilities in Medicare and Medicaid. One major option being considered was a de-emphasis on certification of nursing homes' policies and capacities and an interest in "quality of care and services provided to patients."[89] One revised condition of participation designed to effect this option was that for patient care management. This provision would have called for detailed assessment shortly after admission, revised assessments as appropriate, discharge planning if appropriate, and patient care planning. Assessment would have included "social and background data, diagnoses, physical impairments, functional impairments, behavior, special procedures, care being provided, drug regimen reviews, and an estimate of discharge potential." These are the union of the types of data called for in PSRO nursing home medical care evaluations and in the patient appraisal and care evaluation (PACE) form. As in the case of the PSRO medical care evaluations, gathering the data required to perform patient assessment is a necessary but far from sufficient condition for good long-term care.

Patient care planning was required by the draft conditions of participation; individualized care plans would be revised at least quarterly. To require nursing homes to engage in care planning will formalize what is often done intuitively today. Greater thoughtfulness and consistency may result. But the benefits of this requirement are difficult to gauge in the absence of valid evidence about how to meet the needs of individual patients.

A final issue in institutional care pertains to placement of patients at the correct level. After reviewing this problem, the Moreland Act Commission found only a weak relation between patient needs and level of care.[90] A point system for patient classification that was introduced in response to the commission's criticisms was itself attacked as capricious and insensitive to important differences in individual needs.[92] Foley and Schneider found considerable variation in six different assessment systems' "assignments" of a group of approximately seven hundred patients to either SNF or ICF care.[92] After reviewing issues in assigning institutional long-term patients to proper levels of care, Lawson concluded that this task "far exceeds known observer reliability with regard to a simpler situation, such as reading electrocardiograms or feeling arterial pulses. It will, therefore, not support the observer agreement that is required."[93]

The reported evidence on this question is mixed. Wenkert and others found that:

> Physician–nurse teams using common concepts of levels of patient care can make replicable judgments with respect to the care needs and proper placements of statistically random samples of patients seen in different settings.[94]

Bell, on the other hand, found a considerable range of difference in the estimates by physicians, nurses, and social workers about the proportion of newly admitted nursing home residents who could have been sustained in the community had certain in-home services been available.[95]

Similarly, Seidl and others learned that actual home care case managers judged a substantially higher proportion of their clients to be at risk of institutionalization than did a disinterested (and possibly less knowledgeable) panel.[96] Similar sorts of evidence appear in the work of Pollak[97] and of Williams and others.[98]

In the realm of long-term care generally, the apparent importance of consulting professionals from a number of different fields further complicates the task of learning what care is appropriate for patients with various problems. Such consultation is desirable given the variety of professions assisting the elderly in meeting their multifaceted needs. The frequently reported disinterest by physicians in many of the problems of the aged[99] appears to have led to a disjunction among knowledge, interest, and power. This has probably slowed reduction in the disparity of views about both the requirements of this population and how to meet them. Fragmentation of funding sources has probably had the same effect.

If Lawson is correct regarding the greater difficulty of making accurate clinical judgments in such complex areas of long-term care as level of nursing home placement, how much better is inter-rater reliability in the more straightforward realms of acute care? Koran's comprehensive examination of this subject constitutes a chilling indictment of physician decisionmaking. After reviewing over fifty reports, he concluded that "if the results of these studies are representative of the reliability of clinical data, methods, and judgments, there is little room for complacency."[100] The work of Dunn and Conrath[101] reinforces this conclusion.

Koran was willing to tentatively identify factors influencing physician agreement. One was that "the less severe an abnormality, the lower the inter-observer agreement rate will be." Care planning for patients suffering chronic conditions or general frailty and thus in need of long-term care is likely to suffer from this difficulty. Indeed, Koran's finding parallels that noted in Part III of this study regarding decisionmaking for home care; within this group of long-term care patients, the number of hours of care needed by the least ill and disabled patients was most difficult for professionals to agree about.[102] Further evidence regarding inconsistent decisions by professionals working in areas removed from acute care is found in Liebman's review of disability determinations under federal income maintenance programs.[103]

Characteristics of patients' problems are not the sole influence on how well professionals agree with one another. Characteristics of professionals' training, experience, and information available may be expected to matter as well. It might reasonably be hypothesized, for example, that more and better information would be associated with greater inter-rater reliability, in that sources of uncertainty, requiring assumptions or guesses, would be removed. It is surprising, therefore, to learn that agreement about diagnosis or treatment in one study of ambulatory care did not improve as more information was provided.[104]

Other reasonable hypotheses are that professionals with similar training and experience, filling similar roles, are likelier to agree with one another. Inter-profession agreement is particularly important in long-term care because, while the skills of many different professions seem relevant to patients' problems, budgets are finite, and the costs of preparing team care plans can be considerable. In Chapters 9 and 10 the association of these variables with different levels of agreement about recommended hours of home care will be examined.

In an area related to interprofessional reliability—how well professionals agreed with certain standards—Shapiro found that more clinical experience was associated with better predictive ability.[105] Perrin and Goodman, in a study comparing ability of three groups of professionals to obtain appropriate information and make appropriate suggestions about therapy,[106] found that nurse practitioners generally did better than either house officers or practicing pediatricians. Further, more experience and training did not seem to be associated with the performance of house officers.

Looking beyond long-term care and acute somatic medicine, it is of interest to note that Ennis and Litwack, in an evaluation of the reliability and validity of the judgment of psychiatrists, argue that psychiatrists disagree so badly and predict outcomes so poorly that they should be denied any diagnostic, judgmental, or predictive role in civil commitment proceedings. Judges and juries "could function quite adequately . . . without 'expert' opinion."[107]

But how reliable are the views of judges? Partridge and Eldridge report striking inter-rater dissimilarities in a study of fifty federal judges' hypothetical sentences of twenty defendants.[108] For example, large differences were found in lengths of prison sentences imposed in the same case; and no evidence was found that experience as a judge tended to moderate disparity.

The findings cited above on the reliability of decisionmaking by professionals in home care, institutional long-term care for the elderly, other areas of long-term care, acute medical care, and other fields indicate that before professional views of the hypothetical cost of a home alternative to institutional care can reliably be compared with the cost of institutional care, differences in the consistency of those professional views should be examined. Further, in the larger context—that of who should be permitted to control or influence the allocation of home care and other long-term care resources—a finding that professionals' evaluations of patients' home care needs disagree considerably would open the door to greater influence over resources by patients or families.

Using the terms presented by Bradshaw, disagreement among professionals would weaken the case for permitting standards of "normative need," experts' views, to prevail. Were this to happen, need felt or expressed by patients or families would seem more important. So, too, might comparative measures of need (equity). Lacking a zero point, it might still be possible to decide who should have more help and who should have less.[109]

In this regard, it is worth examining two contrasting findings. Keith identified a considerable divergence between elderly patients' and public health nurses' rankings of the importance of various services.[110] Nagi, by contrast, found high congruence between medical assessment and self-assessment of disability in several types of activities.[111] It will be of interest to learn which pattern will prevail in hypothetical home care planning.

The issue of who controls the allocation or planning of in-home services is important both in itself and because it can affect the cost of that care and its effectiveness. Therefore, it would be well to learn if professionals agree about what is required to sustain an elderly person at home. Further, it would be well to learn if professionals, on average, agree with patients and their families. At what point "agreement" shades off into "disagreement" must, of course, be decided.

NOTES TO CHAPTER 3

1. Letters from Ms. Janet Kline, Legislative Analyst, Congressional Research Service, Library of Congress, 6 March 1976.
2. For Medicaid, see 45 CFR 249.10 (b) (15) (i) (A); 42 USC 1396 a (13), (19), (20), (21). For Title XX, see 42 USC 1397. For the Older Americans Act, see 42 USC 3001. For more extensive treatment, see also Patricia R. Butler, "Financing Non-institutional Long-term Care Services for the Elderly and Chronically Ill: Alternatives to Nursing Homes." *Clearinghouse Review* 13, no. 5 (September 1979): 335-76; and Linden v. King, Civil Action No. 79-862-T (D. Mass., 2 May 1979).
3. Community Health Services Act (S. 234).
4. Section 2176, Omnibus Budget Reconciliation Act of 1981, Report no. 97-205, U.S. House of Representatives, 29 July 1981.
5. Health Care Financing Administration, "Medicaid Program: Home and Community-based Services," *Federal Register* 46, no. 190, pt. 5 (1 October 1981): 48532-42, 42 CFR pts. 431, 435, 440, and 441.

6. Lucien Wulsin, Jr., "Memorandum to Medicaid Coordinators on Commu-
    nity Services Waivers for Individuals Who Would Otherwise Be in Need of
    Institutional Care" (National Health Law Program, Los Angeles, Cal.,
    23 November 1981).

7. Carolyne K. Davis, "Medicaid Action Transmittal on Title XIX, Social
    Security Act: Decisions on Reducing Bias Towards Institutional Care,"
    Transmittal no. 82–8 (Washington: Health Care Financing Administration,
    May 1982).

8. Dennis F. Beatrice, "Case Management: A Policy Option for Long-term
    Care," in James J. Callahan, Jr. and Stanley S. Wallack, eds., *Reforming
    the Long-term Care System* (Lexington, Mass.: D. C. Heath, 1981), pp.
    121–62. See also James J. Callahan, Jr., "The Channeling Demonstration:
    Summary Statement of Issues, Environment, Intervention, and Outcome"
    (Waltham, Mass.: Levinson Policy Institute, Brandeis University, March
    1981).

9. James J. Callahan, Jr., "Single Agency Option for Long-term Care," in
    Callahan and Wallack, pp. 163–83.

10. Larry M. Diamond and David E. Berman, "The Social/Health Maintenance
    Organization: A Single Entry, Prepaid, Long-term Care Delivery System,"
    in Callahan and Wallack, pp. 185–213.

11. By the mid-1970s, the depth of this advocacy warranted compilation of
    two useful bibliographies: Liz Karnes, "Alternatives to Institutionalization
    for the Aged: An Overview and Bibliography," Council of Planning Librar-
    ians Exchange Bibliography no. 877, September 1975; Wendy Garen, et
    al., "Alternatives to Institutionalization: An Annotated Research Biblio-
    graphy on Housing and Service for the Aged" (Urbana, Ill.: Housing Re-
    search and Development, University of Illinois, July 1976).

12. Journalistic accounts are common. Newspaper articles, which number in
    the hundreds, touch on one or more of these areas. See, for example, Jack
    Newfield, "The Last Unspeakable Nursing Home," *Village Voice*, 18 Sept-
    ember 1978. For overviews, see Frank E. Moss and Val J. Halamandaris,
    Too Old, Too Sick, Too Bad (Germantown, Md.: Aspen, 1977); Mary
    Adelaide Mendelson, *Tender, Loving Greed* (New York: Knopf, 1974);
    and New York State Moreland Act Commission, *Regulating Nursing Home
    Care: The Paper Tigers* (New York: Moreland Act Commission, October
    1975). An important newer work is Carol A. Delany and Kathleen A.
    Davies, *Nursing Home Ombudsman Report: The Pennsylvania Experience*
    (Harrisburg: Pennsylvania Advocates for Better Care, January 1979).

13. A suggestion of some of the decency assurance problems under home care
    is offered in Susan K. Kinoy, "Discussion of Problems Concerning the
    Selection of Home Attendants by Patients of Their Families" (Testimony
    before the United State Senate Special Committee on Aging, Washington,
    D.C., 16 May 1977).

14. See David Rothman, *The Discovery of the Asylum* (Boston: Little, Brown,
    1971).

15. Ellen L. Bassuk and Samuel Gerson, "Deinstitutionalization and Mental
    Health Services," *Scientific American* 238, no. 2 (February 1978): 46–53;
    Kim Hopper, Review of Andrew T. Scull, *Decarceration: Community*

Treatment of the Deviant—A Radical View, Health PAC Bulletin, no. 78 (September–October 1977), pp. 24–31; Leona L. Bachrach, "Deinstitutionalization: An Analytical Review and Sociological Perspective," National Institute of Mental Health, ser. D, no. 4, DHEW Pub. no. (ADM) 76–351 (Washington, D.C.: Government Printing Office, 1976). But see Gary J. Clarke, "In Defense of Deinstitutionalization," *Milbank Memorial Fund Quarterly, Health and Society* 57, no. 4 (Spring 1979): 461–79.

16. Robert L. Kane, et al., "Is Good Nursing-Home Care Feasible?" *Journal of the American Medical Association* 235, no. 5 (2 February 1976): 516–19.

17. The Quality of Life Committee, *Draft Report* (Washington, D.C.: Veterans Administration, 15 July 1977). (Mimeo.)

18. Jane Lockwood Barney, "Community Presence as a Key to Quality of Life in Nursing Homes," *American Journal of Public Health* 64, no. 3 (March 1974): 265–68.

19. Susan Rosenfeld Friedman, Lenard Kaye, and Sharon Farago, "Maximizing the Quality of Homecare Services for the Elderly" (Paper presented at the 30th Scientific Meeting of the Gerontological Society, San Francisco, Cal., 21 November 1977).

20. For two examples, see the following: J.P. Costello and G.M. Tanaka, "Mortality and Morbidity in Long-Term Institutional Care of the Aged," *Journal of the American Geriatric Society* 9 (1961): 959 ff; M.A. Lieberman, "Relationship of Mortality Rates to Entrance to a Home for the Aged," *Geriatrics* 16 (October 1961): 515–19.

21. Stanislav V. Kasl, "Physical and Mental Health Effects of Involuntary Relocation and Institutionalization on the Elderly—A Review," *American Journal of Public Health* 62, no. 3 (March 1972): 377–84.

22. Arthur Bigot, "Protective Services for Older People: A Reanalysis of a Controversial Demonstration Project," (Paper presented at the 31st Scientific Meeting of the Gerontological Society, Dallas, 17 November 1978).

23. Margaret Nielsen, "Home Aide Service and the Aged: A Controlled Study," pt. 1 (Cleveland: Benjamin Rose Institute, August 1970).

24. Janet B. Mitchell, "Patient Outcomes in Alternative Long-Term Care Settings," *Medical Care* 16, no. 6 (June 1978): 439–52. For a more detailed view, see Janet B. Mitchell, "Alternatives in Extended Medical Care" (Ph.D. dissertation, Florence Heller Graduate School for Advanced Studies in Social Welfare, Brandeis University, 1976).

25. Sidney Katz, et al., "Effects of Continued Care: A Study of Chronic Illness in the Home," DHEW Pub. no. (HSM) 73–3010 (Washington, D.C.: National Center for Health Services Research and Development, December 1972).

26. Margaret Nielsen, et al., "Older Persons After Hospitalization: A Controlled Study of Home Health Aide Services," *American Journal of Public Health* 62, no. 8 (August 1972): 1094–1101.

27. Alan Sager, et al., *Living at Home: The Roles of Public and Informal Supports in Sustaining Older Americans* (Waltham, Mass.: Levinson Policy Institute, Brandeis University, March 1982).

28. Among the work in this area is that recorded in Battelle Human Affairs Research Centers, "Evaluation of the Outcomes of Nursing Home Care,"

NTIS PB 266–301, prepared for the National Center for Health Services Research (Seattle: Battelle, October 1976); Alan S. Rosenfeld and Milton F. Bornstein, "Quality of Life and Care in Long Term Care Institutions: An Empirical Study" (Worcester, Mass.: Commission on Elder Affairs, 1978); Laurence G. Branch, *Understanding the Health and Social Service Needs of People Over Age 65* (Boston: Center for Survey Research of the University of Massachusetts, 1977); and Sager et al.

29. For useful material on the population in need, see Laurence G. Branch and Floyd J. Fowler, Jr., *The Health Care Needs of the Elderly and Chronically Disabled in Massachusetts* (Boston: Survey Research Program of the University of Massachusetts, March 1975); Laurence G. Branch, *Understanding Health and Social Service Needs*; Levinson Policy Institute, *Alternatives to Nursing Home Care: A Proposal*, Stock no. 5270–1248, prepared for the U.S. Senate Special Committee on Aging, (Washington, D.C.: Government Printing Office, 1971); American Public Welfare Association, "Report on Long-Term Care" (Washington, D.C.: American Public Welfare Association, November 1978); and Laurence G. Branch, James J. Callahan, Jr., and Alan M. Jette, "Targeting Home Care Services to Vulnerable Elders: Massachusetts' Home Care Corporations," *Home Health Care Services Quarterly* 2, no. 2 (Summer 1981): 41–58.

30. Brahna Trager, "Home Health Services in the United States," Report to the U.S. Senate, Special Committee on Aging (Washington, D.C.: Government Printing Office, April 1972), app. 3, Items 1–2, pp. 82–114.

31. Judith LaVor (Williams) and Marie Callender, "Home Health Cost Effectiveness: What Are We Measuring?" *Medical Care* 14, no. 10 (October 1976): 866–72.

32. The literature on this subject is large. See among others, Kathleen Connelly, Philip K. Cohen, and Diana Chapman Walsh, "Periodic Medical Review: Assessing the Quality and Appropriativeness of Care in Skilled Nursing Facilities," *New England Journal of Medicine* 296, no. 15 (April 1977): 878–80; Alan C. Beckman, Linda S. Noelker, and Debra David, "PEER REVIEW: Overt and Covert Factors in the Decision to Institutionalize" (Paper presented at the 1977 meeting of the Gerontological Society, Cleveland, Benjamin Rose Institute, 1977); John Holahan and Bruce Stuart, "The Extent and Cost of Unnecessary and Inappropriate Utilization," in *Controlling Medicaid Utilization Patterns*, U.R.I. 17700, vol. 2, (Washington, D.C.: Urban Institute, 1977).

33. Congressional Budget Office, *Long-Term Care for the Elderly and Disabled* (Washington, D.C.: Government Printing Office, 1977), app. B.

34. Nancy N. Anderson, et al., "A Comparison of In-home and Nursing Home Care for Older Persons in Minnesota," Minneapolis: H.H. Humprey Institute, University of Minnesota, June 1980. See also Frederick W. Seidl, Kevin D. Mahoney, and Carol D. Austin, "Providing and Evaluating Home Care: Issues of Targetting" (Paper presented at the Gerontological Society's 31st Scientific Meeting, Dallas, 20 November 1978).

35. Congressional Budget Office, p. 62; Michael E. Smyer, "Differential Usage and Differential Effects of Services for Impaired Elderly," *Advances in*

Research (Duke University Center for the Study of Aging and Human Development) vol. 1, no. 4 (Winter 1977).

36. Jay Greenberg, "The Determinants of Bias in Observational Studies: A Simulation Study and a Long-term Care Example" (Ph.D. dissertation, Harvard School of Public Health, 1978).

37. A.L. Cochrane, *Effectiveness and Efficiency* (London: Nuffield Provincial Hospital Trust, 1972).

38. John M. McKinlay and Sonja M. McKinlay, "The Questionable Contributions of Medical Measures to the Decline of Mortality in the United States in the Twentieth Century," *Milbank Memorial Fund Quarterly: Health and Society* 55, no. 3 (Summer 1977): 405-28.

39. Victor Cohn, "Science Comes to Medicine – Slowly," *Technology Review*, December 1974, pp. 8-9.

40. Nancy Robinson, et al., "Costs of Homemaker-Home Health Aide and Alternative Forms of Service: A Survey of the Literature" (New York: National Council for Homemaker-Home Health Aide Services, Inc., 1974).

41. "Cost Analysis: Home Health Care as an Alternative to Institutional Care" (Kalamazoo, Michigan: Homemakers Upjohn, October 1975).

42. General Accounting Office, letter to Rep. Edward I. Koch, MWD-76-30, B-164031(3), 17 September 1975.

43. John Craig, "Cost Issues in Home Health Care," in Marie Callender and Judy LaVor, *Home Health Development, Problems, and Potential* (Washington: Disability and Long-term Care Study, Office of the Assistant Secretary for Planning and Evaluation, DHEW, April 1975), pp. 48-55.

44. Applied Management Sciences, "Evaluation of Personal Care Organizations and Other In-Home Alternatives to Nursing Home Care for the Elderly and Long-term Disabled," Contract HEW-05-74-294, Final Report and Executive Summary (Revised), (Silver Spring, Maryland: AMS, 1 May 1976).

45. "Critical Review of Research on Long-term Care Alternatives Sponsored by the Department of Health, Education, and Welfare" (Washington, D.C.: Assistant Secretary for Planning and Evaluation, DHEW, June 1977).

46. LaVor and Callender, "Home Health Cost Effectiveness."

47. Neville Doherty, J. Segal, and Barbara Hicks, "Alternatives to Institutionalization for the Aged," *Aged Care and Services Review* 1, no. 1 (1978): 1-16.

48. Health Care Financing Administration, *Long-term Care: Backgrounds and Future Directions*, HCFA Pub. No. 81-20047 (Washington: HCFA, January 1981).

49. Comptroller General of the United States, "Report to the Congress on Home Health – The Need for a National Policy to Provide Better Care to the Elderly," HRO 78-19 (Washington, D.C.: General Accounting Office, 30 December 1977); William F. Laurie, "Employing the Duke OARS Methodology in Cost Comparisons: Home Services and Institutionalization," in *Multidimensional Functional Assessment: The OARS Methodology*, 2nd ed. (Durham, N.C.: Center for the Study of Aging and Human Development of Duke University, 1978), ch. 12, pp. 110-20.

50. For a general commentary, see Thomas R. Willemain, "Beyond the GAO Cleveland Study: Client Selection for Home Care Services," *Home Health Care Services Quarterly* 1, no. 3 (Fall 1980): pp. 65–83.

51. William Weissert, Thomas Wan, and Barbara Livieratos, "Effects and Costs of Day Care and Homemaker Services for the Chronically Ill: A Randomized Experiment," DHEW Pub. No. PHS–79–3250 (Hyattsville, Md.: National Center for Health Services Research, August 1979).

52. Phillip G. Weiler, et al., "Comments on the Weissert Report," *Home Health Care Services Quarterly* 1, no. 3 (Fall 1980): pp. 97–121.

53. Arnold Arluke and John Peterson, "Old Age as Illness: Notes on Accidental Medicalization," (Paper delivered at the annual meeting of the Society for Applied Anthropology, San Diego, California, April 6–9, 1977).

54. U.S. House of Representatives, Select Committee on Aging, Subcommittee on Health and Long-term Care, "New Perspectives in Health Care for Older Americans" (Washington, D.C.: Government Printing Office, January 1976).

55. Budd N. Shenkin, "Stalking the Irrational," Review Essay, *Journal of Health Politics, Policy and Law* 1, no. 3 (Fall 1976): 355–71; Nelida A. Ferrari, "Freedom of Choice," *Social Work* 8, no. 4 (October 1963): 104–6; Anne R. Somers and Florence M. Moore, "Homemaker Services— Essential Option for the Elderly," *Public Health Reports* 91, no. 4 (July– August 1976): 354–59; M. Powell Lawton, "Social and Structural Aspects of Prosthetic Environments for Older People," (Paper presented at the Third Annual Institute on Man's Adjustment to a Complex Environment, V.A. Hospital, Brocksville, Ohio, 1968), cited in Institute of Medicine, *The Elderly and Functional Dependency: A Policy Statement* (Washington, D.C.: National Academy of Sciences, 1977), p. 9.

56. Amitai Etzioni, Alfred J. Kahn, and Sheila B. Kamerman, "Public Management cf Health and Home Care for the Aged and Disabled," Position Paper (New York: Center for Policy Research, January 1975).

57. Institute of Medicine, *The Elderly and Functional Dependency: A Policy Statement* (Washington, D.C.: National Academy of Science, 1977), p. 9; State Communities Aid Association, "Report of the Arden House Institute on Continuity of Long Term Care" (New York: State Communities Aid Association, 1978), p. 8.

58. Institute of Medicine, p. 9; see also American Public Welfare Association, "Report on Long-Term Care" (Washington, D.C.: American Public Welfare Association, November 1978).

59. For a general discussion, see The President's Commission on Mental Retardation, *The Mentally Retarded Citizen and the Law* (New York: The Free Press, 1976), especially pp. 234–35.

60. 364 U.S. 479 (1960).

61. Cited in The President's Commission on Mental Retardation.

62. Linden v. King, Civil Action No. 79–862–T (D. Mass. 2 May 1979). Generally, see Audrey C. Cohen, *The Citizen as the Integrating Agent: Productivity in the Human Services*, Human Services Monograph Series, no. 9 (Washington, D.C.: Project Share, 1978).

63. George J. Annas, "Homebirth: Autonomy vs. Safety," *Hastings Center Report* 8, no. 4 (August 1978): 19–20.
64. Maurice Tubiana, cited in Francois Dupuis, "France: Restoring Dignity to Death," *Washington Post*, 23 May 1974.
65. American Foundation for the Blind, *Washington Report*, December 1977, p. 2.
66. Stanley J. Brody, "Health Care for Older Americans: The Alternative Issue" (Testimony before the U.S. Senate Special Committee on Aging, 17 May 1977).
67. David Guttman, "Seekers, Takers, and Users – The Elderly as Decision Makers" (Paper presented at the 30th Scientific Meeting of the Gerontological Society, San Francisco, November 1977).
68. Marcella Z. Davis, "The Organizational–Interactional Structure of Patient Participation in Continuity of Care: A Framework for Staff Intervention" (Paper presented at the 30th Annual Scientific Meeting of the Gerontological Society, San Francisco, November 1977).
69. Richard Schulz and Barbara Hartman Hanusa, "Long-Term Effects of Control and Predictability Enhancing Interventions: Findings and Ethical Issues" (Pittsburgh, Pa.: Carnegie–Mellon University Department of Psychology, 1977). (Mimeo.)
70. William G. Bell, "Community Care for the Elderly: An Alternative to Institutionalization" (Tallahassee: Program in Social Policy and the Aging, Florida State University, June 1971).
71. Jane L. Barney, "The Prerogative of Choice in Long-Term Care," *The Gerontologist* 17, no. 4 (July 1977): 309–14.
72. David Mechanic, "The Growth of Medical Technology and Bureaucracy: Implications for Medical Care," *Milbank Memorial Fund Quarterly: Health and Society* 55, no. 1 (Winter 1977): 61–78.
73. Duncan Neuhauser, "The Really Effective Health Delivery System," *Health Care Management Review* 1, no. 1 (Winter 1976): 25–32.
74. Burton D. Dunlop, "Expanded Home-based Care for the Elderly: Solution or Pipe Dream?" *American Journal of Public Health* 70, no. 5 (May 1980): 514–19 offers a clear statement of this general position.
75. Brahna Trager, "In Place of Policy: Public Adventures in Non-institutional Long-term Care," (Paper presented at the American Public Health Association's annual meeting, Los Angeles, November 1981).
76. National Conference on Social Welfare, "The Future of Long-term Care in the United States," Report of the Task Force (Washington, D.C.: The National Conference on Social Welfare, February 1977). (Multilith.)
77. Congressional Budget Office, *Long-term Care for the Elderly and Disabled* (Washington, D.C.: CBO, February 1977), p. 33.
78. Health Care Financing Administration, "Memorandum for July 14, 1978 Briefing, Major Initiative: Long-term Care/Community Service" (Washington, D.C.: HCFA, 1978), app. 9.
79. For one side of the argument see HCFA, "Memorandum for July 14 Briefing" and David A. Hamburg and Sarah Spaght Brown, "The Science

Base and Social Context of Health Maintenance: An Overview," *Science* 200, no. 4344 (26 May 1978): 847–49; for the opposing view, see John Lister, "Training for What?–Winter of Discontent," *New England Journal of Medicine*, 300, no. 12 (22 March 1979): 656–58.

80. Max Weber, *Parliament and Government in Germany*, app. 2, "Bureaucracy and Political Leadership," in Guenther Roth and Claus Wittich, eds., *Economy and Society: An Outline of Interpretive Sociology*, (New York: Bedminster Press, 1968), p. 1395.

81. R.I. Lee and L.W. Jones, *The Fundamentals of Good Medical Care* (Chicago: University of Chicago Press, 1933), cited in David M. Kessner, "Quality Assessment and Assurance: Early Signs of Cognitive Dissonance," *New England Journal of Medicine* 298, no. 7 (16 February 1978): 381–86.

82. Hamburg and Spaght, "The Science Base and Social Context of Health Maintenance"; A.L. Cochrane, *Effectiveness and Efficiency* (London: Nuffield Provincial Hospital Trust, 1972).

83. Robert L. Kane and Rosalie A. Kane, "Care of the Aged: Old Problems in Need of New Solutions," *Science* 200, no. 4344 (26 May 1978): 913–19.

84. William C. McAuliffe, "Measuring the Quality of Medical Care: Process versus Outcome," *Milbank Memorial Fund Quarterly: Health and Society* 57, no. 1 (Winter 1979): 118–52.

85. Witness the large-scale Research Development Consensus Project of the National Institutes of Health conducted since 1977.

86. Nathan Glazer, "The Attack on the Professions," *Commentary* 66, no. 5 (November 1978): 34–41.

87. Bay Area Welfare Consortium, *Final Report of the Homemaker-Chore Study*, (Berkeley: University of California School of Social Welfare, September, 1977). See also U.S. Congress, "Proprietary Home/Health Care," Joint Hearing Before Subcommittee on Long-term Care of U.S. Senate Special Committee on Aging and Subcommittee on Health and Long-term Care of Select Committee on Aging of U.S. House of Representatives, 28 October 1975 (Washington, D.C.: Government Printing Office, 1976).

88. Health Care Financing Administration, "Long-term Care Quality Assurance," Memorandum, 24 June 1978. (Draft.)

89. Health Care Financing Administration, "New Directions for Skilled Nursing and Intermediate Care Facilities," Notice of Public Meetings, n.d.

90. New York State Moreland Act Commission, *Reimbursing Operating Costs* and *Assessment and Placement: Anything Goes*, Reports 5 and 6 (New York: Moreland Act Commission, March 1976).

91. Peter Kihss, "Point System of Reclassifying Nursing-Home Patients is Under Attack," *New York Times*, December 20, 1977.

92. William J. Foley and Donald P. Schneider, "A Comparison of the Level of Care Predictions of Six Long-term Care Patient Assessment Systems," *American Journal of Public Health* 70, no. 11 (November 1980): 1152–61.

93. Ian R. Lawson, "The Antithesis Between Fiscal and Clinical Systems in Geriatric Care," in Edward J. Hinman, ed., *Advanced Medical Systems: The Third Century* (Miami: Medical Books, 1977): 93–101.

94. Walter Wenkert, John G. Hill, and Robert L. Berg, "Concepts and Methodology in Planning Patient Care Services," *Medical Care* 7, no. 4 (July–August 1969): 327–31.

95. William G. Bell, *Community Care for the Elderly: An Alternative to Institutionalization* (Tallahassee: Program in Social Policy and the Aging, Florida State University, June 1971).

96. Seidl, Mahoney, and Austin.

97. William Pollak, "Utilization of Alternative Care Settings by the Elderly: Normative Estimates and Current Patterns," Working Paper 963–12 (Washington, D.C.: Urban Institute, 13 March 1973).

98. T. Franklin Williams, et al., "Appropriate Placement of the Chronically Ill and Aged," *Journal of the American Medical Association* 226, no. 11 (10 December 1973): 1332–35.

99. See for example, Patricia Lee Kasschau and Vern L. Bengston, "The New American Dilemma: Decision-makers View Aging and Social Policy" (Los Angeles: University of Southern California, Andrus Gerontology Center, August 1977).

100. Lorrin M. Koran, "The Reliability of Clinical Methods, Data, and Judgments," *New England Journal of Medicine* 293, no. 13 (25 September 1975): 642–46, and vol. 293, no. 14 (2 October 1975): 695–701.

101. Carl V. Dunn and David W. Conrath, "Primary Care: Clinical Judgment and Reliability," *New York State Journal of Medicine* 77, no. 4 (April 1977): 748–54; see also, Robert H. Brook and Francis A. Appel, "Quality-of-Care Assessment: Choosing a Method for Peer Review," *New England Journal of Medicine* 288, no. 25 (21 June 1977): 1323–29; and Ward Casscells, Arno Schoenberger, and Thomas B. Graboys, "Interpretation by Physicians of Clinical Laboratory Results," *New England Journal of Medicine* 299, no. 18 (2 November 1978): 999–1001.

102. An interesting exception to this pattern, in the field of mental retardation, is reported by Priscilla Pitt Jones and Kenneth J. Jones, "Costs of Ideal Services to the Developmentally Disabled Under Varying Levels of Adequacy" (Waltham, Mass.: Heller School, Brandeis University, 1 July 1976).

103. Lance Liebman, "The Definition of Disability in Social Security and Supplemental Security Income: Drawing the Bounds of Social Welfare Estates," *Harvard Law Review* 89, no. 5 (March 1976): 833–67. Determinations are particularly important under SSDI and SSI because they are yes/no affairs. Gradations, which would have provided safety margins against error, are lacking here.

104. Dunn and Conrath.

105. Alan R. Shapiro, "The Evaluation of Clinical Prediction," *New England Journal of Medicine* 296, no. 26 (30 June 1977): 1509–14.

106. Ellen C. Perrin and Helen C. Goodman, "Telephone Management of Acute Pediatric Illnesses," *New England Journal of Medicine* 298, no. 3 (19 January 1978): 130–35.

107. Bruce J. Ennis and Thomas R. Litwack, "Psychiatry and the Presumption of Expertise: Flipping Coins in the Courtroom," *California Law Review* 62 (1974): 693–752. See also, "Psychiatrists' Views Found Inconsistent," *New York Times*, May 30, 1978; and Dunn and Conrath.

108. Anthony Partridge and William B. Eldridge, "The Second Circuit Sentencing Study: A Report to the Judges of the Second Circuit," (New York: Federal Judiciary Center, August 1974).

109. Jonathan Bradshaw, "The Concept of Social Need," *New Society*, 30 March 1972, pp. 640–44.

110. Pat M. Keith, "A Preliminary Investigation of the Role of the Public Health Nurse in Evaluation of Services for the Aged," *American Journal of Public Health* 66, no. 4 (April 1976): 379–81.

111. Saad Nagi, "Congruency in Medical and Self-Assessment of Disability," *Industrial Medicine* 38, no. 3 (March 1969): 27–36.

STUDY GOALS, METHOD, AND EXECUTION

4 DESIGN OF THE STUDY

GOALS

The goals of the present study emerge from the considerations just discussed. If for political reasons a policy of more generous funding for home care services were chosen—on the condition that only patients for whom home care was no more costly would be eligible—and if, for reasons of method, there are advantages to learning the costs of a hypothetical alternative to institutional care, then a base is necessary on which to estimate the cost of the in-home services. Many possible candidates could be asked their views of the cost of home care for people about to enter nursing homes. This study seeks the recommendations of most of the potential candidates.

This study has four principal goals. Goal One is to learn the extent of agreement among patients, their families, and various professionals about the types, quantities, and providers of hypothetical home care services needed to sustain patients—individually and collectively—at home. This is done by examining closely the service requests of members of the three groups. Goal One is taken up in Chapter 7.

Goal Two is to assess whose views of home care need are more valid, should patients, their families, and professionals disagree about needed services. This goal will be pursued in two ways. First, correlation and multiple regression will be used to gauge the relation of objective patient characteristics to the types of services recommended by members of the three groups (Chapter 8). Second, the extent of agreement among professionals themselves will be explored. The term "agreement" itself will be examined from a variety of directions. Analysis of variance, Kendall's W, Cronbach's Alpha, and factor analysis—supplemented by descriptive statistics—will be used to gauge the extent of agreement within and across professional lines (Chapter 9).

Goal Three is to learn how the various views of hypothetical home care cost compare with the actual cost of institutional care, and what proportion of the patients could be cared for at home at no greater expense. Further, by applying savings, achieved through diversions of some patients to home care, to subsidizing other patients for whom home care is marginally more expensive, how many could be maintained at home with no increase in system cost (Chapter 7)?

Goal Four is to learn more about both long-term care policy and planning for individuals' needs by mining the by-products of data generated to reach Goals One through Three. There is a clear need for better information regarding the association between objective patient characteristics and needed care.[1] The data suggest opportunities for establishing a cooperative model for home care planning, incorporating views of patients, families, and professionals. It appears that the cost of care plans generated through such a model would be reasonable and affordable (Chapter 10).

Disagreement about the control or influence of dependent older persons, their families, and various professionals over long-term services has been in part a product of uncertainties about the goals of those services, their costs and effects, and the legitimacy of professional knowledge. These uncertainties interact. For example, if the principal goal of long-term care is to maximize longevity, physicians or related professionals might be best able to allocate funds. Should these professionals disagree about allocation, or should they agree but their prescribed services prove of little effect, the legitimacy of their control over resources is called into question.

Alternatively, patients, families, and professionals might begin with different goals. In a particular case, the patient, understanding her condition to be terminal, might choose to live at home in relative comfort and reject life-prolonging interventions. Her family might be unwilling to continue to care for her at home and therefore prefer immediate nursing home entry. The patient's physician might argue for aggressive therapy and rehabilitation in hospital. Full real costs or benefits of any choice are seldom borne by, or even visible to, any party. To decide who should have the right to choose setting or type of care involves medical, ethical, legal, and social considerations. What, for example, is a patient's right to choose home care if her family cannot provide it and adequate formal supports are not available? What should a hospital do when its continuing care department believes home care to be unsafe but a patient declines to enter an institution? What are the rights of patient, family, and physician to seek care that is very costly if funds are limited?

Depending on the goal(s) of long-term care for a particular person, the patient, family, or one or more professionals can be supposed best able to allocate available resources to reach the chosen end(s). Today, given poor articulation of goals, various restrictions on spending, and setting of care—and often such exigencies as the need to empty a hospital bed—professionals generally choose sites and quantities of care after little consultation with patients.

Possibly, better goal articulation and cooperative planning should not even be pursued if costs are likely to preclude real choice. This would be regrettable because greater autonomy in long-term decisionmaking can be important to aged persons—particularly to those whose freedom of action generally is contracting. Given the nontechnical nature of most long-term services, the potential for a greater measure of consumer sovereignty certainly exists. Should the three groups disagree, devices are needed to reconcile them.

To help lay a firmer foundation for home care planning for individual patients, the following information should prove to be of help: data on the characteristics of patients about whom professional agreement is relatively good or bad; data on which patients are thought to need more or less home care; data on the services about which agreement is best; and data on which services and providers are thought most useful for which patients by which professionals. Finally, the effects of various types of information on professional prescriptions is measured in the hope that it will shed some light on what constitute appropriate care planning and utilization review procedures (Chapters 8 and 9).

Lacking outcomes measures and given the widespread belief that the long-term care system works badly, a better care planning process—one that is equitable, reasonable, and reliable—may help to convince legislators and bureaucrats that higher appropriations for long-term care in general and for home care in particular would not simply amount to "throwing money at problems."[2]

STUDY METHODS

The method adopted by the present study was to identify a group of patients about to enter nursing homes. There would be no interference in placement or provision of services. These patients would be admitted into nursing homes. The average per diem costs of their institutional care would be measured. But, before entering nursing homes, they would receive a full functional, medical, and psychosocial assessment. Based on this assessment and other information, a group of health and social services professionals—physicians, hospital discharge planners, and home health agency care planners—would individually design detailed home care plans for each patient included in the study.

Data gathering was planned to be accomplished in four phases. These were to: (1) compile the study sample at four Massachusetts hospitals; (2) assess patients; (3) interview patients and a member of their families; and (4) obtain professional home care plans.

The Sample

A total sample of 100 patients was sought for the study: 30 from a Boston-area teaching hospital, 20 from a Boston-area community hospital, 20 from a teaching hospital eslewhere in the state, and 30 from a community hospital elsewhere in the state. These proportions parallel the shares of discharges from these four types of hospitals. Only hospitals of 150 beds or more were included because it was felt only large facilities could generate the volume of discharges needed to complete the sample in adequate time. Of all patients admitted to nursing homes in 1973 to 1974, 34.8 percent had "resided" in acute care hospitals before entry into the homes.[3] The study sample, therefore, represents this group, allowing for differences in types of patients cared for at large versus small hospitals.

Hospitals were to be selected on several grounds. The first was their location and type of facility. The second was whether they seemed typical of their class. (A hospital specializing in care of a certain type of illness had to be excluded.) The third was whether the pertinent staffs and boards of the hospital were willing to grant permission. For the Boston-area hospitals, a fourth criterion—that the facilities be convenient to consultants who would be briefly visiting patients—was added.

The Screening Process

To be included in the study, patients had to meet several requirements. First, they had to have resided in the "community," not in an institution, prior to the hospital admission. This condition was set to assure that, when interviewed about their own home care service requirements, patients had a recent source of information about those requirements.

Patients about to enter nursing homes from the community were preferred to patients already in institutions for another reason. The former plan would be likelier to better mimic real-world policy conditions—making available home care services for patients about to enter institutions. It is relatively difficult to deinstitutionalize older patients who have lived for a long time in nursing homes and have lost their housing and other roots in their neighborhoods.[4]

Second, the discharge planner—social worker or continuing care nurse—in the hospital had to decide that the patient would be discharged to a long-term care facility—rehabilitation hospital, chronic disease hospital, skilled nursing facility, intermediate care facility, or rest home—for a stay of not less than two months. (The stay in a first facility could be less than two months if it was expected that the patient would subsequently be discharged to another long-term care facility, yielding a stay in both institutions of over two months.)

Third, the patient's physician was asked to permit participation in the study. No patient was approached and asked to participate without this permission.

Fourth, the hospital discharge planner was asked to decide if the patient was competent to understand the nature of the study, respond to questions, and give informed consent. Patients judged not competent were not approached.

Fifth, the hospital discharge planner was asked to decide if the patient could cope well enough with the emotional stress of thinking about home care, at the time of discharge to a long-term care institution, to permit participation in the study. Patients judged unable to cope were excluded. Finally, patients and the members of their families who knew the patient best (the caregiver) were approached separately and asked if they were willing to participate in the study. Consent was desired from both patient and caregiver, because each would be interviewed.

Because delays arose in the course of executing this plan, changes were made in the type of patients who could be included, the hospitals they were drawn from, and the size of the sample. These delays, and the reasons for them, will be discussed in Chapter 5. The remainder of the study design was not modified.

Patients who were excluded from the study for any of the reasons noted above were not ignored. The reason(s) for their hospital admissions, their medical diagnoses and disabling conditions, their known hospital and long-term care facility admissions, their sociodemographic characteristics—age, sex, race, ethnicity, religion, education, marital status, living arrangement, occupation, and employment status—were recorded. Based on this information, it was possible to measure how similar the study sample—those screened into the study—is to those screened out of the study (see Chapter 6).

The Patient Assessment Form

Once a patient was included in the study, an assessment form was completed (Appendix A). This included, in addition to the data just described, information about the patient's: (1) functional ability to manage activities of daily living (walking, transferring, dressing, bowel and bladder function, and the like); (2) independence in such instrumental activities of daily living as shopping and housework; (3) architectural barriers in the home; (4) composition of household; (5) capacity of informal support system; (6) psychosocial characteristics; (7) impairments and limb motion; (8) abnormal medical signs; (9) medications; (10) special nursing procedures; and (11) special personality, family, cultural or other characteristics.

The purpose of the assessment form was to assemble objective data about patients—data that would be used by consulting professionals as the base on which to design home care plans. Summary data were not given to consultants. Only information observed about patients in hospital, recorded from their medical records, or reported by them or their families was presented.

Uninterpreted, objective data were presented to professionals to provide a common base for planning individual patients' services. In this way, one potential source of disagreement regarding needed services—patients' characteristics—would be eliminated. Nonetheless, three other sources of disagreement remain. This should be borne in mind when interpreting the meaning of the levels of agreement reported in Chapters 9 and 10.

Given knowledge of patients' history and current status, professions might differ in their views of prognosis absent services.[5] Given agreement about status and prognosis, choice of different goals could lead to service packages of varying size or composition. Finally, even given unanimity about status, prognosis, and goals, professionals might differ in their estimations of the efficacy of various services and, therefore, in recommended types, quantities, or providers of care.

The patient assessment form is a version of the patient appraisal and care evaluation (PACE) form.[6] The form was adapted to home care planning by the addition of information about architectural barriers, household composition, and similar variables. The advantages of the PACE form were thought to be several. First, it seemed at the time that the PACE was going to be extensively used to evaluate federally supported long-term care programs. Study data would, therefore, be comparable with those of large-scale efforts. Second, it presented data about patients in discrete, undigested form, allowing professionals to assimilate information as they wished. Finally, the bulk of the information would be observed and recorded by health care and social service professionals who were well acquainted with patients. The PACE form was designed to perform many functions, among them research. In short, it fills most of the general requirements for good assessment forms.[7]

Several other assessment vehicles were reviewed before the PACE was selected. The one given most serious consideration was the Older American Resources and Services (OARS) inventory.[8] The OARS form had several important assets. It was carefully developed with extensive support, and it appeared likely to be used in a variety of research settings—as indeed it has been.[9] Further, the reliability and internal validity of its components were being measured, and they appeared high. The OARS was ultimately rejected because, first, most data had to be obtained from the patient. It was felt that, under the patients' circumstances in this study, too much time would be demanded. Also, to obtain so much data directly from patients might weaken their validity.[10] Second, the OARS seemed more applicable to a population less ill and disabled than that expected to be included in this study's sample; little detailed data on medical status or nursing needs were called for. Third, it was feared that the OARS was not compact enough to permit the study's consultants to review its raw data in detail in sufficient time to make its use economical.

After data collection for the present study was completed, findings were reported that suggest that medical records, an important source of certain PACE data, are inadequate in some respects. While this presents some difficulty in method for the present study, no harm is caused to patients, for care plans are only hypothetical in that home care is not actually delivered. To rely on similar sources for real-world care planning presents the danger of harming patients by providing them with too little or too much care.[11]

Patient and Caregiver Interviews

The second source of data acquired for the study was to be obtained by conducting separate interviews with patients and with their principal caregivers. In view of the apparent importance to well-being of older people of ability to make decisions for themselves, it was thought useful to ask patients, hypothetically, what services they would need to live at home in a "safe, adequate, and dignified manner." Such questions go beyond patient choice about site of care; they open the door to learning more about how older people regard their needs for service. If patients' control over setting of long-term care is judged important, it seems reasonable to consider control over level of service to be important as well.

To learn what areas patients saw themselves as needing help in, they would be asked, service by service, for forty-one separate areas, whether they needed assistance and, if so, how many times per week they would need that help. These services included several in the area of personal care, such as bathing and dressing; several housekeeping services, such as cooking and cleaning; a range of nursing services; and a set of medical and therapeutic services. A full list of all services is appended to this chapter. In addition, patients were asked how many times per week they thought an unpaid provider would be able to render assistance in each service area. The difference between the total number of episodes of help sought and the number of unpaid episodes would be the number of paid episodes for which formally organized services would be required.

Based on these data, comparisons could be made between patients, between patient and caregiver, and among patient, caregiver, and professionals regarding several variables of interest. These were the types of services where help was thought necessary, how many episodes were requested, and the breakdown of requests into paid and unpaid help. Similar comparisons could be made for total episodes of help sought and for each of the four categories—personal care, housekeeping, nursing, and medical-therapeutic—just mentioned.

Patients' views were sought for several reasons. If patients were to have some sovereignty as consumers of long-term care services, it would be useful to compare the types and quantities of help they thought necessary with the views of caregivers and professionals. This would make it possible to compare, in a rough way, the potential costs of the help requested by patients with that thought necessary by caregivers or professionals.

Episodes of help were the only items requested from patients or family members. Professionals were asked to also indicate the duration of each episode and the preferred provider(s) of care. In this way, the cost of professional plans could be estimated with fair accuracy, but professional-caregiver-patient plans could be compared using only episodes. (This decision was made so as to reduce stress on patients and caregivers by shortening interviews with them to about fifteen minutes.

Agreement among patients, caregivers, and professionals would, as a signal of reliability, induce confidence that the services requested were the services needed. Reliability points to validity. This is not enough to insure validity, but without it, validity (or confidence that selected services would be effective services) is impossible. If there is disagreement among patients, caregivers, and professionals, it must be decided who should be permitted to allocate services. There are several goals to try to reach in making this decision. They include the importance of choice itself to many patients; the need to support caregivers, to sustain their efforts; and the desire to provide the services that will do the most to enhance medical, functional, and emotional well-being of the patient.

Professional Care Plans

Eighteen professionals were asked to write a detailed care plan for each patient in the study sample. The care plan was designed to be completed service by service and provider by provider so as to avoid inducing professionals to overlook services they believed necessary to patients' well-being. For each service, such as bathing, meal preparation, supervision of medications, or physical therapy, the professional was asked to indicate: first, whether the patient required the service; second, how long it would take to provide the service on average on each occasion; third, the total number of episodes per week (or month) the service would be needed; and fourth, who should provide the service and how often (Appendix C). A separate care plan was sought for each of two successive three-month periods following hospital discharge.[12] This would yield an estimate of the types, quantities, and providers of services thought necessary for the patient to live at home in a safe, adequate, and dignified manner.

When first conceived, the study design was to have each professional prepare three separate care plans for each patient. The first was to be an optimal plan, containing all the services from which the patient might be expected to benefit. The second was to be a plan designed to approximate in its effectiveness the care the patient could be anticipated to receive in an institution of average quality that offered the level of service the patient was expected to require at discharge. The third was to be a minimal plan, containing the fewest possible services necessary to safety. The cost of preparing, editing, key-punching, and computing all these data made it necessary ultimately to reduce to one the number of plans sought. It was decided to set as the standard that level of service which the professional thought would yield safe, adequate, and dignified home care.

In asking the professionals to write care plans, it was assumed that any patient could be safely cared for at home, given appropriate care. All conceivable goods or services could be hypothetically brought into the home. It was up to each professional to prescribe the types, quantities, and providers of services necessary. Drugs, appliances, supplies, and equipment were omitted from the care plan. It was assumed that these would vary directly with needed services, and a cost equal to 5 percent of the cost of services was included in calculating the total cost of home care to attempt to reflect these costs.

As originally conceived, the project would employ nine consultant professionals. Each would prepare a care plan on each of one hundred patients. Three of the professionals would be physicians of different specialties, three would be hospital discharge planners, and three would be home health agency care planners. Half of the latter six would, it was hoped, be nurses; the other half, social workers. Members of different professions, carrying out different roles, were sought because each was thought to have an important perspective on patients' needs. It was desired to know how well the three groups—physicians, nurses, and social workers—agreed with one another about patient needs. Two sorts of comparisons were sought: intraprofession (how well physicians agreed with one another, for example) and interprofession (how well physicians agreed with discharge planners, for example). In the subsequent analyses, role rather than training is the variable most frequently used to divide professionals from one another.

It has been desired throughout to obtain from each care planner his or her own, independent views of patient needs. While it might be argued that each sort of professional should be considered expert in his or her field,[13] the present study treats this argument not as given but as a question to be investigated. For example, according to Berg, et al.:

> The decision as to what health care is needed is generally regarded as the physician's responsibility, but he may not always be well informed regarding the availability of the needed services in different settings. In particular for the chronically ill or disabled patient who does not require institutional care, nurse observers can often judge the supervision of services required as well as or better than physicians.[14]

It was decided in the course of the present study that, given the range of problems borne by patients in need of long-term care, it would be a useful exercise to attempt to learn whether different professionals indeed tended to be more consistent in their views of needs in the areas falling within their own fields of specialization or whether all professionals tended to agree equally well across all needs.

In addition to the team approach to care planning, which follows from acceptance of the specialization argument, a Delphi approach to planning was considered and rejected.[15] (In Delphi, a number of persons make independent decisions and then are told how the others decided. Each then makes a new decision. A movement toward consensus usually ensues. There is no way of learning immediately whether the consensus is a valid one.) Again, it was desired to learn the views of the individual professionals now practicing. It should be noted that some professions whose views of patient need are most important (such as physical or occupational therapists) were excluded from the sample simply in the interest of achieving a number of each group included sufficient to permit useful analysis of differences within professions and averages across professions. When it became possible to expand the sample of professionals, it was decided to vary the information available for care planning rather than the number of professions. At the same time, difficulties in securing the desired sample size of one hundred led to more intensive analyses on a reduced sample of fifty.

Each of the nine original professionals was to rely only on the PACE form in prescribing home care. When the opportunity arose to double the sample of professionals, it was decided at the same time to test the effect of the type of information available to professionals on the prescribed types, quantities, and providers of services. Before writing their care plans, six of the additional prescribers would, at the Boston-area hospitals only, review the PACE forms and then briefly (for five-to-ten minutes) visit each patient just prior to hospital discharge. Two of the six were physicians, two were hospital discharge planners, and two were home care planners. Because these professionals would visit only the patients at the Boston-area hospitals, the nature of their care plans could be compared with those of the nine who never visited, to distinguish the effect of visiting from the effect of their individual characteristics as professionals. Dunn and Conrath found that reliability of professional views seemed independent of information levels. It was desired here to see if reliability in home care planning varied with information.

Three additional professionals who knew individual patients well were also asked to write care plans. These were each patient's own physician, discharge planner, and primary care or floor nurse. They were asked to rely on the PACE and their own detailed knowledge of the patient. Each of these three profes-

Table 4-1. A Sketch of the Care Planning Process.

	Professionals Categorized by Information Available			
	Consultants			
Professionals Categorized by Role	Nonvisiting	Visiting	Inhospital	Total
Physicians	3	2	1	6
Discharge Planners	3	2	1	6
Home Health	3	2	—	5
Floor Nurses	—	—	1	1
Total	9	6	3	18

Notes:

Each of the eighteen professionals received a copy of the patient's completed PACE form. The eighteen care planners wrote 50 care plans, yielding a total of 900.

Each care plan indicated prescribed help in each of forty-one services (grouped into four service subtotals). Providers were selected from among fifty-eight titles (grouped into ten provider categories). The dependent variables were episodes, hours, and costs of care.

sionals would be expected to write only a few care plans: physicians and floor nurses might prepare one or two; discharge planners would prepare one for each of their patients screened into the study. By contrast, each of the other fifteen professionals would write a plan for each patient. The fifteen are referred to as "consultants," either "visitors" (six), or "nonvisitors" (nine). The remaining three are called "hospital care planners." Table 4-1 presents an overview of the care planning process, identifying the different groups of professionals and patients.

Of the fifteen consultant professionals, nine relied exclusively on PACE data for all patients; six other consultants visited some patients but relied exclusively on PACE data for the others. The three hospital professionals used PACE data and their own personal knowledge in all cases. The data recorded in each plan were analyzed in total (hours, episodes, and costs of care) and in detail by type of service and by type of provider. These various subtotals will be explained in Part III.

APPENDIX TO CHAPTER 4

The Forty-One Services

Personal Care

Caregiving/Supervision—continuous
Periodic checking
Bathing
Dressing
Toilet
Transferring
Supervision of medication
Turning in bed
Grooming
Eating and drinking

Household

Shopping
Meal preparation
Telephone
Transportation
Socialization
Light housework
Heavy housework
Laundry
Management of personal affairs

Nursing

Bowel/Bladder training
Decubitus care

Nursing (cont'd.)

Wound care
Eye care
Bladder irrigation
Suctioning/chest PT
Inhalation/IPPB therapy
Other oxygen therapy
Range of motion exercises
Nutritional/Diet exercises
Medications administered
Monitoring of vital signs
Mental and neurological status
Foot care
Teaching and other nursing

Other Professional Services

Primary medical care
Medical specialist care
Dentist
Podiatrist
Physical therapy
Occupational therapy
Psychotherapy/Counseling

Categories of Providers

Paid Providers

Medical

M.D.–Primary (G.P., F.P., Internist)
M.D.–Specialist
Dentist
Podiatrist

Nursing

Registered Nurse
Licensed Practical Nurse
Nurse Practitioner
Physician's Assistant
Psychiatric Nurse Clinician

Personal Care

Homemaker
Home Health Aide
Homemaker/Home Health Aide
Personal Care Attendant
Orderly

Support

Social Worker
Escort Service
Sitting Service
Daily Checking Service
Visiting Aide
Community Geriatric Coordinator
Community Mental Health Worker
Companion
Lawyer

Therapy

Inhalation Respiratory Therapist
Physical Therapist
Physical Therapy Aide
Occupational Therapist
Occupational Therapy Aide
Recreational Therapist
Dietician
Dietary Aide
Speech Therapist
Laboratory Technician

Paid Providers (cont'd.)

Miscellaneous

Home Delivery (groceries, etc.)
Meals-On-Wheels
Laundry/Diaper Service
Heavy Chore Service
Cleaning Agency
Ambulance
Medicab
Redi-Van/Chair car
Hairdresser
Talking Books

Unpaid Providers

Resident

Family
Friend

Nonresident

Family
Friend
Clergy
Friendly Visitor
Transportation service – e.g. Minibus
    for Senior Citizens
Building Superintendent

Skilled Providers

M.D.–Primary (G.P., F.P., Internist)
M.D.–Specialist
Dentist
Podiatrist
Nurse Practitioner
Physician's Assistant
Psychiatric Nurse Clinician
Registered Nurse
Licensed Practical Nurse
Lab. Technician
Social Worker
Inhalation/Respiratory Therapist
Physical Therapist
Occupational Therapist
Recreational Therapist

Categories of Providers (cont'd.)

Skilled Providers (cont'd.)	*Unskilled Providers (cont'd.)*
Dietician	Physical Therapy Aide
Speech Therapist	Family- resident
Clergy	Family- nonresident
Lawyer	Friend- resident
	Friend- nonresident
	Transportation Service – e.g. Minibus
Unskilled Providers	for Senior Citizens
Homemaker	Redi -van/ Chair car
Home Health Aide	Ambulance
Homemaker/ Home Health Aide	Medicab
Personal Care Attendant	Meals-on-Wheels
Orderly	Laundry/ Diaper Service
Escort Service	Heavy Chore Service
Sitting Service	Cleaning Agency
Daily Checking service	Building Superintendent
Visiting Aide	Hardresser
Friendly Visitor	Talking Books
Home Delivery Service	Community/ Mental Health Worker
Community Geriatric Coordinator	Companion

NOTES TO CHAPTER 4

1. See, for example, the report on long-term care by former HHS Under-secretary Nathan Stark, *Home Health Line* 5 (28 November 1980): 160–62.
2. It is believed, in sum, that these goals would, if attained, help respond to many of the concerns raised in Anthony Lenzer and Avedis Donabedian, "Needed . . . Research in Home Care," *Nursing Outlook* 10, no. 10 (October 1967): 42–45.
3. National Center for Health Statistics, "Characteristics, Social Contacts, and Activities of Nursing Home Residents, United States 1973–1974," National Nursing Home Survey, *Vital and Health Statistics*, ser. 13, no. 27 (May 1977).
4. On the difficulties of deinstitutionalization, see Barry Siegel and Judith Lasker, "Deinstitutionalizing Elderly Patients: A Program of Resocialization," *The Gerontologist* 18, no. 3 (June 1978): 293–300.
5. Robert H. Brook and Francis A. Appel, "Quality-of-Care Assessment: Choosing a Method for Peer Review," *New England Journal of Medicine*, 288, no. 25 (21 June 1973): 1323–29; and Margaret W. Linn, Lee Gurel, and Bernard S. Linn, "Patient Outcome as a Measure of Quality of Nursing Home Care," *American Journal of Public Health* 67, no. 4 (April 1977): 337–44 offer evidence on disagreement about prognosis.

6. The PACE is the product of collaboration among workers at four universities. See Ellen W. Jones, Barbara J. McNitt, and Eleanor M. McKnight, *Patient Classification for Long-term Care: User's Manual*, DHEW Pub. No. HRA 74-3107 (Washington, D.C.: Bureau of Health Services Research and Evaluation, December, 1973).

7. These requirements are described in: Institute of Medicine, *The Elderly and Functional Dependency: A Policy Statement* (Washington, D.C.: National Academy of Sciences, June 1977), pp. 16-17; M. Powell Lawton, "The Functional Assessment of Elderly People," *Journal of the American Geriatric Society* 19, no. 6 (December 1971): 465-81.

8. Eric Pfeiffer, ed., *Multidimensional Functional Assessment: The OARS Methodology* (Durham, N.C.: Duke University Center for the Study of Aging and Human Development, 1975).

9. *Multidimensional Functional Assessment: The OARS Methodology* (Durham, N.C.: Duke University Center for the Study of Aging and Human Development, 1978), app. C.

10. Janet Plant, "Various Approaches Proposed to Assess Quality in Long-Term Care," *Hospitals* 51, no. 17 (September 1977): 93-98.

11. Linda K. Demlo, Paul M. Campbell, and Sarah Spaght Brown, "Reliability of Information Abstracted from Patients' Medical Records," *Medical Care* 16, no. 12 (December 1978): 995-1005.

12. To ask professionals to look forward six months seemed reasonable. This estimate coincides with that of Linn, et al. No validation of the reasonableness of choosing this duration is yet available.

13. Kathleen Connelly, Philip K. Cohen, and Diana Chapman Walsh, "Periodic Medical Review: Assessing the Quality and Appropriateness of Care in Skilled-Nursing Facilities," *New England Journal of Medicine* 296, no. 15 (14 April 1977): 878-80. On the advantages of team planning generally, see Sidney Katz, Laura Halstead, and Mary Wierenga, "A Medical Perspective of Team Care," in Sylvia Sherwood, ed., *Long-term Care: A Handbook for Researchers, Planners, and Providers* (New York: Spectrum, 1975); John E. Schuman and Harold N. Willard, "Role of the Acute Hospital Team in Planning Discharge of the Chronically Ill," *Geriatrics* 31, no. 2 (February 1976): 63-67.

14. Robert L. Berg, et al., "Assessing the Health Care Needs of the Aged," *Health Services Research* 5, no. 1 (Spring 1970): 36-59, citing R. Walker and C. Frost, "Measurement of Social Restoration of the Mentally Ill by the General Adjustment and Planning Scale," *Health Services Research* 4, no. 2 (Summer 1969): 152ff.

15. Rachel M. Rosser, "The Reliability and Application of Clinical Judgment in Evaluating the Use of Hospital Beds," *Medical Care* 14, no. 1 (January 1976): 39-48; see also the comment and reply in *Medical Care* 15, no. 6 (June 1977): 527-31. For an exciting use of a mechanized Delphi incorporating clinical judgment and empirical observations, see Richard M. Burton, William W. Damon, and David C. Dellinger, "Estimating the Impact of Health Services in a Community," *Behavioral Science* 21 (1976): 478-89.

5 EXECUTION OF THE STUDY

Data gathering was planned to be conducted in six steps: designing forms, introducing the study in hospitals, orienting consultants, screening patients, completing forms, and managing information. Five of these proceeded as expected. The other, screening patients into the study, took much longer than planned. Consequently, certain aspects of the design had to be altered, even though these changes would somewhat affect the analyses planned. This chapter briefly sets out data gathering plans, discusses problems encountered and how they were overcome, and indicates how changes in design affected the methods and products of analyses.

DESIGNING FORMS

The PACE form required some adaptation to enhance its utility to home care planning. A copy of the revised form appears in Appendix A. Additional space was provided to record medical diagnoses. A new section on major disabling conditions and their dates of onset was added. The patient's anticipated site of discharge was indicated, along with expected length of stay at that site. No changes were made in material on functional ability. A new section on instrumental activities of daily living was included. To learn patients' needs for assistance in mobility, inquiry into the presence of stairs and other barriers in the home was made.

Information was requested on the composition of patients' households prior to hospitalization and the hours when family or friends were available in the home. This was followed by the assessment by the discharge planner of the ability and willingness of the family or other informal support to care for the patient in either their home or the patient's home. The PACE's sections on psychosocial functioning and impairment were retained with minor changes. Granger's criteria for evaluating active limb motion were added.[1]

The section on medical status was expanded to leave room for many possible abnormal and normal test results and findings. Purpose of medications was sought. The nursing procedures section was enlarged to include space for recording what teaching had been done. For both medications and nursing procedures, those completing the forms were asked to indicate what was expected to be continued following discharge.

The general design of patient interview and professional care plan forms was described in Chapter 4. These forms inquired about the same services, to permit comparison of requested episodes of care among patients, caregivers, and professionals. The patient and caregiver interview was designed to be completed in fifteen to twenty minutes. The professional care plan was intended to take thirty to sixty minutes to fill out, depending on familiarity with the form and the number of services the patient was thought to need. Because of coding and other requirements, the care planning form was somewhat time consuming to complete for the first patient or two. With practice, it seemed to go well. For hospital professionals, most of whom completed only one care plan, the design of the form probably did not enhance its acceptance. More important, it can be speculated that lack of familiarity with the form may have been a factor influencing these care planners' relatively high level of prescribed hours. Because the hospital professionals were not familiar with the forms, they may have prescribed duplicate care to ensure that patients received needed services, not realizing that such care had already been called for. One piece of evidence weakens the power of this explanation: While hospital discharge planners' mean prescribed hours for fifty patients fell slightly below that of hospital physicians, it exceeded that of floor nurses. Most discharge planners wrote several care plans. Most physicians or floor nurses wrote only one.

INTRODUCING THE STUDY

The task of introducing the study in the hospitals was accomplished in two phases. The first was to secure permission to conduct the project in the hospital; the second was to orient the hospital coordinator and other workers to data-gathering methods.

All of the four hospitals initially approached proved willing to participate. Once permission was obtained, there followed the task of orienting the in-hospital coordinator to study procedures. The coordinator was the person responsible for discharge planning—usually the head of the social service department or the chief continuing care nurse. The hospital coordinator was responsible for supervising all aspects of in-hospital data collection—patient screening, obtaining informed consent, completing the PACE form, obtaining the three hospital professionals' care plans, mailing all completed forms to the study team at the Levinson Policy Institute, and recording the date, site, and level of care of discharge.

Coordinating data collection was a complex job. All forms had to be completed prior to a patient's discharge and, at the Boston-area hospitals, in sufficient time to allow scheduling the six visits by consultants. (To protect patients, coordinators were asked the number of visits per day to be permitted.) After one or two patients had been screened into the study, data collection appeared to run smoothly at most hospitals.

SELECTING CONSULTANTS

While negotiations with hospitals were proceeding, consultants were recruited and oriented to the study. Their selection was purposive. In each category it was desired to request the participation of well-trained professionals who were experienced in dealing with older patients requiring long-term care. Realizing that it would be difficult to perform multivariate analyses of the relation of professional variables (such as age, experience, and attitude) to the magnitude or composition of home care plans, it was decided to seek the involvement of professionals who by reason of training, experience, and reputation seemed likely to represent good present practice in long-term care. It was also decided that the number of full-time equivalent years of direct patient care of the members of the three groups, on average, would be similar. This criterion was met. Physicians averaged 8.2 years of full-time equivalent practice, hospital discharge planners averaged 11.6 years, and home health planners averaged 8.7 years. Of the five consultant physicians, one was a geriatrician, one was a physiatrist, one was a psychiatrist and internist, and two were internists specializing in cardiology and oncology, respectively. All worked at teaching hospitals in Boston. Three of the discharge planners were registered nurses, one was a social worker, and one had degrees in both nursing and social work. Three of the home care planners were nurses; two were social workers. One worked in a hospital-based home care program, one in a neighborhood health center, one in a visiting nurse association, and two in home care corporations (the organizational vehicles for providing Title XX-funded homemaker and chore services to the elderly in Massachusetts). All hospital discharge planners and home care planners were employed in the Boston metropolitan area.

While all consultants were familiar with the needs of patients receiving long-term care, three did not have extensive home care experience. Their home care prescriptions did not, however, differ systematically from those of the remaining twelve consultants.

SCREENING PATIENTS

Several difficulties were identified during the first two months of screening. At some hospitals, some physicians were reluctant to permit their patients to participate. Possible reasons were fear for patients' safety or reluctance themselves to complete forms. Other physicians were willing to allow their patients to be included in the study but were not themselves prepared to complete care plans. To counter the first difficulty, opportunities were identified to present information about the study to physicians. To increase the rate at which patients were screened into the study, it was decided to drop the requirement that physicians be willing to complete care plans. As a result, hospital physicians' care plans are available on only 52 percent of patients.

A second difficulty pertained to the time required to coordinate the study in the hospital. In some institutions, coordinators proved too busy to discharge all tasks. Ways of dividing the work were found. Hospital administrators offered encouragement to help accomplish this.

The third and more serious difficulty concerned the slow rate at which patients were being screened and accepted into the study. At two of the hospitals, coordinators reported that fewer patients were being discharged to nursing homes than in recent years. This may have been attributable in part to a tightening of the Massachusetts long-term care bed supply relative to the population of likely candidates for care.

At all hospitals, the tighter bed supply may have resulted in a change in the distribution of characteristics of patients being discharged to nursing homes. Coordinators reported an increase in the average frailty, disability, and level of illness of patients being placed in institutions.

These changes in both the numbers and characteristics of patients referred from hospitals to nursing homes had three consequences. First, they probably reduced the number of patients who could potentially be screened into the study. Patients had to be cogent and sufficiently robust emotionally to cope with participation. Second, it probably meant a change in the composition of the study sample. Arguably, patients screened into the study were older, more frail, more disabled, and more ill than would have been the case had the study been conducted two years or even one year earlier. Third, it slowed the rate of intake into the study sample. This problem and how it was dealt with affected the size and composition of the sample, its representativeness, and the goals and analyses of the study itself.

In response to the slow rate at which patients were being screened into the study, two steps were taken. The number of hospitals included in the study was increased, and one of the requirements for inclusion in the study was dropped. Two more institutions, one a Boston-area teaching hospital and the other a Boston-area community hospital, agreed to participate in the study. This led to an increase in the study sample's rate of growth. Even more important was the decision to introduce a new class of patients. These patients might be too frail or ill to be interviewed or otherwise disturbed by the study. The role of these "limited participants" in the study was, therefore, entirely passive: they were not disturbed. Assessment data about them were recorded, their principal caregiver was interviewed, and professional care plans were completed. Assessment data that full participants supplied was obtained from the caregivers of limited participants. Of the final sample, 58 percent were full participants, most of whom were interviewed, and 42 percent were limited participants.

Addition of two hospitals and the inclusion of limited participants helped speed intake, but not enough to complete the planned sample of one hundred patients in time to permit processing and analysis of data. Therefore, the sample size had to be cut back to fifty patients.

At the same time, the sample became more representative of the entire population being discharged from Massachusetts hospitals to nursing homes. As planned, the sample would have stood for only those patients alert and emotionally robust enough to cope with full participation. Inclusion of limited participants meant that more frail older persons would be represented as well.

In summary, several aspects of the design and execution of the study, and of the long-term care environment during execution, probably affected the composition of the sample. Some of these influences were consequences of study method; others accompanied reactions to the slow rate at which patients were initially being screened into the sample; and still others followed from the tightened availability of nursing home beds in Massachusetts both generally and—as a consequence of Massachusetts Medicaid reimbursement policies—particularly for Medicaid-funded patients.

Two forces worked toward a relatively healthy, alert, and robust sample, and four countervailing forces worked toward a relatively ill, confused, and frail sample. In the first direction, the initial requirements that all patients must be medically, intellectually, and emotionally able to give informed consent and be interviewed excluded patients who would tend to require more help to remain safely at home. Human subjects protection obligations and other guarantees of safety built into the study's screening process also had this effect.

Several forces, however, worked to offset these. The most important was the introduction of "limited participation." Here, the desire to interview patients was sacrificed in the interests of securing a sample and, to a lesser extent, representativeness. In the final sample, full and limited participants were indeed very different in all important respects. Across all eighteen professionals, a mean of 45 percent more hours of care was recommended for the average limited participant than for the average full participant.

Several other forces acted to include relatively ill, frail, and disabled patients in the sample. Because as a condition of participation, a family member or close friend who knew the patient at home had to be available to be interviewed, some patients in relatively good condition had to be excluded from the study. Patients who lived with someone or who otherwise had help available at home were able to live at home in the face of greater disability than those who lacked such help.

Because of the considerable and growing difficulty of obtaining nursing home beds in Massachusetts during the time when patients were being screened into the study, more patients who in past years would probably have been sent from hospitals participating in the study to nursing homes were sent home instead (Table 5-1). This may also have reflected the growing availability of Title XX-funded home care. Vladeck reported a similar pattern in New York State.[2]

It might be expected that, given tight nursing home bed supply, some nursing homes sought to "cream" patients by taking those requiring relatively little care. This did not seem to have been a common practice in the experience of discharge planners at hospitals participating in the present study.

As the nursing home population became sicker and older, however, and as Medicaid payment levels lagged behind cost increases, increasing numbers of nursing homes in Massachusetts limited the proportion of their beds available to Medicaid patients. Consequently, such patients remained atypically long in hospitals and were therefore likelier to be included in the study sample.[3]

This comes about because a considerable amount of time was required to complete study forms and, at Boston-area hospitals, to arrange for consultant visits to patients. Patients discharged to nursing homes before these steps could be completed tended to be in relatively good condition and to have incomes and assets above the very lowest, in that they did not require Medicaid support at time of nursing home admission.

Changes in screening requirements and methods affected both the composition of the study sample and analyses that were conducted. Some analyses in Part III, such as that concerning the proportion of the sample that could have been cared for at home at no increase in cost, probably were relatively sensitive to sample characteristics. But other analyses, such as that of interprofessional agreement, may have been relatively insensitive to sample characteristics.

Table 5-1. Patient Discharges for Long-term Care from Sample Hospitals, 1975-1977.

Year	Discharge to LTC Facilities[a]	Percentage Change From Previous Year	Discharges to Home Care	Percentage Change From Previous Year
1975	1995		575	
1976	2296	+ 15.1%	806	+ 40.2%
1977	1938	15.6%	1050	+ 30.3%

Source:
Unpublished annual hospital statistical reports.
a. Chronic care and rehabilitation hospitals, SNFs, ICFs, and rest homes.

Several other consequences followed from sampling changes. The smaller sample would represent a more diverse group. It was expected that full participants would be only about 50 percent of the reduced sample. This would permit analyses across a broader spectrum of patient characteristics—an advantage. Relations between patient characteristics and service need across fifty patients could be calculated, but the smaller sample size would reduce reliability of associations between a certain level of need for care and a certain kind of patient. It might be difficult to say much about the care needs of different classes of patients. The smaller sample size might reduce the strength of multiple regression techniques of associating independent patient variables with dependent variables of average hours of prescribed home care, average cost of prescribed home care, or professional agreement about home care needs.

A further consequence of the drop in sample size and the additional limited participation was the diminution of the number of patients to be interviewed. Of twenty-eight full participants, only twenty-three (82%) could actually be interviewed. This restricted the power of the comparison between patient and professional requests for home care services. Finally, the caregivers of only twenty of these twenty-three patients were themselves interviewed. In all, thirty-six (72%) of the caregivers were interviewed, but in only the twenty cases could patient-caregiver-professional comparisons be made. Nonetheless, these results were interesting for what they suggest. The smaller sample size also meant somewhat reduced power of regression analyses of the characteristics of patients for whom home care was cheaper. The same difficulty limited factor analyses of professional clusters of agreement about patient needs.

As the study progressed, the importance of measuring reliability and equity of professional views became increasingly apparent. A final mode of analysis here was to see how well individual professionals agree with themselves about patient needs. All consultants were asked to redo ten care plans on patients for whom they had already written prescriptions. The self-consistency of professionals' judgments over time will be presented in Chapter 9.

COMPLETING FORMS AND MANAGING INFORMATION

PACE forms were completed while patients were in the hospital. Patients and caregivers were interviewed separately during this time. Before discharge of patients to be visited, hospital coordinators phoned study staff at the Levinson Policy Institute (LPI). Staff scheduled consultant visits. When a PACE form was completed, it was mailed to LPI, whence copies were distributed to all consultants who did not visit that particular patient.

Consultants mailed all care plans to LPI. Hospital coordinators collected the three care plans completed by hospital professionals and mailed them, with the patient and caregiver interviews, to LPI. In the entire process, only one form, a care plan, was lost and had to be redone. At LPI, a double-entry log system was established to govern the flow of forms and to serve as a bookkeeping device to insure that all who completed forms were paid in a timely manner. It was also a device to learn which forms might be missing on a given patient or which care plans might be outstanding from a given consultant. The diligence of the study staff in managing data meant that none of over 1,500 forms was misplaced.

At LPI, PACE and screening forms were coded; interviews and care plans were edited and coded. An able staff of Brandeis undergraduates assisted LPI in these jobs. Key-punching was done by contract. Approximately 29,000 cards of data were generated on the study sample of fifty patients. All data were edited and all analyses were run at Harvard University's computer center.

A FOLLOW-UP STUDY

To address some of the issues posed or left unresolved by the study reported here, a follow-up project has been conducted.[4] This new project's findings will be selectively reported in Part III when they bear on analyses undertaken for the first study.

The follow-up project aimed to compare professional views of the home care needs of a sample of about one hundred actual recipients of home care in Massachusetts with the care being provided. Professional prescriptions were compared not wih actual nursing home costs, but rather with actual hours of home care. Major aims of the follow-up project were to gauge the equity and adequacy of in-home care, learn more about the relation of client characteristics to need for care, and assess whether public in-home supports tended to buttress or displace family contributions. Ten of the fifteen professional consultants serving in the first study remained for the follow-up. Once again, client and caregiver views of needed services were sought. The members of the second project's sample were slightly older but less disabled than the members of the first.

In the follow-up, needed long-term care was grouped into nine outcome-related domains of well-being; in the first study, four skill-related subtotals have been employed. This somewhat inhibits detailed comparisons of findings, but relations between the two efforts can still be usefully drawn.

NOTES TO CHAPTER 5

1. For this and other aspects of Granger's work, see Carl V. Granger, Marilyn Kaplan, Richard H. Fortinsky, and Donna A. Dryer, "Long-Term Care: Evaluation and Proposed Model for Delivery of Services to Chronically Ill People in the Metropolitan Providence Area" (Providence, R.I.: Metropolitan Nursing and Health Services Association, 31 March 1978).
2. Bruce C. Vladeck, "Some Issues in the Economics and Financing of Long-term Care" (Paper prepared for the Institute on Continuity of Long-term

Care, Arden House, New York, December 18–20, 1977); See also "Nursing Home Bed Shortage," *New York Times* 13 June 1978; and "Shortage of Space in Nursing Homes Plagues Elderly," *Washington Post*, 16 June 1978; Jean Dietz, "Useless Hospitalizations cited in Report on Nursing Home Beds," *Boston Globe*, 3 May 1979.

3. Leonard Gruenberg and Thomas R. Willemain, "Hospital Discharge Queues in Massachusetts," DP–29 (Waltham, Mass.: University Health Policy Consortium, Brandeis University, November 1980).

4. Alan Sager, et al., *Living At Home: The Roles of Public and Informal Supports in Sustaining Disabled Older Americans* (Waltham, Mass.: Levinson Policy Institute, Brandeis University, March 1982).

6 THE STUDY SAMPLE

This chapter describes the fifty patients who made up the study sample and indicates in some detail how they variously resembled and differed from 1) residents of U.S. and Massachusetts nursing homes and 2) those patients at participating hospitals who were screened out of the study.

Descriptive variables were not chosen because they were interesting in some abstract sense. Rather, patient characteristics were recorded on the PACE form in the hope that they would inform professionals' hypothetical home care plans. While describing the sample, the reasons these variables might influence care planning will be indicated.

FORCES AFFECTING SAMPLING

In 1973 to 1974 34.8 percent of U.S. nursing home residents had been discharged from acute care hospitals directly to nursing homes. For the northeast region of the country, this figure was 41.0 percent.[1] In Massachusetts, however, as indicated in Table 6-1 this proportion was both considerably higher and increasing. Thus, it is reasonable to assume that, because groups who reside in different settings before entering nursing homes have different characteristics, the study sample is more representative of persons newly admitted to Massachusetts' nursing homes than a sample similarly drawn in most other states would be of populations of persons newly admitted to nursing homes in those states. Finally, it should be noted that not all patients in the study sample were discharged to "nursing homes." Seven of the fifty were actually placed in rehabilitation/chronic disease hospitals. Massachusetts has an unusually large number of beds

Table 6-1. Sources of Admission to Massachusetts Nursing Homes and Rest Homes, 1973 and 1975.

Source of Admission	1973[a]		1975[b]	
	Number	Percent	Number	Percent
Acute Hospital	21,448	57.7%	23,859	67.6%
Mental hospital	1,746	4.7	1,159	3.3
Other nursing/Rest home	3,686	9.9	3,383	9.6
Private residence	6,768	18.2	5,856	16.6
Other level of same home	2,616	7.0		
Other	936	2.5	1,024	2.9
Total all sources	37,200	100.0%	35,281	100.0%

a. Figures from the Massachusetts Department of Public Health, *Health Data Annual, 1974* (Boston: Mass. Dept. of Public Health, 30 October 1974), Table 67.

b. Figures from the Massachusetts Department of Public Health, *Health Data Annual, 1976* (Boston: Mass. Dept. of Public Health, 12 May 1977), Table 42.

in such institutions; it is widely believed that many of them would by virtue of their services and their charges be classified as skilled nursing facilities in most other states. Massachusetts has a relative deficit of SNF beds.[2] For these reasons, it was deemed appropriate to include in the study sample these seven patients.

THE SAMPLE: CHARACTERISTICS AND COMPARISONS

Fifty patients were screened into the study sample from six different Massachusetts hospitals over the fifteen months from April 1977 to June 1978. This section will describe these patients in detail to permit comparisons with other samples. It will also describe how patients screened into the study differed from those screened out.

Age and Sex

As Table 6-2 indicates, the sex distribution of the study sample was fairly close to Massachusetts and U.S. patterns. The sample had two or three fewer men than would have been required to conform to the general proportions. As measured by median age, both the men and women of the sample were slightly younger than their state or national counterparts. This is as expected, since age of new entrants is compared with average age of all residents. Greater age is associated with greater functional problems. These problems increase especially after age seventy-five.[3]

Table 6-2. Study Sample versus Massachusetts and U.S. Nursing Home Populations: Sex and Age Comparisons.

	Male	Female	Total
Percentage By Sex			
Sample	24.0%	76.0%	100.0%
Mass.[a]	27.8%	72.2%	100.0%
U.S.[b]	29.6%	70.4%	100.0%
Median Age By Sex			
Sample	75.5	81.0	79.5
Mass.[a]	76.7	81.8	80.7
U.S.[c]	78.2	83.1	81.0

a. Figures from the Massachusetts Department of Public Health, *Health Data Annual, 1976* (Boston: Mass. Dept. of Public Health, 1974), Table 45. Median age of residents, not admissions.

b. National Center for Health Statistics, *Vital and Health Statistics*, ser. 13, no. 28, Table D.

c. Ibid., Table 3. Age of residents adjusted to reflect age at admission.

Marital Status

Sixteen of the patients in the sample (32%) had a living spouse, whereas only 12.4 percent of U.S. nursing home residents have one. The significance of this information is not clear. It may signify that home care for the members of the sample would have cost less than for the average member of the U.S. nursing home population, other things equal, because of greater availability of help. But other things probably are not equal: married patients were likely to be sicker or more disabled because if they lacked a spouse, they would probably not have been able to live outside an institution for as many years as they did. This point will be discussed in Chapter 8. The difference in marital status between the groups is probably attributable at least in part to the study sample's relatively high share of patients headed toward shorter convalescent nursing home stays. Such patients are likelier to be admitted into nursing homes for medical reasons than is the average patient. Patients admitted for short-term medical reasons are likelier to have family members available at home to care for them than are patients admitted for long-term problems of chronic illness or frailty. The study sample is probably not unrepresentative of new nursing home entrants in this regard; rather, new entrants are not representative of the population residing in nursing homes.

Functional Ability

Much of this speculation about correlates of need for care would be unnecessary were data on the functional ability of larger populations available. Functional ability is the capacity to perform such ordinary activities of daily living as bathing, dressing, walking, transferring, eating, toiletting, and the like. It seems clearly to be thought of as the best predictor of the magnitude of need for long-term care.[4]

Regarding mobility status, the members of the study sample were in somewhat better condition than the population of nursing home residents in 1976. Patients studied were less likely to be bedfast, roombound, or homebound (46.0%) than were the national population of nursing home patients (62.3%).[5] Two factors are at work here. Very few members of the study sample could leave their rooms unassisted, but most could be expected to leave them occasionally with assistance. This is probably true of more than 37.7 percent of nursing home residents, but the necessary help is often not forthcoming. Second, nursing home residents are likely to decline in mobility status over the course of their stays, as they deteriorate, withdraw, or are medicated to constrain "management" problems. In sum, the study sample was probably fairly representative in its mobility of nursing home entrants.

The remainder of this section will be devoted to distinguishing the study sample of fifty patients from those 296 patients screened out. It is hoped that this information will fill some of the gaps in our knowledge of the representativeness of the sample left by the present unavailability of national data. Patients screened in and those screened out could be compared using sociodemographic, medical-functional, and discharge-related variables. In general, the two groups were fairly similar.

Greater age, other things equal, is associated with greater need for home care. As recorded in Table 6-3, the sample screened into the study was 0.7 years (0.9%) older than those screened out.

The study sample was disproportionately female. Other things equal, this is associated with reduced availability of spouse to provide care. Further, women tend to be thought of by care planners as more willing to discharge ordinary household maintenance tasks. This would reduce part of the perceived need for help from others.

Despite the sex composition of the sample, its members were just as likely as were those screened out to be married and to reside with at least one other person. The screening process did not seem to have affected this aspect of the sample's attributes as had been feared. About a third of each group was married, about one-third lived with other family, and about one-third lived alone. Great availability of family members indicated that many tasks could be discharged by unpaid providers. Hours of home care recommended by professionals would probably not be affected very much, but the unpaid proportion of total hours

Table 6-3. Comparisons: Patients Screened in and out of the Study.

Patient Variable	Screened In	Screened Out
Median age	79.9	79.2
Percentage female	76 %	56 %
Percentage married	32 %	34 %
Resides:		
Alone	36 %	36 %
With spouse	28 %	34 %
With other relatives	36 %	26 %
With nonrelatives	0 %	4 %
Mean number of:		
Medical diagnoses[a]	4.1	3.5
Disabling conditions[a]	2.6	2.1
Hospital admissions[b]	0.9	0.8
LTC admissions[b]	0.2	0.1
Anticipated discharge site:		
Rehabilitation hospital	2 %	6 %
Chronic disease hospital	6 %	13 %
Level I SNF (Medicare)	24 %	29 %
Level II SNF (Medicaid)	42 %	32 %
Level III ICF	26 %	20 %
Level IV rest home	0 %	1 %
To indefinite placement	68 %	50 %

a. Current-year figure.
b. Past-year figure.

would be increased, and the cost of hypothetical home care would be lowered. Further, patients who lived with others will be shown to be older and more disabled than those living alone. This seems to be because patients with given problems who live with others tend to be able to live at home longer than similar patients who reside alone. Thus, the latter have a lower disability or frailty threshold for institutionalization.

In the medical-functional areas, the study sample patients seemed to have been in slightly worse condition than those screened out. Those screened in had, on average, a slightly higher number of medical diagnoses, disabling conditions, hospital admissions, and long-term care admissions. While medical diagnosis itself has not been systematically related to need for long-term care services, the number of different diagnoses was counted as a possible measure of medical instability or frailty. The number of disabling conditions was counted for the same reason. These data, together with information on admissions to hospitals and long-term care facilities, provided a useful comparison of the medical instability of the study sample and the group screened out.

Regarding anticipated site of discharge, patients screened into the study were substantially likelier than those screened out to be headed to Level II SNF care and somewhat likelier to go to Level III ICF care. Those screened in were less likely to be expected to be placed in rehabilitation or chronic disease hospitals or Level I SNF nursing homes. The concentration of patients screened out in the higher levels of discharge probably included both patients in relatively good shape who left the acute care hospital for short-term rehabilitation too quickly for study forms to be completed on them and patients too ill to be screened in. This was supported by the relatively low proportion of patients screened out who were expected to have indefinite institutional placements.

Still more detailed information was obtained on patients screened into the study. Unfortunately, time and cost limits made it impossible to record comparable data on patients screened out. Three major areas will be discussed: functional ability, instrumental activities, and psychosocial status.

Three measures were made of functional ability or independence in activities of daily living (ADL). The Barthel index was used to measure independence in walking, climbing stairs, wheeling (if patient could not walk), transferring to chair and bed, transferring to tub or shower, bathing, toileting, bladder function, bowel function, dressing, grooming, eating and feeding, and mobility outside room and house.[6] The degree of dependence in these activities suggests the need for many types of supportive services. A score of zero indicates total dependence on other persons in these activities and a score of 100 indicates full independence.

Table 6-4 indicates the prehospital and anticipated distributions of Barthel scores. A clear drop in functional ability in the course of the present illness was

Table 6-4. Functional Ability of the Study Sample.

	Mean	Median
Prehospital Barthel score	77.1	82.5
Barthel anticipated at discharge	49.8	45.8
Barthel change	−27.3	−36.7

	Prehospital Barthel Score		
	0-74	75-94	95-100
Number of patients	17	16	17

	Barthel Anticipated at Discharge		
	0-40	41-60	61-100
Number of patients	17	19	15

indicated. For members of the study sample, important declines in functional ability were associated with the decision to institutionalize. On average, such factors as change in family willingness to help sustain a patient at home do not seem to have operated alone to yield such a decision.

Pearson product-moment correlations indicated that higher prehospital Barthel scores were associated with larger drops in scores ($r = 0.32$; significant at $< .001$) and higher anticipated Barthel scores were associated with smaller drops ($r = -0.15$; significant at .01). These relations were expected.

A measure related to ADL is that of patients' independence at eight instrumental activities of daily living (IADL): shopping, housework, meal preparation, laundry, taking medication, transportation, managing money, and using the telephone. Patients were asked whether, prior to this hospitalization, they did or were able to do these IADL tasks without help. Eight patients could do none of these independently, twenty-five could do one to four tasks, and seventeen could do five to eight tasks. These data suggest further the frailty of the members of the sample. They appear more dependent on the IADL than on the ADL activities. In general, prehospital Barthel and IADL scores correlated moderately well ($r = 0.54$; significant at $< .001$).

Discharge planners were also asked to assess patients' psychosocial characteristics. These included such items as whether the patient talked with other people, smiled or laughed, was lethargic, or was abusive to self or others. Twenty-two patients were scored positively on fewer than half of the seventeen characteristics.

Of the fifty patients, twenty-four were originally sought from Boston-area hospitals and twenty-six from elsewhere in Massachusetts; twenty-five were to be from teaching hospitals and twenty-five from community hospitals. Table 6-5 indicates how closely these overall targets were struck. At a finer level of detail, however, certain disparities appear. Boston-area teaching hospitals and non-

Table 6-5. Actual Versus Planned Sources of Patients.

Type of Hospital	Actual	Planned
Boston area	23	24
teaching	7	14
community	16	10
Non-Boston area	27	26
teaching	21	11
community	6	15
Total	50	50
teaching	28	25
community	22	25

Table 6-6. The Sample: Participation by Visit Status.

	Participation		
Visit Status	Full	Limited	Total
Visited	10	6	16
Not visited	18	16	34
Total	28	22	50

Boston community hospitals were unable, for a number of valid reasons, to contribute their share of the study sample in sufficient time. Boston-area community hospitals and non-Boston teaching hospitals picked up the slack. Thus, while the sample does not simultaneously represent type and location of hospital, it does represent both variables viewed overall.

The participation and visit statuses of patients are somewhat less well balanced. Most of the patients (29 of 50) are full participants, but only sixteen of fifty were visited (see Table 6-6). The low number of visits is owing to the initial difficulty of securing patients at Boston-area hospitals. A community hospital subsequently added proved too inconvenient for visiting. Despite this disproportion, the number of patients visited was sufficient to suggest whether or not this brief visit affected planning.

NOTES TO CHAPTER 6

1. National Center for Health Statistics, "Utilization of Nursing Homes, United States: National Nursing Home Survey, August 1973–April 1974," *Vital and Health Statistics* ser. 13, no. 28 (July 1977), Table 5.
2. Office of State Health Planning, Commonwealth of Massachusetts, "Report of the Long-Term Care Task Force" (Boston: Office of State Health Planning, August 1977).
3. See the discussion in Thomas T.H. Wan, William G. Weissert, and Barbara B. Livieratos, "Determinants of Outcomes of Care in Two Geriatric Service Modalities: An Experimental Study" (Paper presented at the 31st Annual Scientific Meeting of the Gerontological Society, Dallas, 16–20 November, 1978).
4. Kenneth M. McCaffree, Sharon Winn, and Carl A. Bennett, "Final Report of Cost Data Reporting System for Nursing Home Care" (Seattle: Battelle Human Affairs Research Centers, 1 October 1976); Granger, et al.; Sidney Katz, et al., "The Index of ADL: A Standardized Measure of Biological and Psychosocial Function," *Journal of the American Medical Association* 185 (21 September 1963): 914–19.

5. Bureau of the Census, "1976 Survey of Institutionalized Persons," *Current Population Reports*, ser. P-23, no. 69 (Washington, D.C.: Government Printing Office, June 1978).

6. For information on the Barthel index, see Florence I. Mahoney and Dorothea W. Barthel, "Functional Evaluation: The Barthel Index," *Maryland State Medical Journal* 14, no. 2 (February 1965): 61–65; Carl V. Granger, Gary L. Albrecht, and Byron B. Hamilton, "Outcome of Comprehensive Medical Evaluation: Measurement with the Barthel Index and the PULSES Profile" (Providence, R.I.: Brown University School of Medicine, 1978). (Mimeo.) This study's version of the Barthel index is Granger's modification (see Appendix B).

III FINDINGS AND WHAT THEY SUGGEST

7 COMPARING THE COSTS OF HOME AND INSTITUTIONAL CARE

THE COST OF INSTITUTIONAL CARE

The cost of institutional care for the members of the study sample was estimated by a straightforward method. The actual charges for care in patients' site of discharge was acquired. A weighted average was computed for any patient residing in two or more institutions during the six months following hospital discharge.[1] Excluding administratively necessary days (time spent in hospital by a patient ready for discharge because no nursing home bed was available), the average cost of institutional care for the forty-five patients for whom data could be obtained is $373 per week. When administratively necessary days (ANDs) are included, institutional cost rises to $410 per week. ANDs are excluded from most cost comparisons because they reflect the cost of—hopefully—transient and conceptually easy-to-eliminate inefficiencies in the present system. Taken at the hospitals' actual base per diem rates, they represent a cost equal to 9.9 percent of actual nursing home costs. For interested readers, comparisons between home care costs and institutional costs both with and without the extra cost of ANDs are occasionally provided.

Patient Characteristics and Nursing Home Cost

Multiple regression analysis was performed relating sixteen variables characterizing patients to the actual cost of their institutional care. Table 7-1 lists these variables and indicates their correlation with nursing home cost excluding ANDs.

Table 7-1. Patient Characteristics and Nursing Home Cost.

Patient Variable[a]	Correlation with N.H. Cost[b]
Age	−.130
Number of persons patient resided with	.053
Marital status (yes/no)	−.126
Anticipated site of LTC discharge	−.684[c]
Indefinite LTC placement (yes/no)	−.206
Number of medical diagnoses	.242
Number of disabling conditions	.054
Number of hospital discharges in past year	.025
Number LTC admissions in past two years	−.231
Number of medications, in hospital	.111
Percentage of nursing services used, in hospital	.152
Psychosocial score	−.072
Anticipated Barthel score at hospital discharge	.055
Change in Barthel score: pre-admission to discharge	.198
Prehospital IADL score	.155
Family willing to maintain patient at home (yes/no)	.015

a. These variables are defined in Appendix B.

b. Omits administratively necessary days.

c. Significant at .001.

Variables are defined in some detail in Appendix B. Of the sixteen variables, ten had a positive relation to institutional cost and six had a negative relation. Only one relationship was statistically significant: the patients' anticipated discharge site—the level of long-term care that the hospital discharge planner thought the patient would receive after leaving the hospital—bore a strong negative relation to actual institutional care costs. This was expected. As this independent variable was coded, the negative relation indicates that patients expected to be placed in facilities providing more care (rehabilitation hospitals, skilled nursing facilities) did indeed cost more to care for than patients placed in intermediate care facilities. This relation was significant at the .001 level. What is somewhat surprising is that no other variable bore a statistically significant relation (at the .05 level) to actual nursing home cost.

Table 7-2 reports the results of regression analysis of the relation of the sixteen variables to actual nursing home cost. Four variables—anticipated discharge site, marital status, number of disabling conditions, and number of medical diagnoses—together "explain" about 57 percent of the variation in nursing home cost. Only the first plays an important role. Of the other three, being married and having more disabling conditions and diagnoses were all positively associated with nursing home costs. Being married is also associated, in this sample, with being in need of more home care, probably because presence of a spouse permits

Table 7-2. Regression Results: Patient Characteristics and Nursing Home Cost.

Patient Variable[a]	Significance[b]	Unique Variance[c]
Anticipated discharge site	< .001	.437
Marital status	.012	.079
Number of disabling conditions	.040	.051
Number of medical diagnoses	.237	.016

Note:

R^2 = .573 (< .001).

   a. Stepping in stopped when last variable not significant at .07.

   b. F-test.

   c. Proportion of variation in dependent variable explained by this independent variable if it had been entered last.

patients to remain at home longer, with given disability, than the spouse's absence.

These variables contrast sharply with those explaining average levels of hypothetical home care cost. This clearly indicates that the costs of institutional care and hypothetical home care relate in very different ways to patient characteristics. The costs of home care vary more systematically with patient qualities that reasonably should be associated with cost. Institutional care costs have only a haphazard relation to patient variables. This indicates that the cost of institutional care may in individual cases be largely a product of such factors as the location or age of the nursing home rather than the care it provides. (Newer facilities in metropolitan areas tend to cost more.) Further, patients might be placed in facilities unrelated to their needs, or the facilities, though able to, may not be responding to those needs.

Alternatively, it might be argued that patients are being placed in a reasonable way, but the variables employed in this study do not appropriately represent care needs or their costs. A companion to this argument is that patients' nursing home cost, taken here as average charge by level, does not reflect the cost of care for individuals. It is likely that a mixture of these explanations is at play.

THE COST OF PROFESSIONALLY PRESCRIBED HOME CARE

A large number of home care hours were prescribed for the patients in the study sample. For the fifty patients, mean prescribed home care across eighteen professionals was 125.4 hours weekly. The weekly cost of home care would therefore seem very high.

Table 7-3. Total Mean Prescribed Hours: Paid versus Unpaid and Skilled versus Unskilled.

	Hours per Week	Percent
Payment Status		
Paid	84.3	67.2%
Unpaid	41.1	32.8%
Total	125.4	100.0%
Skill Status		
Skilled	7.3	5.8%
Unskilled	118.1	94.2%
Total	125.4	100.0%

Note:

Almost all skilled providers are paid, but most of the paid providers are unskilled. Lists of the titles of paid, unpaid, skilled, and unskilled providers recommended by prescribing consultants are appended to Chapter 4.

However, of these hours, about two-thirds were paid and over 90 percent were unskilled. Table 7-3 presents these breakdowns in prescribed hours. Because only some of the hours were paid (the remainder of the prescribed hours were to be provided by informal supports—generally relatives or friends residing with the patient) and because almost all hours of care were to be delivered by unskilled providers, the weekly cost of prescribed home care is less than the total prescribed hours might suggest.

The cost of home care was calculated first by taking the mean, across fifty patients, of the mean of the eighteen professionals' care plans for each patient. The cost of these prescribed home care services is $514 per week. Since an average of 84.3 paid hours of care are prescribed weekly, the average hourly charge for home care is $6.10. (Appended to this chapter is a list of the hourly rates used to calculate the cost of prescribed home care.) This relatively low hourly charge reflects the predominance of unskilled services in the package of paid care.

This mean service cost does not fully reflect the expense of maintaining a patient at home. Nonservice costs can be important.[2] It is necessary to include spending on housing and other goods in the total cost of home care. Based on the U.S. Department of Labor's lower budget for a retired couple for the Boston standard metropolitan statistical area, this cost was estimated to be $50 per week for patients whose families were willing to maintain them at home and $76 per week for patients who would live alone.[3] The average for all fifty patients is $60 per week.

Table 7-4. Total Home Care Costs Using Different Measures.

Measure of Service Cost	Mean Service Cost	Mean Non-service Cost	Total Cost
Mean of 50 means	$514	$60	$574
Mean of 50 medians	$453	$60	$513
Mean of 50 thirty-third percentiles	$335	$60	$395

Including nonservice requirements, the mean total hypothetical cost of home care is $574 per week. Two other methods of calculating total costs of home care have been used. One has been to take the mean across fifty patients of the median of the eighteen professionals' plans for each patient. The other has been to take the mean across fifty patients of the thirty-third percentile of home care costs for each patient.[4] To each of the three is added the nonservice costs for individual patients. These results are compared in Table 7-4. The mean of the medians, $453 per week, is 88 percent of the mean of the means. The mean of the thirty-third percentiles is only 65 percent of the means.

Patient Variables and Home Care Costs

The relation of sixteen independent variables to different measures of home care cost has been examined by multiple regression analysis. The results of one such examination are now presented. Table 7-5 indicates the correlation between each of the sixteen variables and the median total cost of home care. (Median total cost, for each patient, is the median of the eighteen professional views of service cost, plus nonservice cost for that patient.)

Half of the variables are positively related to hypothetical home care cost and half are negatively related. Five of the variables are significantly (at the .05 level or better) related to median total home care cost. The number of persons with whom the patient resided prior to hospitalization, better psychosocial status, and better anticipated Barthel score (functional ability) are negatively related to home care cost. The percentage of nursing services used in hospital and the size of decline in Barthel score are positively associated with home care cost. Each of these relations appears entirely reasonable. It should be noted further that anticipated site of institutional discharge has only a weak relation to home care cost, though a more expensive institutional placement is associated with more expensive home care.

The results of multiple regression analysis on median total home care cost indicate a pattern quite different from that reported in the previous section, where actual institutional cost was the dependent variable. In the present case,

Table 7-5. Patient Characteristics and Median Total Home Care Cost.

Patient Variable[a]	Correlation with Home Care Cost
Age	.197
Number of persons patient resided with	-.316[b]
Marital status (yes/no)	.089
Anticipated discharge site	-.204
Indefinite placement (yes/no)	.164
Number of medical diagnoses	.178
Number of disabling conditions	.184
Number of hospital discharges (past year)	-.025
Number of LTC admissions (past year)	.045
Number of medications in hospital	-.079
Percentage of nursing services used in hospital	.291[b]
Psychosocial score	.315[b]
Anticipated Barthel score at discharge	-.459[c]
Barthel change from pre-admission	.359[b]
Prehospital IADL	-.040
Family willing to maintain at home (yes/no)	.074

a. Variables are described in Appendix B.

b. Significant at .05.

c. Significant at .01.

three variables were significant at the .05 level or better. Regression results appear in Table 7-6. Together, the three characteristics explain about 42 percent of the variation in home care cost. Anticipated Barthel score is the most important of the independent variables, followed by the number of persons with whom the patient resides and age. This list contrasts with those variables — anticipated discharge site, marital status, number of disabling conditions, and number of medical diagnoses — which explained 57 percent of the variation in actual institutional costs.

For the reasons set out in the preceding section, it is not possible to decide whether the relation of patient variables to cost is more sensible in the home care case or the nursing home case. Certainly, some of the variables relevant to the cost of home care, such as the number of persons with whom the patient lived at home, have only an indirect bearing on how much institutional care should cost. The variable functional ability should have a stronger relation to the actual cost of institutional care. It certainly has been taken into account by home care planners. Its weak impact on institutional costs may be reasonable because: 1) the cost of institutional care is closely tied to reimbursed level (SNF, ICF, and the like); and 2) overall need for help, suggested by functional ability, has relatively little to do with level of placement, which is mandated by regulation to be made largely in light of medical considerations.

Table 7-6. Regression Results: Patient Characteristics and Median Total Home Care Cost.

Patient Variable[a]	Significance[b]	Unique Variance[c]
Barthel score anticipated at discharge	$< .001$	.225
Number of persons patient resides with	.003	.138
Age	.019	.078

Note:

R^2 = .422 ($< .001$).

  a. Stepping stopped when last variable not significant at .07.

  b. F-test.

  c. Proportion of variation in dependent variable explained by this independent variable.

In the area of home care costs, another regression was run using the same sixteen patient variables. Here, the dependent variable was each patient's coefficient of variation (CoV) in prescribed costs across eighteen professional care planners. The purpose of this analysis was to learn the relation of patient variables to professional agreement about home care service cost. The CoV is the relative standard deviation. This is the standard deviation in cost, divided by the mean of cost for that patient. It thus controls agreement for the base of costs, serving thereby as a standard for comparison across patients. It is interesting to note that the average CoV is 55.5 percent, indicating that for the average patient, the standard deviation equals 55.5 percent of the mean. This suggests a fairly high level of disagreement among professionals about the average cost of care. Table 7-7 sets out the relation of patient variables to CoV in service costs, and Table 7-8 contains the results of the regression itself.

The patients about whose home care costs the professionals agree best are the more disabled patients—those whose functional ability dropped most over the course of their current illness, who needed many nursing services, who were older, and who had suffered more acute episodes in recent months. Thus, greater age and more change in functional ability and medical status are associated with more agreement among professionals. It should also be noted that patients whose anticipated functional ability at discharge was better were harder to agree about.

COST COMPARISONS

The average cost of institutional care, excluding ANDs, was $373 per week. For total home care cost, the mean of the individual means was $574 per week; the mean of the medians was $513; and the mean of the thirty-third percentiles was $395. (These are the costs of professionals' home care plans. Costs of patients'

Table 7-7. Patient Characteristics and Coefficient of Variation[a] in Home Care Service Costs.

Patient Variable[b]	Correlation with Coefficient of Variation of Service Cost
Age	−.224
Number of persons patient resided with	.013
Marital status (yes/no)	.045
Anticipated discharge site	.149
Indefinite placement (yes/no)	−.023
Number of medical diagnoses	.222
Number of disabling conditions	−.091
Number of hospital discharges (past year)	−.110
Number of LTC admissions (past two years)	.032
Number of medications in hospital	.051
Percentage of nursing services used in hospital	−.361[c]
Psychosocial score	.085
Anticipated Barthel score at discharge	.352[c]
Barthel change from pre-admission	−.428[d]
Prehospital IADL	−.035
Family willing to maintain at home (yes/no)	−.157

a. Coefficient of variation = standard deviation divided by mean.
b. Variables are described in Appendix B.
c. Significant at .05.
d. Significant at .01.

Table 7-8. Regression Results: Patient Characteristics and Coefficient of Variation[a] in Home Care.

Patient Variable[b]	Significance[c]	Unique Variance[d]
Barthel change	.005	.128
Percentage of nursing services used	.006	.125
Age	.037	.068
Number known hospital discharges	.112	.038

Note:
R^2 = .377 (< .001).

a. Coefficient of variation = standard deviation divided by mean.
b. Stepping stopped when last variable not significant at .07.
c. F-test.
d. Proportion of variation in dependent variable explained by this independent variable.

Table 7-9. Patients for Whom Home Care is Less Expensive.

	Mean			Standard for Calculating Home Care Cost Median			Thirty-third Percentile		
	Number	Mean Home Care Cost	Mean Nursing Home Cost	Number	Mean Home Care Cost	Mean Nursing Home Cost	Number	Mean Home Care Cost	Mean Nursing Home Cost
Patients for whom home care is less expensive	8	$448	$763	9	$408	$727	14	$309	$604
Patients for whom home care is more expensive	37	$622	$289	36	$562	$284	31	$461	$268
Total	45	$591	$373	45	$531	$373	45	$413	$373

Note:
Administratively necessary days (ANDs) are excluded from the cost of institutional care.

and families' plans are taken up in the next section.) Table 7-9 presents the numbers of patients for whom care was more and less expensive under each of these standards.

While institutional care is always cheaper for most of the patients for whom data are available, there is always a subset of people for whom home care is cheaper. As would be expected, the size of this group rises as the standard for calculating home care costs changes from the mean to the median to the thirty-third percentile of care planners. Its size is somewhat greater when institutional costs include ANDs.

It is noteworthy that even in this very ill and disabled sample of patients who are being referred to institutions, there is a substantial number for whom home care is less expensive.

The savings that would accrue from placing each patient in the cheaper setting are set out in Table 7-10. (Institutional costs are given both including and excluding ANDs, thereby indicating their unimportance.) A substantial savings in total long-term costs follows, under each of the six comparisons, after patients for whom home care is cheaper are in fact diverted. These savings range from 11.3 percent to 25.6 percent depending on the standard of comparison. They represent the decreased cost of care for the individual patients directed to home care. They do not represent net system savings. The latter would depend on how the total costs of home and institutional care were affected by changes in the numbers and characteristics of patients receiving care in the two sites.

The impact of the diversion of individual patients on the long-term care system at large must be considered. If patients are diverted to home care and the nursing home beds they would have occupied are filled by others, who would not be eligible for home care, then total long-term care costs would rise by the costs of home care for those diverted plus or minus the difference in the cost of nursing home care for the two groups. If the beds that would have been occupied by diverted patients are closed, a net savings is likely. This would depend on whether the drop in total nursing home cost is or is not offset by the rise in total home care cost. This, in turn, would partly depend on the relations of marginal to average costs of nursing home and home care for the patients diverted.

Institutional care is cheaper for the majority of patients in the study sample regardless of the standard used to calculate home or institutional costs. By each standard, however, some patients are identified for whom home care is less expensive. Even greater numbers of patients could be cared for at home with no increase in system cost if the savings on the patients diverted to home care were used to subsidize care for those for whom home care was marginally more expensive.

Using a standard of diverting to home care only the nine patients (Table 7-9) whose median prescribed cost fell below institutional cost excluding ANDs, $1,889 would be saved weekly (Table 7-10). If this sum were applied to subsidizing home care for patients whose institutional care was marginally

Table 7-10. Total Weekly Costs in Various Settings ($).

| Standard of Cost | All Patients in | | | Savings Accompanying Diversion (2) − (3) | Percentage Saved over (2) |
	(1) Home Care	(2) Institutional Care	(3) Less Expensive Care		
Exclude ANDs[a]					
Mean home care costs	$26,595	$16,785	$14,277	$2508	14.9%
Median home care costs	23,895	16,785	14,896	1889	11.3%
Thirty-third percentile	18,585	16,785	12,634	4151	24.7%
Include ANDs					
Mean home care costs	26,595	18,450	15,665	2785	15.1%
Median home care costs	23,895	18,450	15,111	3339	18.1%
Thirty-third percentile	18,585	18,450	13,721	4729	25.6%

a. Administratively necessary days.

cheaper, an additional fifteen patients could have been diverted. Thus, twenty-four of forty-five patients (53%) could have been cared for at home with no increase in cost.

What are the characteristics of the patients for whom hypothetical home care was thought cheaper versus the characteristics of those for whom it was thought more expensive? The standard of comparison used to categorize patients is the thirty-third percentile of total home care costs versus institutional costs that excluded ANDs. There were fourteen patients for whom home care was cheaper and thirty-one for whom nursing home care was cheaper. The home care group was somewhat less likely to have resided alone prior to this hospitalization; its members were less likely to be married; but the family was somewhat likelier to be willing to maintain the patient at home. The Barthel score anticipated at discharge was ten points (12%) higher for the home care group. This group was taking more medications in-hospital, but it received fewer nursing services. The home care patients were slightly more likely to be full participants. Perhaps the most important distinction is that fully nine (62%) of the fourteen home care patients were being referred to rehabilitation or chronic disease hospitals or Medicare SNFs while only seven (23%) of the nursing home patients were being referred to these more intensive and costly facilities. Table 7–11 displays in

Table 7–11. Characteristics of Patients for Whom Home Care is Cheaper versus Those for Whom It Is More Expensive.

Variable	Home Care Cheaper	Nursing Home Care Cheaper
Number of patients	14	31
Age (mean)	80.0 years	78.8 years
Female	71.4%	74.2%
Residing with others	71.4%	58.1%
Married	21.4%	41.9%
Family willing to maintain at home	85.7%	71.0%
Anticipated Barthel score (mean)	54.5	44.6
Barthel change (mean)	−30.6	−30.2
IADL positive	44.0%	38.5%
Number of diagnoses (mean)	4.1	3.8
Number of hospital discharges (mean)	0.7	0.9
Number of current medications (mean)	6.6	5.1
Current nursing services (mean)	29.0%	34.0%
Indefinite institutional placement	71.4%	67.7%
Rehabilitation, chronic, Medicare SNF placement	64.3%	23.3%
Medicaid SNF placement	14.3%	43.3%
Medicaid ICF placement	21.4%	33.3%
Full participants	54.1%	51.6%

detail the characteristics of the two groups. Home care seems to have fared relatively well in the cases of patients whose institutional care is quite expensive. As Willemain has noted, it is not so much that home care is cheaper for these patients as that their institutional care is more expensive.[5]

This pattern is quite different from that argued[6] or found[7] in other studies. The usual pattern is that home care is likelier to be less expensive than institutional care for the less ill or disabled. This may well be true among the general population of older citizens who need help, but, at least in the sample studied here, who were about to be institutionalized, the reverse is likelier to hold. This suggests that real opportunities may exist in caring at home for persons with serious functional or medical problems. For them, institutional care may have become so expensive that home care is cheaper.

Figure 7-1 graphs these possible relations. In the range between points A and B, home care is more expensive for the average patient. If the range of disability of the members of the study sample extends between points X and Y, some of the above cost findings would be explained.

The relation of patient characteristics to the relative costs of home and institutional care has been analyzed by multiple regression. Home care costs and institutional costs together were formed into two dependent variables. One was the difference between the two; the other was their ratio. Results under the two

Figure 7-1. One View of Home and Institutional Care Costs.

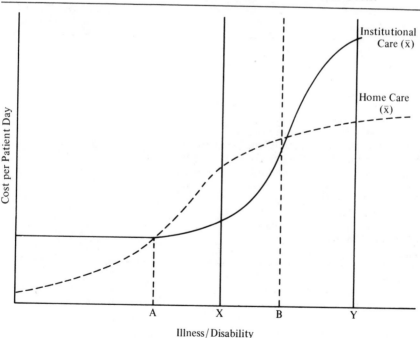

analyses are generally similar so, for the sake of coherence, only regressions on median total home care cost minus institutional cost (excluding ANDs) will be discussed. A higher value for this dependent variable means that home care is more expensive; a lower value means that institutional care is more expensive.

How do the different patient variables influence the direction of the cost comparison? This question is answered by the data in Table 7-12, which presents the correlation coefficients between each of the patient characteristics and the difference between home and institutional care costs. A positive relation means that a higher value for the independent variable is associated with a probable increase in the relative cost of home care. Anticipation that the patient will be discharged to a more intense level of care is strongly associated with home care being cheaper. Conversely, a higher Barthel score anticipated at discharge is fairly strongly associated with home care being cheaper. Both of these relations hold when other variables are not controlled. Table 7-13 displays the regression results themselves. They indicate that more intense levels of anticipated institutional placement, higher anticipated Barthel score, and greater numbers of residents in the patient's household are all associated with greater likelihood that

Table 7-12. Patient Characteristics and the Comparative Costs of Home and Institutional Care.

Patient Variable[a]	Correlation with Home Care Cost Minus Nursing Home Cost[b]
Age	.151
Number of persons patient resides with	-.272
Marital status (yes/no)	.125
Anticipated discharge site	.398[c]
Indefinite LTC placement expected (yes/no)	.266
Number of medical diagnoses	-.290
Number of disabling conditions	.215
Number of known hospital discharges (past year)	-.041
Number of known LTC admissions (past 2 years)	.166
Number of medications in hospital	-.150
Percentage of nursing services used in hospital	.097
Psychosocial status	-.156
Anticipated Barthel score at discharge	-.332[d]
Change from preadmission Barthel	.049
Prehospital IADL	-.120
Family willing to maintain at home (yes/no)	.085

a. Variables are described in Appendix B.

b. Home care costs rise relative to institutional costs as value for dependent variable rises; a negative correlation means that as value of independent variable rises; it is probable that cost of home care falls relative to cost of institutional care.

c. Significant at .01.

d. Significant at .05.

Table 7-13.   Regression Results: Patient Characteristics
and the Comparative Costs of Home and Institutional Care.

Patient Variable[a]	Significance[b]	Unique Variance[c]
Anticipated discharge site	.001	.236
Anticipated Barthel score	.002	.156
Number of persons patient resides with	.013	.098
Number of disabling conditions	.087	.044

Note:

$R^2 = .465 \ (< .001)$.

a. Stepping in stopped when last variable entered not significant at .07.

b. F-Test.

c. Proportion of variation in dependent variable explained by variation in this independent variable, if entered last.

home care will cost less than institutional care. Conversely, the greater the number of disabling conditions the patient suffers from, the higher the likelihood that home care will cost more than institutional care. The last relation is not strong, but it does offer support for the conventional view that people who need more help are cheaper to care for in institutions. The host of factors confounding appropriate placement or actual cost of institutional care, which were discussed earlier in this chapter, may dim the conventional view's perspicacity in regard to the study sample.

In general, these regression results support the earlier analysis of the characteristics of patients for whom home care is likely to be less expensive. In this study sample of patients about to enter Massachusetts long-term care facilities, it appears that real opportunities for savings might be found by diverting to home care selected patients bound for relatively intensive levels of institutional care. The study sample is far too small to permit even the suggestion that policies should be remade to permit greater diversion of such patients. But these findings do suggest the desirability of looking more closely at the possibilities for home care for selected patients in this group.

PROFESSIONAL, PATIENT, AND FAMILY VIEWS OF COST

All analyses of cost to this point have concerned only professionals' views of cost of hypothetical home care. Means, medians, and thirty-third percentiles of professionals' views have been examined. This has followed largely from the composition of the available data. The cost of professionals' prescribed plans could be accurately estimated because, as noted in Chapter 4, each home care plan called for a service-by-service statement of the episodes, hours, and providers of care. To protect patients and family members from the stress of a lengthy interview, they were asked only the service-by-service episodes of help required and whether these episodes would need to be delivered by paid or unpaid providers. Thus, a rough measure of the comparative costs of professionals', patients', and families' requests for help may be gained by considering episodes of paid services sought.

There are only twenty patients for whom both patient and family interviews could be completed. For these patients, the median cost of professionals' home care plans was less expensive than institutional care in five of the eighteen cases (28%) in which institutional cost data were available. The median number of paid episodes prescribed by professionals for the twenty patients was eighty-eight episodes of care weekly. Patients sought only seventy-five paid episodes; family members sought seventy-two. Patients sought less help than professionals in eight cases (40%); family members sought less than professionals in thirteen cases (65%). As will be seen in Chapter 8, this seems to have been due more to greater reliance on *unpaid* providers by patients and families than to any meaningful reduction in total episodes thought necessary.

On this basis, it seems reasonable to conclude (barring differences in average durations of episodes for the three groups) that patients' and families' care requests would probably cost a bit less to meet than would the care plans of the median professional. If the mean of professional views were employed, patient and family requests would look cheaper still.

The follow-up project has come to roughly similar conclusions. While professionals did recommend about 20 percent fewer hours of in-home care, in total, than clients were actually receiving, professionals thought that an increase of 22.5 percent in paid help was called for. Professionals sought only about two-thirds as much help from family members for the clients included in the follow-up study as those family members were actually providing. Professionals thought that roughly two-fifths of the total help needed should have been provided by paid helpers; actually, only about one-quarter of all help was being given by paid providers. This suggests that even very experienced long-term care professionals may have a tendency, on average, to underestimate the willingness and ability of informal supports to aid disabled relatives or friends. Alternatively, assessment data provided to professionals, on which they based their care plans, may have systematically misled them. Finally, professionals' views of what families would and should do may be either more realistic long-term levels of support or a better reflection of what is good for families to attempt.

BREAKDOWN OF HOME CARE COSTS

The total cost of home care has been categorized by characteristics of prescribing professions, services prescribed, and providers recommended. In the two discussions that follow, costs of different professionals' views of hypothetical home care need are cross-cut first by services and then by providers.

Professional prescribers are the five physicians, hospital discharge planners, and home health agency care planners (who together constitute the group of fifteen consultants) and the three hospital care planners (the patient's physician, discharge planner, and floor nurse). Service subtotals are personal care, housekeeping, nursing, and medical-therapeutic ("other"). The forty-one individual services, sorted into the four subtotals, appear in a list appended to Chapter 4.

As Table 7-14 indicates, the three hospital care planners prescribed more expensive care than the fifteen consultants. By analysis of variance, this $105 per week difference is significant at .005. It is not clear which of these views of need is more appropriate or valid; this question will be taken up in subsequent chapters.

Among the consultants, a difference of $145 was found between the weekly costs of physicians' and hospital discharge planners' views. Home health planners fell almost exactly in between. These differences were significant at .001.

A most striking pattern that emerges across the various means of the groups of professionals is the similarity in the proportion of total cost allotted to each of the four categories of service (see Table 7-15). This suggests agreement about allocation of home care services, even in the face of disagreement about volume.

By calculating the average coefficient of variation across all patients within each professional group, it was found that hospital consultants agreed best about costs, followed by consultant physicians, discharge planners, and home health planners. For no group, however, was agreement about cost very good. The average coefficient of variation across all care planners was 40.9 percent.

Table 7-14. Professional Views: Weekly Cost of Care Distributed Across Service Subtotals.

Professional Care Planner	Service Subtotal ($/week)[a]				
	Personal Care	Housekeeping	Nursing	Other	Total
Physicians	$395	$81	$39	$30	$545
Discharge planners	264	76	40	20	400
Home health	293	107	49	26	475
Consultant Subtotal	331	90	44	26	491
Hospital Subtotal	401	104	59	32	596
Total	$343	$92	$47	$27	$509

a. Mean ($\bar{X}$) for each group.

Table 7-15. Professional Views: Percentage of Weekly Cost Distribution Across Service Subtotals.

Professional Care Planner	Percentage of Cost				
	Personal Care	Housekeeping	Nursing	Other	Total
Physicians	72%	15%	7%	6%	100%
Discharge planners	66%	19%	10%	5%	100%
Home health	62%	23%	10%	5%	100%
Consultant Subtotal	67%	18%	9%	5%	99%
Hospital Subtotal	67%	17%	10%	5%	99%
Total	67%	18%	9%	5%	99%

Costs can be broken down into a large number of provider subtotals. For this analysis, only a distinction between the costs of skilled and unskilled providers will be drawn (see appendix to Chapter 4 for lists of providers by subtotal).

Among the consultants, physicians recommend the most skilled help, followed by discharge planners and home health planners. Differences among consultants are significant at .04. Consultants generally recommend substantially less costly skilled care than do hospital professionals; this difference is significant at .015 and far exceeds the disagreement between consultant and hospital professionals regarding unskilled services. These data are reported in Table 7-16.

The relatively high cost of unskilled providers, 82 percent of the total across all professionals' care plans, suggests real opportunities for reducing the costs of in-home care. Skilled providers tend to be busy in the course of their visits. By caring for more than one patient in a given location, the only saving would be reduced travel time (an important home care overhead cost). Unskilled providers are busy in much of what they do, but much other unskilled care is devoted to delivering continuous supervision for patients who should not have been left alone.

This single service required an average of $293 per week, across all prescribers, patients, and providers. Almost all providers were unskilled. This sum was 70 percent of the cost of all unskilled care and 47 percent of the total cost of care. The costs of home care per person would be markedly reduced by a shared housing scheme. Further, in other areas of personal care and in housekeeping as well, there exist opportunities for economies of scale. These suggestions run be-

Table 7-16. Professional Views: Costs of Skilled and Unskilled Providers.

| Professional | *(dollars per week)* | | |
	Skilled Providers[a]	*Unskilled Providers[b]*	*Total*
Physician	$100 (18%)	$445 (82%)	$545
Discharge planner	67 (17%)	334 (83%)	401
Home health	62 (13%)	414 (87%)	476
Consultants	79 (16%)	412 (84%)	491
Hospital	153 (26%)	442 (74%)	595
Total	$ 91 (18%)	$417 (82%)	$508

a. Difference among consultants significant at .04; between consultants and hospital professionals at .015.

b. Difference among consultants significant at .001; between consultants and hospital professionals at .235.

yond home care for individuals into shared housing, foster care, and domiciliary arrangements. These all carry difficulties in quality assurance and, in general, they fall beyond the scope of this study. But the clear and predictable opportunities for savings in these areas indicate the need for continuing investigation into the alternatives mentioned. Up to the present, shared housing and foster care seem to have been suggested largely for frail older persons without serious medical difficulties. They may also be suitable sites of care for older citizens who, like many members of the study sample, have problems requiring supervision by skilled professionals.

SUMMARY AND IMPLICATIONS

This chapter has looked at several aspects of the comparative costs of home and institutional care. First, very different constellations of patient characteristics explained actual institutional costs and hypothetical home care costs. This would be appropriate if different aspects of patients actually affected real costs of care in the two settings. Alternatively, if professionals' views of home care need are accurate, the relation of patient variables to institutional costs could well reflect distortions that accompany regulating financial and practical aspects of nursing home placement and payment. There is little relation between hypothetical mean home care costs and real institutional costs: $r = 0.02$. Further, median home care hours, which would perhaps better reflect the real burden of providing home care, correlate with institutional costs at only 0.05.

Several important patient variables were identified that predict whether home care or institutional care would tend to be more (or less) expensive. More intense level of institutional placement, higher Barthel score anticipated at discharge, and greater number of persons residing with the patient at home and independently predict increased likelihood that home care will cost less than institutional care.

Care in both settings is expensive. By diverting to home care those patients for whom it is markedly cheaper, substantial savings may be won. When these savings are applied to subsidizing the home care of patients for whom it is marginally more expensive, a total of about half of the sample could be cared for at home with no increase in overall spending on these patients.

Patient and family views about episodes were compared with the median of professional views. Patients and family members generally requested a bit less paid help than professionals thought necessary. This suggests at least that the cost of permitting patients or family members control or influence over service allocation would probably be no greater than the cost of professional control.

The impact on long-term care system cost of diversion to home care of patients for whom home care is no more expensive is unclear. Impact depends on the size and savings accrued from diversion of individuals, on how these savings are spent, on the characteristics of patients diverted and of those who replace them in nursing home (if any), and on the types of controls placed on entry into the expanded home care benefit structure. These important issues fall beyond the scope of the present study.

Another subject deserving further examination is whether the savings suggested by the hypothetical diversion of some patients do not in fact reflect actual overplacement of these patients in rehabilitation or chronic disease hospitals. Of course, this can be turned around: some study patients placed in ICFs may be at too low a level due to unavailability of appropriate beds. These questions follow from the method used in the current study—that of relying on the average rate by level of care—for all patients in a given institution.

Differences in costs recommended by professionals for the various services and provider groups are clearly statistically significant in most cases. The predominance of unskilled hours in all care plans suggests opportunities could be realized through shared housing, foster care, or other arrangements. In this way, the large share of home care cost that is owing to the need to have a caregiver in place, to prevent or contain harm to patients, is spread over many patients. Clearly, however, moves in this direction must be made with the dangers in mind that the growth of small and unsatisfactory semi-institutions might thereby be nurtured.

APPENDIX TO CHAPTER 7

Provider Charges

Provider Category	Hourly Rate[b]
Medical	
M.D.–primary[a] (internist, G.P., F.P.)	$55.00
M.D.-specialist[a]	60.00
Dentist[a]	40.00
Podiatrist[a]	24.00
Nursing	
Registered	12.47
Licensed practical nurse	10.05
Personal Care	
Homemaker	4.85
Home health aide, homemaker-home health aide	5.17
Personal care attendant	5.74
Support	
Social worker	9.62
Escort service	4.25
Visiting aide	4.00
Therapy	
Physical therapist	14.00
Physical therapy aide	7.50
Occupational therapist	14.00
Dietician	20.00
Miscellaneous Services	
Meals-on-Wheels[c]	1.67[c]
Heavy chore service	8.00
Cleaning service	7.00
Medicab[c]	37.50[c]

a. Where applicable, a visit or episode rate equal to one-half the hourly rate was used in calculating costs.

b. Based on Medicare, Medicaid, Title XX, and other home care charges in effect during period for which institutional costs were calculated.

c. This service was delivered on an episode basis only.

NOTES TO CHAPTER 7

1. To allow for patients' personal allowance, drugs, medical-therapeutic professionals, and other goods and services not included in the nursing home daily rate charged to Medicare or Medicaid, an additional 15 percent was added. (This was not done where the institutional rate was all-inclusive.) Similarly, on the home care side of the cost comparison, prescribed service costs were inflated by 5 percent to cover drugs, supplies, and appliances. Both of these proportions are best guesses, based on available data and off-the-record estimates by knowledgeable persons of average costs. They may be in error, but the possible consequences of even fairly large errors for the analyses in this chapter do not seem to be serious.
2. Bruce C. Vladeck, "Some Issues in the Economics and Financing of Long-term Care" (Paper prepared for the Institute on Continuity of Long-term Care, Arden House, New York, December 18–20, 1977), p. 9.
3. U.S. Department of Labor, "Three Budgets for a Retired Couple, Autumn 1977," USDL *News*, 78–698, 13 August 1978. Acute medical care costs were omitted from the cost comparison on both the home care and nursing home sides. For patients whose families were willing to maintain them at home, a factor of 55 percent was applied to the food budget and a factor of 50 percent was applied to all other categories. For patients living alone, a factor of 67 percent was applied to housing costs. All costs were inflated by 6 percent to reach an estimated 1 July 1978 level. These proportions were chosen because they reasonably reflect one person's share of the retired couple's budget. Readers may adjust these as desired, but, because of non-service costs' relatively small share (12 to 18%) of total home care costs, these assumptions will not greatly affect cost comparisons.
4. This standard was chosen arbitrarily. It was desired to learn the cost of home care based on the care plan of the sixth least costly prescriber for each of the fifty patients.
5. Personal communication, Thomas R. Willemain, February 1979.
6. Jay Greenberg, "The Costs of In-home Services," in Nancy N. Anderson, ed., *A Planning Study of Services to Non-institutionalized Older Persons in Minnesota* (Minneapolis: Governor's Citizens Council on Aging, 1974, pt. 2).
7. Comptroller General of the United States, "Report to Congress on Home Health—The Need for a National Policy to Better Provide for the Elderly," HRD–78–19 (Washington, D.C.: General Accounting Office, 30 December 1977). A probable limitation of the applicability of this approach lies in its use of average institutional cost across all levels of disability.

8 PROFESSIONAL, PATIENT, AND FAMILY VIEWS OF HOME CARE NEEDS
Their Relation to Patient Characteristics

DO PROFESSIONALS, PATIENTS, AND FAMILY MEMBERS AGREE ABOUT NEEDED HOURS OF HOME CARE?

Whenever possible, the patient and the family member (or other caregiver) who knew the patient best were separately interviewed to learn how much help they thought was required to permit the patient to live at home in a safe, adequate, and dignified manner. Each was asked, service by service, how many episodes of help would be necessary. A total of twenty-three (79% of the full participants) patients and thirty-six family members were interviewed.

Overall, the two groups agreed with one another well in most respects. This was especially true of the twenty cases where both patient and family members were interviewed. As seen in Table 8-1, patients requested a mean of 118 discrete episodes (such as being bathed or receiving physical therapy) of service weekly. Family members thought that 130 episodes were necessary. Most of the professional groups, and the professionals on average, recommended slightly more episodes in total than the patients requested, and about as much as the families requested. Professional groups agreed well among one another.

In the area of paid services, however, as indicated in Table 8-2, both patients and family members sought considerably less paid help than professionals prescribed. Further, regardless of their views of the number of total episodes needed, patients and families—particularly the latter—felt that unpaid providers could carry an appreciably greater share of total episodes than did professionals. This was pronounced even in the personal and housekeeping areas, where legislators often fear patient or family greed. Patients believed that unpaid providers

Table 8-1.   Professional-Patient-Family Views of Total Need.[a]

Need as Viewed by	Total Weekly Episodes Needed in				
	Personal Care	Housekeeping	Nursing	Other	Total
Physicians	80	34	22	4	140
Discharge planners	75	38	27	2	142
Home health planners	60	29	18	3	110
All consultants	72	34	22	3	131
Hospital professionals	67	30	23	3	123
All professionals	71	34	22	3	130
Patients	60	32	23	3	118
Families	70	29	27	4	130

a. N = 20 patients.

Table 8-2.   Professional-Patient-Family Views of Paid Episodes Needed.[a]

Need as Viewed by:	Paid Weekly Episodes Needed in				
	Personal Care	Housekeeping	Nursing	Other	Total
Physicians	63	21	19	4	107
Discharge planners	54	21	19	2	96
Home health planners	46	20	15	2	83
All consultants	54	21	18	3	96
Hospital professionals	40	18	14	3	75
All professionals	52	20	17	3	92
Patients	43	16	13	3	75
Families	36	15	17	4	72

a. N = 20 patients.

could deliver an average of forty-three episodes weekly (36% of the total). For family members and professionals, these figures were fifty-eight (45%) and thirty-eight (29%), respectively. Thus, compared to both patients and families, professionals underestimated both the quantity and proportion of episodes that unpaid providers could deliver.

It is particularly noteworthy that family members were highest in their estimates of availability, ability, and wllingness of the informal support system to help sustain patients at home. It might be argued that families are overstating how much help they and other informal supports would provide because they felt guilty at the prospect of their relative being institutionalized or because they would not be held responsible for their estimates. In response, others might assert that family members are best informed about how much the informal supports would be available, able, and willing to do. Predictions would have to be compared with behavior to learn whose views of family effort are correct, but the above data, on a small subsample, suggest that if professionals were to negotiate with family members about the relative contribution of the latter to home care plans fulfilled jointly by paid and unpaid providers, family members would be forthcoming.

This discussion rests on the assumption that the average episode prescribed by professionals is of a duration similar to that requested by patients or their families. Implications of these findings for costs of care sought by the three groups may be suggested if the parallel assumption that the average cost per episode of care by paid providers would be similar across the three groups is made.

The relatively low imputed value of unpaid help prescribed by professionals themselves can be estimated without such assumptions. Across fifty patients, a mean of 40.7 hours per week of unpaid help was prescribed by professionals. This figure represents the mean across patients of the mean of eighteen individual professionals' prescriptions for unpaid hours for each patient. For this help to be delivered in the absence of family and other unpaid help, paid providers would be required. Perhaps, the most appropriate paid provider to substitute for unpaid help is the generalist homemaker-home health aide. In this study, as noted in the appendix to Chapter 7, the hourly cost of a homemaker-home health aide's care is estimated at $5.17. Thus, the average cost of replacing unpaid help with that of a homemaker-home health aide is estimated to be $210 per week. Table 8-3 summarizes these data and presents quintile values for the cost of substituting paid providers. It can be seen that for many patients, even the relatively low professional estimates of hours of unpaid help represent a considerable contribution to home care.

Table 8-3. The Imputed Value of Unpaid Help Prescribed by Professionals.

A. *Value Unpaid Help*	*Mean of Means*	*Mean of Medians*
Hours per week	40.7	35.3
Value per week	$210	$182

B. *Distribution of Mean Hours and Value*	*Hours per Week*	*Value per Week*
Patient with highest prescribed hours	85.7	$443
10th	72.4	374
20th	57.0	295
30th	30.7	159
40th	8.6	44
Patient with lowest prescribed hours	1.5	8

To this point, the examination of the extent of agreement among professionals, patients, and family members about needed home care episodes has compared only the averages of each group's recommendations. When the number of episodes recommended for individual patients is examined using Pearson product-moment correlation analysis, agreement fades badly in many cases. In general, the patient-family diad showed best agreement. Patient-professional and family-professional agreement about total episodes of care needed was only fair; about paid or unpaid episodes, it was worse still (Table 8-4). These data indicate that disagreements about individual patients across patient-family-professional lines can be obscured when averages alone are considered. For program or budgetary purposes, congruence among the three groups is excellent; when planning care for individuals, conflicts may well be anticipated.

PATIENT CHARACTERISTICS AND DIFFERENT VIEWS OF NEED

It was argued in Part II that Barthel score anticipated at discharge, a reliable and valid measure of independence in functional ability (in activities of daily living),

Table 8-4. Patient-Family-Professional Agreement About Needed Episodes of Home Care.

	Pearson Product Moment Correlation		
	r	r-squared	P^a
A. Total Episodes			
Patient-Family	.67	.45	.002
Patient-Professional[b]	.50	.25	.030
Family-Professional[b]	.57	.32	.010
B. Paid Episodes			
Patient-Family	.70	.48	< .001
Patient-Professional[b]	.26	.07	.266
Family-Professional[b]	.35	.12	.141
C. Unpaid Episodes			
Patient-Family	.74	.55	< .001
Patient-Professional	.43	.19	.061
Family-Professional	.25	.06	.283

Note:
In several cases, patients or family members deferred to professional judgment for various technical services. Professional views of these deferrals have been included in the appropriate patient or family totals, slightly inflating apparent agreement.

a. Two-tail test.
b. Mean of 18 professional care planners.
N = 20.

is probably the best single predictor of need for home care services. Pearson correlations were performed for patients' anticipated Barthel scores and the number of episodes of home care requested by patients, family members, and the mean of professionals. Each group sought reasonable and equitable numbers of episodes of home care; requested episodes bore a clearly negative relation to functional ability (Table 8-5). Each group considered that patients with greater functional ability indeed needed fewer episodes of home care. According to each of the three groups, the relation was roughly linear. Professionals appeared to adhere closest to this pattern although the use of an "average" professional care plan makes comparability of correlation values difficult.

It is not possible to say, on the basis of this analysis, that any one of the three groups of prescribers can be trusted to write care plans that are clearly most equitable. All three can distinguish patients who seem to need more care from those who need less; professionals are best able to do this. The nature of the relation of anticipated Barthel score to needed episodes of care has not, however, been established well enough to say with assurance that professionals are more likely to have been right. It is, for example, possible that professionals are on average overly rigid in their use of the anticipated Barthel score standard.

Because interviews with both patients and family members could be obtained in only twenty cases, the above analysis of equity of care planning by members of the three groups is certainly limited in its generalizeability. For the same reason of sample size, only the relation of professionals' prescribed hours of home care to patient variables will now be examined in detail. The purposes of this examination are first, to learn how predictable and equitable are professionals' views in light of patient characteristics, and second, to compare this predictability across different areas of home care services and providers.

The Equity of Professional Views

Sixteen different patient characteristics, the same as those employed in Chapter 7, were selected as independent variables for multiple regression analyses.

Table 8-5. The Relation of the Number of Episodes of Home Care Requested by Patients, Their Families and Professionals to Patients' Anticipated Barthel Scores.

Anticipated Barthel Score at discharge with number of home care episodes requested by:	Pearson Product-Moment Correlation		
	r	r-squared	P^a
Patient	−.62	.39	.005
Family	−.57	.32	.010
Professionals[b]	−.76	.58	< .001

a. One-tail test.

b. Mean of 18 professionals.

(These variables are specified in Appendix B.) Dependent variables considered first were hours of care prescribed by the average of the eighteen professionals in eight service areas, five different subtotals of services, and total hours.

Several findings are salient. First, given the small sample size, it is interesting to note that from three to six independent variables bore statistically significant relations to each dependent variable. Second, these variables explained a high proportion of the variation in the dependent variables, as shown by the R^2 results. The high R^2s thus indicate that just a few independent variables are useful in predicting hours of home care prescribed by the mean of professionals. This means that professional views are, on average, relatively predictable – a finding of no small importance. Professionals' plans may or may not be effective, but they do at least seem reasonable. Further, the integrity or reasonableness of average professional views is reinforced by the *selective* predictive utility of different variables for different services and service subtotals. That this selectivity seems reasonable will be shown by the nature of association between classes of variables. This suggests a high level of equity in professional care plans.

The dependent variables selected for analysis are the four service subtotals, certain of the individual services making up each subtotal, total prescribed hours, and total minus continuous supervision hours. The last item was included because about 51 percent of all hours prescribed by professionals were on average allotted to the one service, continuous supervision. The eight individual services analyzed were selected as interesting illustrations of the care planning process and because it was thought that they were important and fairly representative services.

For personal care services (Table 8-6), the proportion of variation in prescribed hours explained by just a few independent variables (R^2) is quite high. While this explanation does not go so far as to indicate that care plans would be appropriate and effective, it does indicate that the "average professional" used this information about patients in a consistent manner. Patients with lower functional ability were thought clearly to need more help; younger patients, less help; and so on. It is, however, surprising that the family's willingness to maintain the patient at home should be negatively associated with prescribed total hours. A negative relation of family willingness with paid hours or total cost would be expected; with total hours, it would not be.

Professionals were not able to use data about patients to prescribe needed hours of household help in so consistent a manner. The R^2s in this group are measurably lower. In each case, however, prescribed hours of care appear most sensible. This is particularly true for transportation (Table 8-7), which at first glance seems to suffer from reversal of coefficients' signs: high Barthel and psychosocial status, for example, are associated with greater prescribed help with transportation. The most reasonable interpretation here is that some patients were thought safe to transport more frequently because they were in better condition.

Table 8-6. Regression Results: Personal Care: Mean Prescribed Hours and Patient Variables.

Patient Variable	Personal Care Subtotal			Bathing			Eating–Drinking		
	Standard Coefficient	Signifi-cance[a]	Unique Variance[b]	Standard Coefficient	Signifi-cance	Unique Variance	Standard Coefficient	Signifi-cance	Unique Variance
Anticipated Barthel	-.657	$< .001$	.346	-.855	$< .001$	.686	-.547	$< .001$	.232
Resides with				.134	.051	.017			
Maintenance at home				-.123	.074	.014	-.177	.115	.025
Age	.349	$< .001$	.106						
Psychosocial	-.239	.013	.046				-.245	.037	.045
Number of disabling conditions							.280	.011	.069
R^2	.707			.821			.582		
Significance	$< .001$			$< .001$			$< .001$		

a. F-test.
b. Proportion of dependent variable explained by this variable alone.

Table 8-7. Regression Results: Household Services: Mean Prescribed Hours and Patient Variables.

Patient Variable	Household Subtotal			Transportation			Light Housekeeping		
	Standard Coefficient	Signifi-cance	Unique Variance	Standard Coefficient	Signifi-cance	Unique Variance	Standard Coefficient	Signifi-cance	Unique Variance
Anticipated Barthel	-.267	.062	.056	.392	.004	.123			
Anticipated discharge site				.374	.004	.122			
Age				-.279	.027	.068			
Psychosocial	-.238	.095	.045	.215	.096	.037	-.302	.015	.076
Marital status							.411	.002	.144
IADL	-.256	.061	.057				-.396	.004	.112
Number of diagnoses							-.267	.026	.062
Indefinite placement							-.247	.049	.048
R^2	.325			.450			.523		
Significance	<.001			<.001			<.001		

The pattern of professional prescribing in the nursing field also indicates that appropriate variables informed decisions. Witness the importance of nursing services used in hospital to total prescribed hours of nursing care, and the importance of Barthel *change* to the need to monitor vital signs (Table 8–8).

In the medical-therapeutic area, patients whose institutional placement was expected to be indefinite (probably because they had suffered too much harm or lacked informal support permitting them to go home) were thought by professionals to need markedly less care overall and less physical therapy in particular (Table 8–9). It cannot be said whether this represents reasonable resource allocation or a tendency to invest too little effort in actively caring for patients not expected to improve.

The prescribed total need for home care, and for the total less continuous supervision, is explained very well by only a few patient characteristics—anticipated Barthel score, age, and psychosocial status (see Table 8–10). This high R^2 suggests that "cookbook" formulas might be useful in establishing guidelines for ranges of budgeted home care hours for patients with given characteristics. Only a few such characteristics might have to be recorded and incorporated into possible care planning or utilization review equations. Of course, this should not be done until the average of the professionals' views or some other standard of home care need is actually validated.

Regression results on mean prescribed hours have, to this point, concerned only individual services or service subtotals. Regressions were run as well on the provider subtotals. R^2 coefficients and their significance are the only results on providers that will be discussed. These are presented in Table 8–11. Worth noting are these points: patient characteristics generally have better power in explaining differences in average prescribed hours for the unskilled providers or for the unpaid providers (particularly residents of the patient's household) than for the skilled providers or the paid providers. Thus, for example, in light of families' declared willingness to provide more episodes of care than professionals prescribed—both absolutely and proportionately—it is of interest to note the high R^2 relating patient variables to mean hours of unpaid help prescribed by professionals. Professionals may be underestimating family ability or willingness to provide help, but they are doing so in a most reasonable and consistent manner, given the information made available to them.

These regressions on mean prescribed hours suggest that, on average, the eighteen professionals were prescribing home care in reasonable relation to objective patient characteristics. About three-fourths of interpatient variation in total prescribed hours were explained statistically by just a few patient variables. Curiously, the lowest level of explained interpatient variation was found in the housekeeping subtotal, an area in which patients and members of their families might reasonably be expected to be competent to exercise a fair measure of consumer judgment about needed in-home help.

Table 8-8. Regression Results: Nursing Services: Mean Prescribed Hours and Patient Variables.

Patient Variable	Nursing Subtotal			Monitoring Vital Signs		
	Standard Coefficient	Significance	Unique Variance	Standard Coefficient	Significance	Unique Variance
Barthel change				.516	.001	.188
Number of disabling conditions				.275	.032	.070
IADL				-.268	.066	.051
Anticipated discharge site	-.372	.002	.099	-.228	.073	.048
Anticipated Barthel	.382	<.001	.128			
Percentage of nursing services	-.367	<.001	.108			
Psychosocial	.168	.076	.027			
Reside with						
R^2	.653			.388		
Significance	<.001			<.001		

Table 8-9. Regression Results: Medical–Therapeutic Services: Mean Prescribed Hours and Patient Variables.

Patient Variable	Medical–Therapeutic Subtotal			Primary Medical Care			Physical Therapy		
	Standard Coefficient	Signifi-cance	Unique Variance	Standard Coefficient	Signifi-cance	Unique Variance	Standard Coefficient	Signifi-cance	Unique Variance
Indefinite placement	-.568	<.001	.269	.240	.080	.057	-.609	<.001	.356
Anticipated Barthel	-.330	.012	.077				-.489	<.001	.229
Marital status	.260	.041	.049						
Number of disabling conditions				.345	.018	.108	-.184	.082	.033
Number of current medications				.285	.046	.075			
R^2	.527			.225			.546		
Significance	<.001			.011			<.001		

Table 8-10. Regression Results: Totals: Mean Prescribed Hours and Patient Variables.

Patient Variable	Total			Continuous Supervision			Total Minus Continuous Supervision		
	Standard Coefficient	Signifi- cance	Unique Variance	Standard Coefficient	Signifi- cance	Unique Variance	Standard Coefficient	Signifi- cance	Unique Variance
Anticipated Barthel	-.670	< .001	.359	-.524	< .001	.220	-.596	< .001	.209
Age	.317	< .001	.088	.396	< .001	.137	.175	.023	.025
Psychosocial	-.276	.003	.061	-.244	.038	.048	-.287	< .001	.065
Anticipated discharge site	-.142	.086	.018						
Number of nursing services							.224	.004	.042
R^2	.754			.553			.813		
Significance	< .001			< .001			< .001		

Table 8-11. Regression Results: Provider Subtotals (*Mean Hours*).

Category of Providers[a]	R^2	Significance
Medical	.190	.009
Nursing	.383	< .001
Care	.530	< .001
Support	.412	< .001
Therapy	.477	< .001
Miscellaneous	.395	< .001
Paid	.475	< .001
Unpaid	.640	< .001
resident	.674	< .001
nonresident	.368	< .001
Skilled	.421	< .001
Unskilled	.711	< .001
Total	.754	< .001

a. See appendix to chapter 4 for categorization.

In the follow-up project, strikingly parallel findings were made. For a somewhat less disabled group, recipients of in-home care, about three-fourths of the interclient variation in total prescribed service hours was again explained by a small number of objective variables. And once again, the household area showed the lowest level of explained variation. The follow-up project reinforces the findings of the current study regarding professional ability to relate objective client characteristics to estimated hours of needed in-home care in consistent ways. In the follow-up project, client variables were also associated with actual hours of in-home care. Only slightly lower levels of explained interclient variation were obtained, suggesting that professionals, on average, were able fairly well to reconstruct prevailing care plans from assessment data. These findings generally support the position that professionals are able equitably to relate older citizens' characteristics to needed in-home services such that more help is assigned to those who seem to need more.

WHAT ARE THE CHARACTERISTICS OF PATIENTS ABOUT WHOM PROFESSIONALS AGREE?

Across the fifty patients of the study sample, an average of 124.8 hours of home care weekly was prescribed by the mean of the eighteen professional care planners. One measure of agreement among professionals about an individual patient's needs is the standard deviation across the eighteen professionals' hours of care prescribed for that patient. The standard deviation ranged from 11.9 to

67.1 hours weekly. The mean standard deviation across patients was 48.8 hours weekly.

But is the standard deviation a good yardstick for measuring how well professionals agree about one patient versus another? A general trend has been observed in many areas that standard deviations tend to increase with the mean. In these instances, variability may be compared by using the relative standard deviation or "coefficient of variation," the standard deviation's proportion of the mean.

In the present study, it has been decided to use the standard deviation to examine the characteristics of patients about whom professional agreement is best and to use the coefficient of variation for interservice and interprovider comparisons. This is because, across patients, the standard deviation does not increase with the mean. Rather, the relation between the two is slightly negative: $r_s = -0.129$ (Spearman rank-order correlation). Thus, to use the coefficient of variation as the interpatient yardstick would inappropriately overcontrol the standard deviation in prescribed hours per patient.

Patient characteristics have been found to explain between 13.5 percent and 41.2 percent of the differences in standard deviations in professionally prescribed hours. In personal care, lower age, lower prehospital IADL independence, and greater family willingness to maintain the patient at home characterized patients about whom professional agreement was better (Table 8-12). Among the household services, professional agreement was better for patients whose Barthel scores had fallen relatively little and for patients whose psychosocial status was judged relatively good. Good psychosocial status, high anticipated functional ability, and use of fewer nursing services in hospital were associated with better professional agreement about hours of nursing care needed. Agreement about medical-therapeutic services (Table 8-13) was better for patients whose institutionalization was not expected to last indefinitely, whose anticipated Barthel score was expected to be high, and whose psychosocial status was relatively good.

For the important service called continuous supervision, agreement was good for patients who were younger, had lower prehospital IADL scores, and used more nursing services in hospital. The category all hours of care other than continuous supervision presents a similar picture: higher Barthel score meant lower agreement, as did discharge to a more intensive level of care.

Agreement about total home care hours was predicted principally by greater family willingness to maintain patients at home and lower patient age (Table 8-14).

Generally, agreement about the more disabled patients was better, perhaps because their needs were more obvious. Why presence of particular characteristics enhances agreement in some areas but not others cannot be answered by this exploratory discussion. But there is a wide range in the standard deviation

Table 8-12. Regression Results: Patient Characteristics and Professional Agreement: Subtotals.

Patient Variable	Personal Care			Housekeeping			Nursing		
	Standard Coefficient	Significance	Unique Variance	Standard Coefficient	Significance	Unique Variance	Standard Coefficient	Significance	Unique Variance
Age	.340	.014	.116						
Maintenance at home	-.251	.066	.062						
IADL	-.194	.153	.037						
Psychosocial									
Barthel change				-.302	.034	.091	-.346	.010	.098
Anticipated Barthel				-.235	.097	.055	-.319	.022	.076
Percentage of nursing services							.224	.074	.045
R²	.235			.143			.412		
Significance	.008			.032			.001		

Table 8–13. Regression Results: Patient Characteristics and Professional Agreement: Subtotals.

Patient Variable	Medical–Therapeutic			Continuous Supervision			Total Minus Continuous Supervision		
	Standard Coefficient	Signifi-cance	Unique Variance	Standard Coefficient	Signifi-cance	Unique Variance	Standard Coefficient	Signifi-cance	Unique Variance
Indefinite placement	-.424	.003	.167						
Anticipated Barthel	-.308	.035	.078				.295	.042	.084
Psychosocial	-.199	.175	.031						
Age				.262	.062	.065			
IADL				-.334	.019	.106			
Percentage of nursing services				-.234	.102	.049			
Anticipated discharge site							.172	.228	.029
R^2	.276			.229			.135		
Significance	.003			.010			.039		

Table 8-14. Regression Results: Patient Characteristics
and Professional Agreement: Total.

Patient Variable	Total		
	Standard Coefficient	Significance	Unique Variance
Maintain at home	−.283	.052	.071
Age	.276	.044	.076
Number of known LTC admissions	.180	.210	.029
R^2		.225	
Significance		.011	

in prescribed hours across individual patients. Better information about the factors enhancing agreement about particular service needs of particular patients might help yield improved understanding of how professionals plan care. This sort of detailed look at the building blocks of the home care plans might help professionals make manifest their own views of service need and expected effectiveness. The importance of this incremental approach to care planning will be more apparent after the material in the following chapter has been presented.

This is one area in which the follow-up project's findings contrast with those of the study reported here. In the follow-up project, interprofessional agreement, again measured by standard deviation, was superior for the less disabled clients. In acute medicine and in the study reported here, professional agreement is generally superior for the clients in greater need. One possible explanation of the divergence in findings may be that the relation between reliability and agreement in curvilinear. In the study reported here, average Barthel score anticipated at discharge was 49.8; in the follow-up project, it was fully 74.7. Thus, the samples are quite different, and the finding of entirely different slopes may therefore signify either an anomalous research result, or a suggestion of an underlying curvilinear relationship (Figure 8-1). Professional agreement may be easier to obtain for the most and least disabled persons, with the moderately disabled group hardest to agree about. Those who are very disabled may be expected to need a great deal of help to do many things; those who are relatively independent may need very little; both judgments may be relatively easy to make. The needs of citizens of moderately severe disability may well be more difficult to determine reliably. Further investigation is clearly called for here to examine what must for now be only a tentative hypothesis.

Earlier in this section, the intention was stated to employ the coefficient of variation to compare agreement among professionals about need for specific services, service subtotals, and provider subtotals. Appendix E presents these data. Selected patterns are now briefly identified.

Figure 8-1. Functional Ability and Professional Agreement:
A Hypothesis.

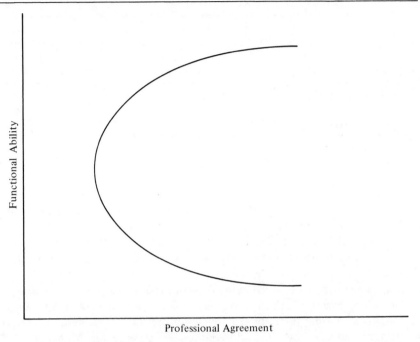

Professional Agreement

Among the service subtotals themselves, the lowest coefficient of variation is found for household services, followed by personal care, nursing, and medical-therapeutic (in that order). Average coefficients of variation across fifty patients are lower for subtotals than for individual services. This probably reflects a canceling of the individual differences.

Among the personal care services, bathing's coefficient of variation was lowest; that for periodic checking was highest. Among household services, best agreement was about shopping; the worst was about assistance with telephoning. For nursing, best was monitoring of vital signs, and the worst was decubitus care. For medical-therapeutic services, best was primary medical care, and worst was dentists' services.

The pattern that emerges here is that professionals generally agreed best about hours of care required to discharge more necessary and pressing functions. This might have been expected; its presence is nonetheless a reassuring sign pointing toward the reasonableness of professional decisionmaking. It should also be noted, however, that while agreement is better about the more necessary and pressing services, it is perhaps not as great as might be hoped. Across fifty patients, a mean coefficient of variation equal to 41.7 percent of prescribed hours suggests wide confidence intervals. The extent and nature of interprofessional agreement about patients' care needs is the subject of Chapter 9.

SUMMARY AND IMPLICATIONS

On average, agreement was good among professionals, patients, and family members about needed episodes of home care. This agreement was not very good in individual cases, but differences tended to average out. That averaging out occurs is important because it suggests that the preferences of the three groups could be accommodated within a single program budget. Agreement about planning care for individual patients—how to carve up the budget—is by no means as good (as indicated by the Pearson product-moment correlations).

Of particular interest was the finding that family members' estimates of the number of episodes unpaid providers would deliver was the highest of the three groups—both absolutely and as a proportion of total episodes. Because the number of hours of unpaid help could be calculated only from professional care plans, these were used to estimate the imputed values of unpaid help. These values for most patients were significant, pointing to the potential importance of family effort on behalf of a group even so ill and disabled as the study sample.

Members of all three groups—professionals, patients, and family members—sought more episodes of care for more disabled patients. This negative relation points to the reasonableness of all three groups of care planners. A more detailed look at the relation of professional prescriptions to patient characteristics was made possible by the larger sample size available for this analysis. Multiple regressions were performed on the mean number of hours prescribed per patient (across eighteen professionals) for a group of different services and service and provider subtotals. Mean professionally prescribed hours could be approximated with fair accuracy (R^2s typically greater than 60 percent were found) using only a relatively small number of objective patient characteristics. The particular characteristics varied in sensible relation to the dependent variable in most cases, further testifying to the overall reasonableness of the average professional's prescription. This reasonableness may be taken as an indication of *equity* in care planning, in that patients who by their objective characteristics seem to need more care, have more care prescribed for them. A similar pattern was identified earlier, in which episodes of care sought by patients, family members, and professionals all bore equitable relations to anticipated Barthel score. This evidence on equity is not overwhelming, but it does point in an encouraging direction.

Agreement about the more disabled patients seemed superior, but more careful work in this area would help to build a firmer foundation for professional agreement. The same can be said about the extent of professional agreement about particular services and providers. Here, consistency seemed better about the more necessary or pressing services, but it was not strikingly impressive in most areas.

9 AGREEMENT AMONG PROFESSIONALS
Patterns of Consistency and Variation

If professionals agree well about the home care needs of the elderly, such reliability points to the possibility that prescribed services would be effective. And, given the difficulty of measuring effectiveness of long-term care services, this pointer would be most welcome. If professionals do not generally agree well, it would be desirable to explore when they do agree and, if possible, why. This would indicate opportunities for improving reliability in the future. Multiple clusters of views (as opposed to random scattering), if found to exist, would point to opportunities for clinical trials or natural experiments to attempt to learn who is right. Finally, low levels of professional agreement in certain areas could help open the door to greater patient and family influence over the design of home care plans.

There are four potential sources of disagreement among professionals about the hypothetical home care needs of the elderly patients who constitute the sample of the present study:

1. The phrase "safe, adequate, and dignified" may be interpreted to mean service at different levels in different areas of home care. Goals may vary; household services may matter more to one professional; continuous supervision and medical monitoring may matter more to another.

2. Given agreement about goals, professionals may synthesize the discrete objective data on the PACE form into varying pictures of patients' overall condition.

3. Given agreement about goals and current status, professionals may disagree about prognosis—the path the patient might take absent care.

165

4. Even given agreement about all the foregoing, professionals could still disagree about the types, quantities, and providers of home care required to move the patient from current prognosis along a desired trajectory toward particular goals.

In view of these opportunities for disagreement, the reader will not be surprised to learn that the following sections report much variety in professional prescriptions. What is surprising is the extent of agreement about home care needs and the depth of these agreements, particularly given all the reasons for disagreement in long-term care discussed in Chapter 3.

Failure to define the word "agreement" is not the source of this apparent paradox, although different meanings will emerge below. There is no a priori way to identify when agreement fades to disagreement. Rather, it must be decided in specific instances whether the extent of agreement that may be expected is sufficient for the purpose at hand. Even weak agreement is enough to support parimutual wagering on horse races; somewhat better agreement on rules of ordinary behavior is adequate to govern Boston-area auto drivers (except at rotaries); but only excellent agreement among engineers will persuade public authority bond underwriters that a bridge will support investors' financial risks.

The first section of this chapter will present progressively disaggregated views of the extent of professional agreement about the hypothetical home care needs of the members of the study sample. In the course of disaggregation, various groups' views of different needs will be presented and contrasted. The relation of professional variables — role, training, information, and experience — to types and quantities and providers of care prescribed (and to agreement about them) will be analyzed. Such questions as, Do professionals recommend more care or agree better about care in their own disciplines? will be addressed. Better agreement in a professional's field of expertise might reassuringly point to validity. (It might, alternatively, point to blind worship of in-bred error, but this is less likely.) A related question is whether intraprofession agreement exceeds interprofession agreement. Techniques of analysis of variance and factor analysis are employed to begin to re-aggregate the data into understandable patterns.

The need to build such patterns is considerable. For example, any attempt to understand how well individual professionals agree about which providers should deliver what proportions of individual service to individual patients would require examination of an $18 \times 58 \times 41 \times 50 \times 3$ ($= 6,420,600$-celled) matrix.

The following section continues the task of re-aggregation and analysis. The techniques of Cronbach's Alpha and Kendall's W are used, in conjunction with certain regression results introduced in Chapter 8, to seek patterns of professional agreement about patients' home care needs. Areas of relatively good and bad agreement are identified, along with possible explanations for the various patterns.

PATTERNS OF PROFESSIONAL CARE PLANNING

This section will begin by presenting progressively disaggregated views of professionals' home care plans. It will consider different groups of professionals' prescriptions about total need, need for various categories of service and care providers, and need for individual services. At the same time, the content of the care plan is sliced finer. The study sample will be disaggregated as well.

By means of disaggregation, the relation of professional variables to care plans' content and to agreement about that content will be measured. Analysis of variance and factor analysis will aid in this measurement, which at the same time begins the task of reaggregating professional care plans into analyzable levels of generalization.

Service Groupings

Table 9-1 presents the number of hours per week prescribed by different care planners grouped by role for the mean of the fifty patients who make up the study sample. It will be seen that the means of the three groups of consultant professionals are very similar in total and fairly similar for the various subtotals. Agreement between the mean of the fifteen consultants and the mean of the hospital professionals is not as good either in total or for the various subtotals.

Also noteworthy in Table 9-1 is the distribution of the proportion of total hours assigned by the means of the three consultants to different subtotals. Physicians are highest on personal care and medical-therapeutic hours; home health care planners are highest on household and nursing hours. Hospital discharge planners fall in between on most subtotals and are lowest on total hours. Hospital professionals recommended more hours of care than consultants in all categories.

Table 9-2 contains the results of one-way analysis of variance (means comparison, repeated measures) tests of the extent of agreement among consultants and between consultants and hospital care planners. The prescriber variable is significant for most service groupings for both comparisons. Disagreement about needed household services and about total hours minus continuous supervision was particularly strong.

A somewhat different picture emerges when agreement by type of training is examined. (This concerns only consultants, so hospital consultants are excluded to avoid repetition.) Disagreement among consultants by training is considerably greater than by role when specific categories of services are examined, but agreement about total hours of home care needed is just as good as when consultants were grouped by role. It should be noted that both nurses and physicians tended to recommend more care in their own areas of specialization (Table 9-3).

Table 9-1. Prescribed Hours[a] by Professional Role and Service Grouping.

Service Grouping	Professional Role: Weekly Hours Prescribed By:					
	$\bar{X}MDC^b$	$\bar{X}DPC^c$	$\bar{X}HHC^d$	$\bar{X}C^e$	$\bar{X}H^f$	$\bar{X}All$
Personal care subtotal	93.2	81.5	77.5	87.3	96.4	85.6
Household subtotal	24.7	28.1	33.1	29.0	36.4	29.7
Nursing subtotal	6.0	7.6	7.7	7.4	9.7	7.4
Medical-therapeutic subtotal	2.5	1.5	2.1	2.1	2.4	2.1
Continuous supervision	74.5	56.4	55.8	64.8	69.8	63.1
Total minus continuous supervision	51.9	62.3	64.6	57.0	75.1	61.7
Total	126.4	118.7	120.4	121.8	144.9	124.8

a. N = 50 patients.
b. MDC = physician consultants.
c. DPC = discharge planner consultants.
d. HHC = home health consultant.
e. C = mean of all consultants.
f. H = hospital consultants.

Table 9-2. Prescribed Hours by Professional Role and Service Grouping: Significance and Explanatory Power of Prescriber Effect.

Service Grouping	Among Consultant Groups		Between Consultants and Hospital Professionals	
	Significance[a]	Explanatory Power[b]	Significance[a]	Explanatory Power[b]
Personal care subtotal	< .001	3.4%	.055	1.47%
Household subtotal	< .001	34.7	.001	13.58
Nursing subtotal	.002	2.4	.017	3.04
Medical-therapeutic subtotal	< .001	7.6	.272	0.66
Continuous supervision	< .001	8.3	.296	0.62
Total minus continuous supervision	< .001	9.8	.001	8.92
Total	.015	0.7%	.001	4.71%

a. Of prescriber effects in one-way analysis of variance.
b. Percentage of total sum.

Table 9-3. Prescribed Hours[a] by Professional Training and Service Grouping.

| Service Grouping | Weekly Hours Prescribed By: | | | Significance and Explanatory Power of Prescriber Effect | |
	MD[b]	RN[c]	SW[d]	Significance	Explanatory Power
Personal care	93.2	80.3	92.5	.003	2.2%
Household	24.7	34.6	22.7	< .001	51.7
Nursing	6.0	9.3	5.0	< .001	13.4
Medical-therapeutic	2.5	2.2	1.2	< .001	14.2
Continuous supervision	74.5	53.9	74.8	< .001	7.5
Total minus continuous supervision	52.0	72.5	46.9	< .001	32.0
Total	126.4	125.4	121.8	.392	0.2%

a. N = 50 patients.
b. MD = consultant physician.
c. RN = consultant nurse.
d. SW = consultant social worker.

Professional agreements about specific care needs of patients for specific services have been analyzed. Seven services were selected from among the forty-one for a closer look at interprofessional agreement. Considering first the role of the professionals, no one group consistently prescribed more hours of care across the services. Rather, group ranking of consultant group varied from service to service. In all cases, however, the hospital professionals continued to recommend more care than did the mean of consultants (Table 9-4). The explanatory power of the prescriber variable among consultants was generally greater for specific services than it was in the case of service subtotals (Table 9-5). Between the means of consultants and hospital planners, however, it was lower, indicating better agreement between the two groups of professionals about these specific services than about the subtotals.

When consultants are regrouped by their training, a more dramatic set of differences emerges (Table 9-6). For several of the specific services, the explanatory power of the variable of professional training is very great indeed. This is particularly true for the services in which none of a fairly wide range of views might be expected quickly to harm patients—housework, transportation, or bathing. Agreement about specific care needs for services such as monitoring of vital signs and primary medical care remains relatively good. In general, agreement is better for services requiring skilled providers.

Table 9-4. Prescribed Hours[a] by Professional Role and Specific Service.

	Professional Role: Weekly Hours Prescribed By:					
Service	$\bar{X}MDC^b$	$\bar{X}DPC^c$	$\bar{X}HHC^d$	$\bar{X}C^e$	$\bar{X}H^f$	$\bar{X}A11$
Bathing	2.1	2.7	3.3	2.7	3.6	2.8
Eating/drinking	2.3	2.6	2.2	2.3	2.8	2.4
Transportation	2.1	1.9	0.6	1.5	2.1	1.6
Light housework	3.5	4.6	6.9	5.0	5.8	5.1
Monitoring vital signs	0.6	0.6	0.9	0.7	0.7	0.7
Primary medical care	0.08	0.07	0.07	0.08	0.12	0.08
Physical therapy	1.8	0.8	1.4	1.3	1.6	1.4

a. N = 50.
b. MDC = physician consultant.
c. DPC = discharge planner consultant.
d. HHC = home health consultant.
e. C = mean of all consultants.
f. H = hospital consultants.

Table 9-5. Prescribed Hours by Professional Role and Specific Service: Significance and Explanatory Power of Prescriber Effect.

	Among Consultant Groups		Between Consultants and Hospital Professionals	
Service	Signifi-cance	Explanatory Power	Signifi-cance	Explanatory Power
Bathing	< .001	23.6%	.003	8.6%
Eating/drinking	.317	0.2	.276	0.3
Transportation	< .001	31.5	.013	5.9
Light housework	< .001	54.0	.110	2.6
Monitoring vital signs	< .001	6.5	> .500	0.1
Primary medical care	.024	3.2	< .001	12.1
Physical therapy	< .001	10.4%	.260	0.7%

The descriptive review of agreement about means of patients' needs now concludes with a brief examination of the consistency of professional views of which groups of providers are needed. Inspection of the data in Table 9-7 indicates that there is some disagreement among consultants grouped by role and only a bit more disagreement between consultants and hospital care planners. Discharge planners sought 22.8 percent less paid help than physicians and expected families would provide 38.2 percent more. Although most differences among and between the means are statistically significant, the explanatory

Table 9-6. Prescribed Hours by Professional Training and Specific Service.

Service	Weekly Hours Prescribed By:			Significance and Explanatory Power of Prescriber Effect	
	MD^a	RN^b	SW^c	Significance	Explanatory Power
Bathing	2.1	3.7	1.7	< .001	52.6%
Eating/drinking	2.3	2.7	1.9	.034	0.7
Transportation	2.1	1.1	0.8	< .001	33.9
Light housework	3.5	7.5	2.5	< .001	73.3
Monitoring vital signs	0.6	0.7	0.8	.082	2.1
Primary medical care	0.8	0.6	0.8	< .001	6.2
Physical therapy	1.8	1.4	0.7	< .001	13.2%

a. MD = consultant physician.
b. RN = consultant nurse.
c. SW = social worker.

Table 9-7. Prescribed Hours by Professional Role and Selected Provider Subtotals: Weekly Hours Prescribed.

Provider Subtotal	$\bar{X}MDC^a$	$\bar{X}DPC^b$	$\bar{X}HHC^c$	$\bar{X}C^{d,e}$	$\bar{X}H^{e,f}$	$\bar{X}All^g$
Paid	92.2	71.2	83.2	85.2	97.5	84.2
Unpaid	34.3	47.4	37.2	40.5	47.4	40.7
Skilled	8.0	5.7	5.0	6.4	12.8	7.1
Unskilled	118.4	113.0	115.3	119.3	132.1	117.8
Total	126.4	118.7	120.4	125.7	144.9	124.8

a. MDC = physician consultant.
b. DPC = discharge planner consultant.
c. HHC = home health consultant.
d. C = mean of all consultants.
e. N = 48.
f. H = hospital consultants.
g. N = 50.

power of the prescriber variable is weak in most cases (see Table 9-8). A similar pattern holds for consultants grouped by training (Table 9-9). For all skilled providers, grouped together, agreement is not as good as for unskilled providers. This difference, however, is minor in all cases. Agreement about unpaid services was somewhat superior. By the measure of Kendall's W, discussed shortly, professional agreement across all fifteen consultants about paid hours was 0.444;

Table 9–8. Prescribed Hours by Professional Role and Selected Provider Subtotals: Significance and Explanatory Power of Prescriber Effect.

Provider Subtotal	Among Consultant Groups		Between Consultants and Hospital Professionals	
	Significance	Explanatory Power	Significance	Explanatory Power
Paid	< .001	5.5%	.018	2.3%
Unpaid	< .001	3.6	.045	1.1
Skilled	.127	1.7	.020	3.6
Unskilled	.193	0.3	.017	2.6
Total	.015	0.7%	.001	4.7%

Table 9–9. Prescribed Hours by Professional Training and Selected Provider Subtotals.

Provider Subtotals	Weekly Hours Prescribed By:			Significance and Explanatory Power of Prescriber Effects	
	MD^a	RN^b	SW^c	Significance	Explanatory Power
Paid	92.2	81.1	78.3	.001	2.4%
Unpaid	34.3	45.3	43.5	.002	2.2
Skilled	8.0	4.9	4.3	.038	2.9
Unskilled	118.4	121.5	117.5	.500	0.2
Total	126.4	126.4	121.8	.392	0.2%

a. MD = consultant physician.
b. RN = consultant nurse.
c. SW = social worker.

about unpaid resident hours, 0.725; and about unpaid nonresident (visitor) hours, 0.404.

It has been shown that agreement regarding total hours of needed care among and between professional groups about the needs of the members of the study sample as a whole is fairly good. When total hours of need are split into service and provider subtotals and into specific services, however, intergroup agreement falls. Agreement is particularly poor among consultants when they are grouped by training. This indicates that training is a more important influence on the prescriptions of study consultants than is role. Another clear pattern is that hospital professionals generally prescribe more care, by all measures, than do consultants.

Prescribed Care and Professional Experience

The relation between consultant professionals' years of practice in direct patient care and the number of hours of home care service they recommend has been measured by Pearson product-moment correlation. A slight negative relation has been found ($r = -0.35$; $R^2 = .12$; significance = .199), indicating that prescribed hours generally decline as professional experience increases. This relation is so slight that it could have been found by chance about one time in five. It does, however, point to the possibility that experience encourages or permits professionals to be less cautious or conservative. With greater experience, they may learn or believe that patients may remain safely at home with a bit less care than they had thought necessary earlier in their careers. The seven less-experienced professionals recommended an average of 131 hours weekly; the eight more experienced, 115 hours. This was a difference of 14 percent or one hour in seven.

Variations in Intragroup Agreement

Which groups of professionals, defined in what ways, show the strongest consistency in their views of patients' needs? Using group coefficient of variation as the standard for comparison, consistency among hospital professionals is seen to be superior to that among the consultants collectively (Table 9-10).

A possible influence here may be one of method. In the hospitals, the three consultants may have had opportunities to discuss the content of their care plans, perhaps while assisting one another in understanding how to complete the form. This is not considered likely. What remains then is to suspect that the better information about patients gained by hospital care planners in the course of their personal associations enhanced the consistency of these professionals' prescriptions.

Whether consultants are grouped by role or by training, only small differences among intragroup coefficients of variation in total hours are found. The most noteworthy distinctions appear when consultants are grouped by training. Social workers' coefficients of variations are lowest across almost all service categories. Social workers distinguished themselves best in the nursing services subtotal. It could reasonably have been expected that nurses would have agreed best in their own field, but they may have held differing though well-grounded views of need (based on different experience) while social workers adhered to a common pattern perhaps based on elements in past training.

Agreement and Information

It will be recalled that the three hospital care planners relied on PACE data plus their own detailed personal information about all patients. At the other extreme,

Table 9-10. Coefficient of Variation[a] in Prescribed Hours: Selected Prescriber Groups: Service Subtotals.

Prescriber Group	Area of Service				
	Personal Care	Household	Nursing	Medical Therapeutic	Total
Physicians	56.2	27.1	77.1	76.9	36.7
Discharge planners	59.7	24.8	67.4	69.1	39.0
Home health	71.7	40.0	79.3	83.1	41.0
Physicians	56.2	27.1	77.1	76.9	36.7
Nurses	57.5	31.8	67.0	80.9	34.0
Social workers	49.3	29.0	53.5	71.3	31.0
Consultants	65.7	37.1	82.8	95.7	40.3
Hospital	34.3	28.5	48.8	46.7	23.7
All	67.6	41.3	87.5	100.3	41.7

a. Coefficient of variation = standard deviation divided by mean.

nine of the fifteen consultants had access only to PACE data in all cases. For the six "visiting" consultants, this pattern was deliberately altered. These six briefly visited patients at the Boston-area hospitals and wrote care plans based on this information and the PACE data. For the remaining patients in the study, from the hospitals outside Boston, these six "visiting" consultants relied only on PACE data. Thus, by three-way analysis of variance, it has been possible to control for the effects on care planning of both information available to prescribers and characteristics of patients.

Across all fifty patients, as Table 9-11 makes clear, an average of 125.4 hours of care was prescribed weekly by the mean of the eighteen care planners. The mean across patients for the three hospital consultants was above 141 hours; for the six "visitors," 129.8 hours; and for the nine PACE-only "nonvisitor" consultants, 117.1 hours. A pattern has emerged that shows more information about patients to be associated with higher prescribed hours. Is this in fact the case?

Hospital professionals clearly prescribed more hours of care. It might be speculated that this was due to relatively poor familiarity with the care planning form, or perhaps due to inexperience with care planning in general, and the interpatient tradeoffs that are often involved. Consequently, it might be thought, hospital professionals tried to write even hypothetical plans that would seek to obtain for patients all possible resources. Reduced familiarity with the care planning form may have led to some duplications as professionals inexperienced with the form sought to ensure that needed services were delivered. But one group of hospital professionals is well experienced in this study's methods of care planning and in weighing the needs of one patient against those of another; they thereby test this hypothesis. These are the hospital discharge planners, whose mean prescribed hours (147.6) was slightly above the average for hospital professionals. Moreover, these care planners were fairly well acquainted with the care planning form, having had the job of explaining its use to other hospital professionals. A final point in support of hospital care planners' view of need comes from their relatively low intragroup coefficients of variation across the different categories of service.

The positive relation between information and prescribed hours of home care probably does not extend into the consultant category. It seems rather that the higher hours prescribed by visitors is a consequence of the characteristics of the professionals as individuals rather than of the better information available to them (on some patients).

How is this known? First, the reader can see by inspecting Table 9-11 that the visitors prescribed more care for both groups of patients—the thirty-four not visited and the sixteen visited. (More care, that is, than the nine nonvisitors prescribed for the two groups of patients.) Second, as indicated in Part B of Table 9-12, the interaction between patient status (visited or not) and prescriber status (visitor or not) has absolutely no measurable influence on prescribed hours of home care. Rather, visiting status of prescribers, particularly in interaction with prescribers' professional role, has considerable impact on prescribed hours and is statistically significant beyond .001. The explanatory power of visitor status alone was only 1.9 percent; but visitor status interacting with professional role explained 6.6 percent of the total sum of squares in this three-way analysis of variance. It seems that the more discretely care planning by various professionals is examined, the greater the disagreement among professionals. Complete disaggregation of a representative care plan is discussed following a brief summary of this discussion of the effects of information on professionals' prescribed hours of care.

Professionals with the best information about patients tended to prescribe the greatest amounts of care. But the brief visit made by some consultants to some patients does not seem to have affected the magnitude of the care plans at all. Visits may have led to more sensitive allocations of hours of care within the total, but this cannot be measured. Hospital prescribers recommended more hours of care in almost every service or provider category (see Tables 9-1, 9-4, and 9-7). This raises the suspicion that the greater number of hours may be more than the product of better information. It may also follow from a relatively indiscriminate belief that older people need more home care of all types. Such a suspicion indicates a need for a closer examination of hospital planners' views before it is decided that these may be valid.

Complete Disaggregation

In this section, increasingly discrete looks have been taken at care planning—by professional role, training, information; by service and provider subtotals; and by

Table 9-11. Total Prescribed Hours by Patient Visit Status and Information Available to Professionals.

Patients	Professionals										
	Nonvisitors (9)[a]				Visitors (6)[a]				Consultants (15)[a]	Hospital (3)[b]	Total (18)
	MDC[c] (3)	DPC[d] (3)	HHC[e] (3)	$\bar{X}$ (9)	MDC (2)	DPC (2)	HHC (2)	$\bar{X}$ (6)			
Nonvisit (34)	123.3	132.2	112.5	122.7	151.1	106.6	146.1	134.6	127.5	148.2	130.9
Visit (16)	103.3	122.7	102.8	109.6	137.6	104.7	130.8	124.4	115.5	127.1	117.5
Total (50)	117.2	129.3	109.5	117.1	146.9	106.0	141.4	129.8	123.8	141.4	125.4

a. N = 49.
b. N = 50.
c. MDC = physician consultant.
d. DPC = discharge planner consultant.
e. HHC = home health consultant.

Table 9-12. Total Prescribed Hours by Information Available to Professionals and Visit Status of Patients: Significance and Explanatory Power.

Variable	Significance (F-test)	Percent of Total Sum of Squares Explained
A. *Eighteen care planners:* *Nonvisiting, Visiting, Hospital (9-6-3)*		
Visited-Nonvisited Status (patients)	.155	3.3%
Nonvisiting, Visiting, Hospital Professionals	< .001	3.9%
Patient Visited Status by Professional Visiting Status	> .500	0.1%
B. *Fifteen consultants only:* *Visiting Status by Professional Role by Patient Visited Status*		
Visited-Nonvisited Status (patients)	.322	1.4%
Professional Role	< .001	1.1%
Patient Status by Professional Role	.165	0.2%
Visiting-Nonvisiting Consultants	< .001	1.9%
Patient Status by Visiting Status of Consultants	> .500	0.0%
Professional Role by Visiting Status of Consultants	< .001	6.6%
Patient Status by Professional Role by Visiting Status	> .500	0.1%

individual service. When to these is added distinctions among patients, the extent of agreement among professionals appears by inspection to break down entirely. Refer to Appendix D for a copy of a complete care plan on one patient, selected at random. The four sheets form one care plan with services down the left hand margin (with appropriate subtotals and total) and individual prescriber labels across the top (with various group means). There appears to be little agreement about any aspect of the care plan either within a profession or across professional boundaries.

In the course of attempting to analyze these data, it was realized that the mass of data about patients, prescribers, services, and providers could obscure patterns of agreement and disagreement of some importance to better understanding patient needs or to building firmer future foundations for care planning. Similarly, it was feared that important differences could be masked by inspection of grouped data alone; distinctive patterns of variation could be hidden by averaging. This has undoubtedly been the case to some extent for the grouped data discussed earlier. To reaggregate discrete pieces of information about individual patients, to seek patterns of agreement and difference among professionals, several statistical tests have been employed. These are factor analysis, Cronbach's alpha, and Kendall's W.

It is of interest to see how seemingly formless data, those that appear in the individual care plans, actually constitute very definite and consistent patterns. While these patterns are not quite strong enough to inspire wholehearted confidence in reliability of professional views (which has been posited as a pointer toward validity), they do indicate that professional care planning is a deliberate, thoughtful, and internally consistent process. These results are encouraging.

Aggregation Through Factor Analysis

Factor analysis was performed on the hours of care recommended by different groups of professionals to learn from another vantage point whether intraprofession agreement (by role or training) was stronger than interprofession agreement. Did nurses, for example, agree better among themselves than some nurses agreed with social workers? Clusters of consultant care planners were formed in interesting patterns.

Using varimax rotation and .5000 as the cutoff for assignment of consultants to groups, four factors were formed on total prescribed hours; from three to six factors were formed on the various service subtotals. Factors were included only if their Eigenvalues exceeded 1.0. By this standard, only a few consultants were left outside all groups; this happened in only two of the subtotals. In a few cases, individual consultants were loaded onto more than one factor.

Inspection of the members of factors formed by these procedures indicates no consistent pattern of agreement within boundaries of professional role or training (Table 9-13). Physicians, discharge planners, and home health planners cluster together, but *across* roles and training. Professional roles and training are thus not associated with agreement about needed home care—either in total or in most of the four service subtotals. (An exception is the nursing subtotals; discharge planners and home health planners sorted themselves into two groups here, and nurses in particular clustered together.)

In sum, patterns of agreement, while moderately strong in many instances seem idiosyncratic and fluid from service to service. Certain professionals agree with certain others about a given service, such as personal care, but form new patterns of agreement for household, nursing, and medical therapeutic services. Few linkages last. These observations hold whether professional affiliations are considered by role or by training. Nurses or social workers did not group any more tightly than did discharge planners or home health care planners. Agreement within a profession is no better than agreement across professional boundaries.

Factor analysis indicates that the seemingly inchoate mix of prescribed hours—as it appears after successive disaggregation to the level of individual care planners, services, and patients—in fact yields definite but shifting associations.

Table 9-13. Consultant Groupings Formed Through Factor Analysis: Service Subtotals.

Service Category	Factor and Members[a]						Loners
	1	2	3	4	5	6	
Personal care	MD-2 DP-4 HH-1	MD-1 DP-1 HH-3	MD-4 DP-3 DP-5	MD-3 DP-2 HH-4			MD-5 HH-5
Household	DP-5 HH-2 HH-5	MD-1 MD-5 DP-2	HH-1 HH-3 HH-4	MD-4 DP-3	MD-3 DP-4	MD-2	
Nursing	MD-2 MD-3--MD-3 DP-1 DP-2 - - - - - - DP-3 --DP-3 DP-4 DP-5 HH-2 HH-3--HH-3	MD-1 MD-5 DP-2 HH-1 HH-4 HH-5--HH-5	MD-4				
Medical-Therapeutic	MD-1 MD-5 DP-2 DP-5 HH-2	MD-3 DP-3 DP-4 HH-3	MD-2--MD-2 DP-2 HH-5	MD-4 HH-4			HH-1

Consultant Groupings Formed Through Factor Analysis: Total Hours of Care

	Factor and Members			
	1	2	3	4
Total hours	MD-4 MD-5--MD-5 DP-3 DP-5 HH-5	MD-1 DP-1	MD-2 DP-4 HH-1 HH-2 HH-4 HH-3---------HH-3	MD-3 DP-2

a. MD = physician; DP = discharge planner; HH = home health care planner.

These patterns are formed separately for each service subtotal, much as major European powers of the eighteenth century or Balkan states of the early twentieth formed new alliances for each war.

THE RELIABILITY OF PROFESSIONAL VIEWS: CRONBACH'S ALPHA AND KENDALL'S W

A useful description of Kendall's W, also known as Kendall's "coefficient of concordance" is that by Siegel.[1] This technique can be thought of as the extension of Spearman's rank-order correlation—how well two people agree about the ordering of any set of data—to how well more than two people agree about that ordering. In the present study, Spearman's correlation could have been used to measure agreement between any two professionals about the ranking of patients by hours of home care needed. In both Spearman's and Kendall's measures, a score of 1.0 indicates complete agreement on ranking; 0.0 indicates total disagreement.

Cronbach's alpha, on the other hand, can be thought of roughly as an interval equivalent of the ordinal Kendall's W. Alpha is to W, then, as the Pearson product-moment correlation is to Spearman's rank-order correlation.[2]

An alpha score of 1.0 would indicate that any one rater's judgment of needed home care across all clients was a perfect linear transformation of any other rater's scores, and a score of 0.0 would reflect the absence of linear relationships. If Kendall's W and a Cronbach's alpha were calculated on the same data, W could be expected to exceed alpha if curvilinear relations obtained. Alpha can be expected to exceed W, on the other hand, if small departures or disagreements in rankings were common. We have found alpha scores consistently higher than W's, indicating fairly frequent but small departures in rankings. But it has been reassuring to find that the two measures themselves have been highly correlated across service domains and providers.

In the present study, alpha and W have been applied to the same sets of data. This was done because the first test of reliability that was performed, alpha, yields unexpectedly high scores. Suggested agreement among individual professionals about individual patients seemed too high; the results did not "feel" right in view of the observed patterns of disagreement about patients. One pointer toward sensible results, however, was the relatively low alpha calculated for prescribed hours of care in the subtotal household services (Table 9-14). This confirmed the high interprofession disagreement in household services uncovered by analysis of variance (see Tables 9-1, 9-2, and 9-3). A strong direct relation was found in general between alpha and the explanatory power of the prescriber variable in one-way analysis of variance across the various service subtotals.

Kendall's W tests on these data tended to confirm the alpha scores. Relatively high alphas were associated with relatively high Ws (and low with low); $r = 0.85$; significance $< .001$. Figure 9-1 graphs this relation. The parallel movements of

Table 9-14. Professional Consistency: Alpha and W Compared.

Service subtotal	Alpha	W
Personal subtotal		
MDC	.72	.43
DPC	.79	.54
HHC	.79	.55
Hospital	.51	
Consultants	.90	.38
Household subtotal		
MDC	.24	.25
DPC	.46	.33
HHC	.51	.33
Hospital	.35	
Consultants	.59	.15
Nursing subtotal		
MDC	.73	.63
DPC	.81	.62
HHC	.76	.60
Hospital	.36	
Consultants	.91	.56
Medical–Therapeutic subtotal		
MDC	.76	.58
DPC	.85	.67
HHC	.78	.58
Hospital	.73	
Consultants	.91	.52
Total		
MDC	.75	.50
DPC	.84	.57
HHC	.83	.56
Hospital	.53	
Consultants	.93	.45

the two sets of data, alpha and W, are clear. The alphas are very high. They point to extraordinary linear relations among professionals' views of need. The Ws are only fairly high, suggesting a somewhat weaker pattern of agreement about ranking of patients by needed hours of home care.

For present purposes both sets of scores have similar practical consequences for interpreting the reliability of professional views of the home care needs of the elderly. What the alpha and W analyses tell us is that the care plans of individual professionals about individual patients for specific service subtotal and

Figure 9-1. Alpha and W Compared.

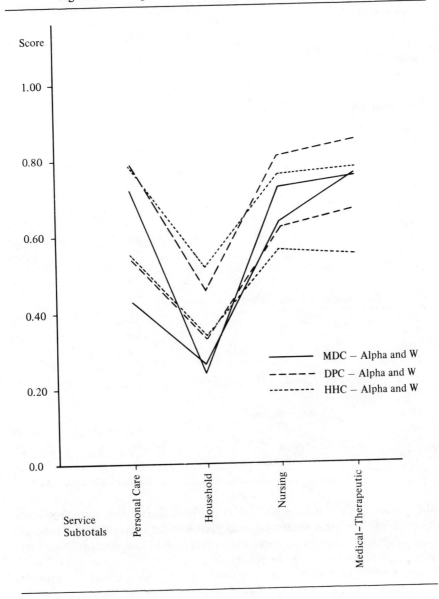

total hours signify good agreement about which patients need more care and which patients need less—by each individual professional's yardstick. Professionals are consistent with themselves. That is, one who usually recommends a relatively high number of hours of care seldom prescribes a low number (relative to other professionals).

Professionals agree, by their own personal yardsticks, about which patients need more help and which need less. If a patient were thought by one care planner to need more hours of service than other patients, a second care planner also would tend to recommend more care for this patient than he or she would recommend for other patients. Thus, professionals tend to agree well about which patients need more care and which need less, but they disagree about how many hours of care are sufficient to sustain individual patients at home. Figure 9-2 graphs this pattern by presenting five professionals' views of five representative patients' home care needs.

The meaning of this analysis for understanding the reliability of care planning by professionals in the present study is important. Individual professionals do not plan care arbitrarily. They are quite consistent with their own views of patient need. This argument is reinforced and extended by the very reasonable relation between average hours of care prescribed across all eighteen professionals and patient characteristics (as was shown in Chapter 8). If the average view of need relates equitably and reasonably to patient characteristics, and professionals are individually consistent, it then follows that professionals as individuals probably do well at relating prescribed hours to patient need. This proposition could be tested by using individual care planners' prescribed hours as regressions' dependent variables.

What remains to be decided in the midst of this consistency and reasonableness is: (1) why professionals disagree and (2) whose views of patients' needs are valid. While these tasks largely fall beyond the scope of the present study, it has been possible to perform two analyses that attempt to learn which of the individual professionals' views of need are more valid. One analysis involved a look at how each of the care planners employed patient characteristics to write care plans. The second analysis considered how well individual professionals agreed with themselves (on the theory that intraprofessional reliability may point to validity).

Individual regression analyses were run on each of the fifteen consultants' prescribed hours for the patients ($N = 50$). A multiple correlation squared (R^2) was calculated for the proportion of difference in hours prescribed for the various patients that could be explained by patient characteristics. R^2 scores ranged from 0.68 to 0.18, indicating the varying degrees to which consultants consistently considered patient characteristics to be important.

Twelve patient characteristics (independent variables) were used (were statistically significant) in at least one of the consultant's regression equations. Antici-

Figure 9–2. Five Physicians' Views of Five Patients' Needs.

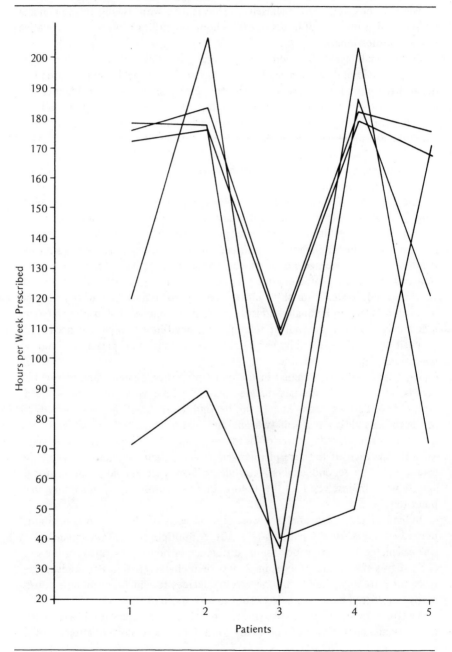

pated Barthel score at discharge was used by all consultants, psychosocial status by eight, and so on (see Table 9–15).

An individual consultant's R^2, indicating consistent use of patient character- istics in prescribing hours of home care, was not associated with professional experience (Pearson product-moment correlation, r = -0.09).

Of interest, however, is the association between consultant's R^2 scores and their self-consistency in total prescribed hours between original and repeat care plans. Individual consultants' R^2 scores correlated moderately well with their individual standard deviation across the ten patients whose care plans were re- peated. (Pearson product-moment correlation = -0.47.) This means that pro- fessionals who relied on patient characteristics in a consistent manner when assigning hours of home care tended to agree better *with themselves*, as mea- sured by the standard deviation between their original and repeat care plans for the same patient. It must be decided for present purposes whether the ex- tent of professional agreement identified in this chapter (on a sample of eighteen care planners and fifty patients) is sufficient to argue in favor of increased or diminished professional control over home care planning.

Why do professionals tend to disagree in such consistent patterns? One gen- eral factor may be professional experience. Professionals with more years in practice tend to recommend somewhat fewer hours of care. Another such factor may be choice of goals. Some professionals may value patient safety and recom- mend generous home care plans even at the risk of engendering avoidable depen-

Table 9–15. Individual Professionals' Multiple Correlation with Prescribed Hours and Number of Significant Variables.

Consultant	$R^{2\,a}$	Number of Significant Variables
MDC 1	.66	6
2	.36	2
3	.52	3
4	.36	2
5	.44	3
DPC 1	.68	5
2	.48	1
3	.33	2
4	.68	4
5	.41	4
HHC 1	.67	2
2	.44	3
3	.47	3
4	.18	1
5	.51	3

a. All significant at .001 except HHC 4 (.003), by F-test.

dence. Other professionals are perhaps willing, in order to encourage or permit greater self-reliance, to be less cautious in assuring patient safety.[3]

Further, professionals may differ in other aspects of home care goals. Some emphasize rehabilitation more than others. Average hours of physical therapy across all patients ranges from 0.25 to 2.70 hours weekly. This indicates different attitudes toward rehabilitation and perhaps toward prognosis as well. Finally, as noted earlier in this chapter, professionals may well differ in their views of the efficacy of services generally or about the meaning of objective data describing patients.

A separate analysis has been performed of intraprofessional consistency. This refers to how well each of the fifteen individual consultants agrees with him- or herself. Ten patients not visited by any of the consultants were selected. They represented the range of prescribed home care hours, from high to low, and the range of professional agreement, also from high to low.

Professionals proved consistent with themselves, on average. The mean of the fifteen consultants' original hours, averaged across the ten patients, was 115.2. The mean repeat prescription was 119.2 hours of home care per week. The standard deviation in prescribed hours from time one to time two, for the average of the consultants, was 7.4 hours weekly. The consultants' mean hours, time one versus time two, correlated at the very high level of $r = 0.91$ (Pearson product-moment correlation).

For individual care planners, the standard deviation ranged from a low of 17.5 hours to a high of 68.4 hours. There was little difference in consistency over time by professional role. Physicians were slightly less self-consistent (standard deviation, time one to time two, 42.2 hours) than were discharge planners (35.6 hours) or home care planners (33.6 hours).

The more experienced professionals were a bit more self-consistent: the Pearson product-moment correlation between individual standard deviation, time one versus time two, and professional experience was $r = -0.20$; $R^2 = 0.04$.

Professional self-consistency was higher for the more disabled patients with more initial prescribed hours. The mean absolute difference in prescribed hours across the fifteen professional consultants correlated (Pearson product-moment correlation) at -0.72 with initial prescribed hours, again indicating that professional self-consistency was better for patients needing more help.

Further, patients about whom professionals disagreed the most (high standard deviation across professionals) were the very patients about whom professionals' self-consistency tended to be weak. The Pearson product-moment correlation between initial standard deviation across professionals and professionals' own self-consistency, measured by the mean absolute difference in prescribed hours across the fifteen consultants, was 0.48.

Finally, to assess overall professional consistency from time one to time two, Cronbach's alpha and Kendall's W were calculated for the fifteen professionals' views of the ten patients' needed hours of home care in the various services and service subtotals analyzed above. These results, reported in Table 9-16, indicate strong agreement among professionals across the two sets of prescriptions. Alpha on total hours for time one was 0.95; for time two, 0.93. Kendall's W on total hours for time one was 0.58; for time two, 0.61.

Professional Agreement About Longevity

At the end of each care plan, professionals were asked to evaluate how many months that particular patient would live if he or she went home with the prescribed care plan and how many months if discharged to the most appropriate long-term care institution, where he or she would receive care of average quality and effectiveness.

Taking the average of all professional views, it was felt that only one of the fifty patients in the study sample would live longer in an institution. Validity of professional predictions of longevity is uncertain, but there is little reason to expect different validity by site of care—unless a bias toward home care influences these estimates. Most professionals did consider the home to be the preferred site of discharge. While predictions about longevity may be influenced by this preference, the reverse is believed to be likely.

On average, professionals believed that patients would live nine months longer at home—an increase of 27.5 percent over institutional longevity.

Table 9-16. Professional Consistency: Time One versus Time Two.

Service	Time One		Time Two	
	W		W	
Continuous supervision	.25		.19	
Bathing	.39		.47	
Eating	.78		.78	
Transport	.45		.51	
Light housekeeping	.12		.17	
Monitoring vital signs	.27		.30	
Primary medical care	.34		.23	
Physical therapy	.57		.53	
Subtotal	W	Alpha	W	Alpha
Personal care	.50	.93	.41	.91
Housekeeping	.18	.65	.05	.77
Nursing	.71	.93	.76	.94
Medical–therapeutic	.57	.92	.47	.89
Total minus continuous supervision	.72	—	.73	—
Total	.58	.95	.61	.93

Table 9-17.   Predicted Life Expectancy: Home versus Nursing Home.

Professional Group	Predicted Life Expectancy (months)		
	Home	Nursing Home	Difference Between Home and Nursing Home
MDC (5)	39.2	30.7	8.5
DPC (5)	34.4	32.2	2.2
HHC (5)	46.1	30.5	15.6
Consultants (15)	39.9	31.1	8.8
Hospital (3)	62.3	49.4	12.9
All (18)	43.6	34.2	9.4
RN (6)	40.1	27.1	13.0
SW (3)	37.9	30.2	7.7
Nonvisitor (9)	35.9	26.8	9.1
Visitor (6)	46.1	37.9	8.2

Table 9-17 presents longevity predictions by site of care and profession, role, and visit status of the care planner. Home health planners and hospital professionals predicted the highest advantage to home care; hospital discharge planners predicted the lowest.

Professional Agreement About Preferred Site of Discharge

All professionals rated the patient's home (or a relative's home) as the most appropriate site of care, though the proportions varied from group to group (Table 9-18). One average, 61.0 percent of the patients were thought most appropriately placed at home immediately following hospital discharge. Home health planners were the likeliest to prefer the home, and hospital professionals and discharge planners were the least likely to prefer the home. Discharge planners' relatively low preference for home care is in line with their judgment that home care only slightly enhances longevity. But the hospital professionals were both the least likely to prefer the home as the immediate discharge site and the group predicting the largest longevity benefit accruing to home care. This inconsistency is difficult to explain.

THE NATURE, EXTENT, AND MEANING OF PROFESSIONAL RELIABILITY

When professional views of home care needed by patients are first examined, agreement seems good. Progressively closer looks reveal increasing apparent dis-

Table 9-18. Preferred Discharge Site by Professional Group.

(proportion rating different site as preferred discharge option, three months following hospitalization)

Professional Group	Home	Special Housing	Rest Home	Intermediate Care Facility	Skilled Nursing Facility		Chronic Disease Hospital	Rehabilitation Hospital	Acute Care Hospital	Total
					Medicaid	Medicare				
MDC	51.7%	2.9%	0.4%	7.7%	11.2%	4.9%	2.8%	17.3%	1.2%	100.1%
DPC	52.4	5.6	0.4	3.7	8.4	13.2	1.8	12.8	1.7	100.0
HHC	87.7	0.0	0.0	3.2	5.7	0.0	0.9	2.1	0.4	100.0
Consultants Hospital	64.0	2.8	0.3	4.8	8.5	6.1	1.8	10.7	1.1	100.1
	42.0	2.7	0.7	12.7	9.0	12.3	7.3	12.0	1.3	100.0
ALL	61.0%	2.7%	0.3%	6.0%	8.6%	7.0%	2.6%	10.7%	1.2%	100.1%
RN	70.2	3.7	0.3	3.0	7.1	8.1	1.1	5.1	1.4	100.0
SW	71.3	0.7	0.0	5.3	9.3	4.7	2.0	6.0	0.7	100.0
Nine non-visitors	64.9	2.2	0.4	3.8	6.9	6.7	2.0	12.0	1.1	100.0
Six visitors	62.1	3.8	0.0	6.5	10.8	5.1	2.1	8.7	1.0	100.1

agreement. Reaggregation via summary measures, however, yields a moderately encouraging picture of professional agreement.

There is good agreement among consultants, whether grouped by training or by role, about total hours of home care needed by the members of the study sample. As the care plans are split into categories of service subtotal and then into individual services, consistency among the means of the professional groups steadily falls. Agreement about nontechnical household services is clearly weakest. Overall agreement is slightly better for unskilled providers and for unpaid providers.

Interprofessional disagreement is only moderate. Professional role (physician-discharge planner-home health planner) generally has little relation to prescribed hours. Professional training has a somewhat stronger relation; physicians and nurses, for example, prescribe more hours of home care in their areas of specialization. More special knowledge of field seems to be associated with more prescribed hours.

Further, more knowledge about patients is associated with higher prescribed hours across almost all services. Hospital professionals prescribed considerably (20%) more care than did consultants. The brief visit made by some professionals to some patients did not affect prescribed hours at all. What therefore seems important is extended personal acquaintance with the patient. It may be wondered whether higher prescribed hours more validly reflect patient need or whether they are the consequence of a personal attachment to the patient—as higher nursing hours prescribed by nurses *might* be a consequence of attachment to the field of nursing. The relative usefulness of special knowledge and objectivity is at issue; it demands empirical investigation in this instance. Indirect support for the utility of greater information about patients is found in the stronger intragroup consistency in prescribed hours generated by hospital care planners.

General knowledge or skill acts in the opposite direction. More experienced consultants tended to prescribe slightly *fewer* hours of home care. The sample size of consultants (fifteen) and of all professionals (eighteen) precludes simultaneous testing of the effects of professional role, training, information about patient, and general experience on prescribed hours. The types and directions of influences identified in this chapter will hopefully be studied in years to come.

When prescribed home care hours are considered not by groups of prescribers, patients and services but rather by individual prescribers' views of individual patients' needs for individual services or individual providers, interprofessional agreement appears terrible. Inspection of these data reveals little commonality of recommended service hours. The discreteness of this information, however, hides strong and interesting patterns of association.

Factor analysis—treating as units of analysis the hours prescribed by individual consultants for individual patients in distinct service categories—uncovers fairly strong interprofessional similarities. These cross lines of role, training, and experience. Agreement within a profession seems no better than agreement across professional boundaries. Professionals join together in agreement about hours of care required for individual service subtotals and then break apart to agree with other professionals about other service subtotals. Thus, professionals do not randomly prescribe home care. Several common views of need can be identified for each service; the validity of each of these shared views can be tested.

Consistency of professional views was demonstrated further by use of Cronbach's alpha and Kendall's W. While some discrepancies were found between these two measures of interjudge reliability, both point to important patterns of care planning. Individual care planners agree about which patients need more care and which need less, by each care planner's yardstick. They are consistent both with themselves and relative to other professionals. Some professionals consistently recommend much in-home service; others recommend less service. Each professional's views seem sensitive to patient characteristics. Professionals are thus well able to rank patients by needed hours of home care. What professionals disagree about, however, is how much care a particular patient requires. Professional reliability appears excellent, as far as it goes, but stops short of perfect consistency.

Findings from the follow-up project in the area of professional agreement reinforce those of the study reported here. Professional consistency in the follow-up was even better than that obtained here. This was perhaps owing to more complete information about clients or to an improved care planning form, in which all professional recommendations for needed in-home care were made on a single matrix, provider by service domain, rather than service-by-service (as in the present study). Professional training remained more important in influencing recommended in-home care than did role.

In the follow-up project, an additional indication that professionals could identify appropriate levels of in-home care was found. Clients in this project who were believed by professionals to be underserved were disproportionately likely to be hospitalized or admitted into nursing homes during the course of the study. Together, the study reported here and the follow-up project strongly suggest a very considerable measure of consistency and equity in long-term care professionals' views of needed in-home care.

In light of these findings and in the context of the present study, what must be asked is, how much control or influence over the allocation of in-home services should professionals receive? Is this agreement sufficient to retain in professional hands the allocation of in-home services? For some observers, no amount of agreement could be enough; for others, no amount could be too little. This question will be the principal focus of Chapter 10, in which findings reported throughout Part III will be assembled to answer the question: Whose views of home care need are more valid?

NOTES TO CHAPTER 9

1. Sidney Siegel, *Nonparametric Statistics for the Behavioral Sciences* (New York: McGraw-Hill, 1956), pp. 229–38.
2. For descriptions of Cronbach's alpha, see Lee J. Cronbach, "Test 'Reliability:' Its Meaning and Determination," *Psychometrika* 12, no. 1 (March, 1947): 1–16; William W. Rozeboom, *Foundations of the Theory of Prediction* (Homewood, Ill.: Dorsey, 1966), pp. 410–15, 445–47.
3. This perspective on care planning was clearly articulated by Andrew S. Dibner, personal communication, 12 February 1979.

10 FINDINGS AND CONCLUSIONS

Critics of public long-term care policy in the United States have complained of its heavy emphasis on institutional care for the elderly. Many who would like to see the elderly permitted choice among a variety of alternative sites of care, including their own homes, are fearful of the cost of more generous public funding of these alternatives.

The comparative costs of home and institutional care have been difficult to measure experimentally because of problems in controlling for the initial characteristics of the two samples, in measuring outcomes, and consequently, in learning what services are indeed effective. Given our present knowledge of how well various types, quantities, and providers of long-term care services enhance well-being, costs and effects of long-term care in various settings have not usually been measured well.

For these and other reasons, this study has tried to consider the interactions and interdependence between policy and planning. The power to plan services—to decide the types, quantities, and providers—affects the cost and effectiveness of home services. Reciprocally, the likely cost and effectiveness of services sought by different groups—patients, families, and professionals—is likely to affect which group(s) are empowered. Finally, probable cost and effectiveness affect the likelihood of more generous public funding for home care. Without increased funding, the power to plan is limited to control over today's relatively meager resources.

To decide whether patients, families, or professionals should be permitted control or influence over home care planning should be considered in light of the likely cost and effectiveness of care recommended by each of the three groups. Within the professional group, the appropriateness of control by various types of care planners deserves examination.

There is a second interaction of power and choice, cost, and effectiveness: Should patients always be guaranteed the right to choose home care, at a cost no greater than institutional care, even though fewer hours of care (or less specialized care) might be available at home at this cost—leading to the possibility of reduced safety or effectiveness? Once eligibility is decided, permitting this choice about site cannot produce greater public costs. But such a policy might expose some older people to harm. Nonetheless, it can be argued, (1) that the right to choose site of care may itself enhance effectiveness in whichever site is chosen, and (2) that given doubts about the comparative effectiveness of home and institutional care, the public may have relatively little interest in regulating where older people decide to live out their years. The study professionals' expectation that patients would live 27 percent longer if they went home with the hypothetical services prescribed suggests a safety margin for home care—one that engenders confidence in permitting some consumer choice about site of care and needed services.

SUMMARY

This study was designed to improve our knowledge about the effectiveness and costs of home care selected by patients, their families, and various professionals. It begins with a sample of patients about to enter nursing homes, obtains many hypothetical estimates of the costs of an in-home alternative believed to be of equal or greater effectiveness, and then compares these costs with those of institutional care actually provided.

If the greater availability of public funds for home care in the future will depend in large part on the costs of care at home and in institutions, then the cost of home care itself, in the present research design, depends on the hypothetical care plans written. Given our weak ability to measure effectiveness of long-term care services, how is it to be decided which view of hypothetical home care need is valid?

In this scheme, home care costs clearly depend on the types, quantities, and providers chosen by the care plans' designers. But the question of who should control the allocation of in-home services is an important issue in itself. Arguments may be advanced on behalf of competing claims of various professionals, patients, and patients' families. These claims may be judged by comparing the likely effectiveness and costs of services sought by the three groups. Some of the analyses presented suggest the relative effectiveness and cost of the home care plans of the three groups.

The hypothetical nature of the present study permits members of the three groups of claimants to prepare home care plans independently. One measure of the validity of the different views is how well and equitably they relate to patients' characteristics: whether more care is prescribed for patients who might "reasonably" be thought to need more. A second measure that points toward validity, for professional plans only, is that of reliability—how well professionals agree with one another about individual patients. Agreement may be in error, but its marked absence would certainly weaken the case for professional control over home care planning and, therefore, for relying on costs of professionals' home care plans as the standard of comparison with the costs of institutional care.

A principal interest has therefore been in deciding who should be permitted to influence or control the allocation of in-home services. On this foundation, the costs of home and institutional care can be compared. Four specific goals have been articulated:

1. To learn how well patients, their families, and various health and social service professionals agree about the types, quantities, and providers needed to sustain patients at home in a safe, adequate, and dignified manner.

2. To assess whose views of home care need seem more valid, should the three groups of hypothetical care planners disagree.

3. To compare the costs of home and institutional care for a group of patients who are about to enter nursing homes.

4. To mine the results and by-products of data gathered to reach the preceding goals, in order to learn how to better plan home care for individual patients. This means first, learning more about which patients seem to need which services, and second, devising a sensible model for cooperative care planning should this seem appropriate.

The costs of home and institutional care were reported in Chapter 7. Several useful points emerged from various analyses of the data.

For the patients studied, care in both settings is expensive. *By diverting to home care those patients for whom it is (hypothetically) cheaper, substantial savings may be gained.* For the members of the study sample, such savings were likeliest to be achieved by diverting patients bound for relatively intensive and costly levels of institutional care, such as rehabilitation hospitals, chronic disease hospitals, and Medicare-funded skilled nursing home care. This pattern is quite different from that usually expected—that the less ill or disabled patients can be cared for at home at less expense. In the present study, the pattern of savings found may partly reflect rigidities or vagaries of institutional placement and reimbursement.

Very different groups of patient characteristics explained actual institutional costs and hypothetical home care costs. *Not surprisingly, therefore, there is almost no predictable relation between hypothetical home care costs and real nursing home costs.* Prescribed hours of home care, which might represent the real burden of home care better than does cost (because unpaid family contribution is included only in hours of care), correlate with institutional costs only marginally better. The real-world forces and decisions that determine the cost of institutional care work in very different ways than the decision about home care costs made by study professionals.

Several important patient characteristics were identified that predict which long-term care setting would be less expensive. More intense level of institutional placement, higher patient functional ability (controlling for level of placement), and greater number of persons residing with the patient at home each predict increased likelihood that home care will be less expensive than institutional care. Thus, other things being equal, less disabled patients do tend to be less expensive to care for at home. This is particularly true when these patients are in fact being discharged to a relatively intensive level of care.

By employing savings, won by diverting to home care those patients for whom it is markedly cheaper, to subsidize the home care costs of patients for whom it is markedly more expensive, it is estimated that a total of about half of the sample could be cared for at home at no increase in overall spending on the sample patients collectively. This is not to say that system costs would necessarily be unaffected. If, for example, nursing home beds emptied by diversion are not filled by other patients, overhead must be spread over a smaller denominator, yielding some increase in the average cost per patient-day for those who remain in institutions. If those diverted require less intense care than the average nursing home patient, as may well be the case, then average variable costs of institutional care will rise following diversion. But, on the other hand, diversion will reduce the need to build new nursing home beds in the face of the rising demand for all forms of long-term care that is certain to materialize in coming years and decades. If the beds emptied by those patients diverted to home care are soon filled by persons needing institutional care, very real systems savings may accrue from diversion, as some new construction is delayed or obviated.

Family members and patients typically requested less paid help than did the median of professionals (using episodes of care as the unit of measurement). This suggests that the cost of permitting patients or their families to influence or control home care planning would probably be no greater than the cost of professional control.

Unskilled care generates the great bulk of costs of prescribed services. A great part of this is owing to one service—continuous supervision. If these costs could be spread over more than one patient, home care would appear still more attractive financially. Vehicles such as adult foster care or shared housing have been proposed to do this. The dangers of creating small and unsatisfactory quasi-institutions must be avoided, however; one of the chief purposes of establishing today's nursing homes, ostensibly under medical-nursing control, was to banish the identified evils of just such arrangements.

If older citizens live with their families or with others in similar circumstances, cost of shelter (including heat, maintenance, cleaning, and the like) can be shared. If older persons in need of care remain in their own communities, it is easier to organize unpaid helpers than would be the case if these persons entered institutions. When older people remain in their own homes or neighborhoods, potential helpers—relatives and friends—can both perceive needs for care and, in many cases, conveniently provide help.

Potentially powerful schemes for summoning greater contributions of unpaid help are being developed. These include housing shared by persons initially aged perhaps forty-five to sixty-five, in which the able care for the disabled, as needed, and are in turn cared for by younger entrants as they themselves age. Another organizing device would involve the use of tokens to reward those who provide "unpaid" help. These tokens could be saved to pay for home care as their holders came to need it.

By providing home care more efficiently or by substituting unpaid for paid providers, the future budget costs per person of home care may be markedly reduced.

The goal of learning the extent of agreement among patients, families, and professionals about needed home care services was pursued in Chapter 8.

Patients, family members, and professionals agreed fairly well on average but somewhat less well in individual cases. The averaging is important in itself because it suggests (and even "suggest" may be too strong a verb in view of the small size of the subsample that could be analyzed) that the preferences of the three groups of care planners could be accommodated within a single budget. The sum might, with allowances for particular individual circumstances, be set in relation to variables proven to predict service needs. Only the proof is needed.

Agreement about the care needs of individual patients was not as good as the overall average might indicate. Patients and family members agreed better between themselves than either group did with professionals. Thus, patients and family members might tend to unite against professionals' analyses of needed home care because the three groups disagree in important respects about the scope and composition of individual home care plans. Control over the content of these plans is therefore of considerable significance.

Surprisingly, family members' estimates of episodes of unpaid help available to patients were the highest of the three types of care planners—both absolutely and as a proportion of total episodes. This is important in itself, as it indicates that families do not seem, by their plans, to be shirking whatever responsibilities they might be thought to have in caring for their older members. This is important also because it suggests that one potential source of conflict among patients, families, and professionals—how much the family should do—might not in practice present a great difficulty. Family plans presupposed certain levels of paid support, but these were below those prescribed by professionals. Therefore, families' predictions of their contributions might well be realistic. Of course, it is possible that family members, facing the prospect of their relative's institutionalization, may have been exaggerating their own willingness to provide home care. But the follow-up project found that families were actually providing 52.3 percent more hours of help than professionals expected.

The goal of assessing the validity of various views of home care needs was pursued in Chapters 8 and 9.

All three of the groups sought less care for those patients with higher antici-pated functional ability. This relation appears on its face to be reasonable and equitable. All three groups thus seem able to distinguish in general ways between patients needing more home care and those needing less.
Because professional care plans were available in greater detail and for a larger sample than patient or family recommendations, the relation of patient characteristics to professionally prescribed home care hours could be examined with some rigor.

By means of multiple regression, it was found that *fairly high proportions of the difference in mean hours prescribed for individual patients* (across eighteen professionals) in most areas of service, *could be explained by only a few patient characteristics.* The particular characteristics that proved useful in predicting interpatient variation related reasonably to the particular area of service in question. This finding lends further support to the view that professionals, on average, plan care in a sensible manner

The possible validity of professional views was explored further by examining patterns of agreement, among professionals themselves, about patients' home care needs, both individually and collectively. The relations of several variables to patterns of interprofessional reliability and to specific hours of care recommended by different professionals were analyzed.

When professional views of home care needed by patients are first examined, agreement seems good. Consultants, whether grouped by training or by role, agree fairly well about the home care hours required on average by patients.

Professional role has little relation to total prescribed hours. Professional training has only a slightly stronger relation. There is some tendency for profes-sionals to prescribe more hours of care in their own field. Physicians and nurses, for example, tend to prescribe more hours of care in their special areas—medical and nursing services respectively—than other professionals prescribe in those areas. Special training in a given field may indicate that the higher hours prescribed here by physicians and nurses represent more valid views of patients' needs. Alternatively, professionals may be inappropriately emphasizing the importance of their own fields. While the former explanation is the more reasonable, this question demands careful investigation. Multidisciplinary team planning for long-term care, as practiced today, usually grants authority or special influence to each member in his or her own field. The appropriateness of doing so should be confirmed. If inappropriate, this study's results would indicate that present patterns of influence in team care planning may yield inflated home care prescriptions.

While more knowledge in a speciality is mildly associated with greater prescribed home care hours, *more familiarity and contact with patients themselves is fairly strongly associated with more prescribed care.* Hours prescribed by hospital professionals were 20 percent greater than those prescribed by consultants. The brief visits made by some consultants to some patients do not seem to have influenced the outcome of care planning.

In this case, as in that of special training, the validity of care plans based on increased familiarity must be confirmed. Hospital professionals become familiar with patients at times of greater disability. Do higher prescribed hours more validly reflect patient need or might they be in part a consequence of personal attachment to a patient or to a residual perception of disability—or, in the case of some in-hospital professionals, a consequence of hospitals' own conservative style of providing services that might be even of marginal benefit? Alternatively, might the difference in prescribed hours only reflect the personal or systematic forces governing selection of the consultants?

More experienced consultants tended to prescribe slightly fewer hours of care across all patients than did the less experienced consultants. In sum, familiarity with patients or knowledge about a field of learning are directly related to prescribed care; general professional knowledge (correlated with experience) is inversely related. The effects of these forces should be studied simultaneously by means of a larger sample of professionals combined with a narrower scope for care planning and, to contain cost, possibly with a smaller sample of patients than those in the present study.

Beyond the associations of certain variables with different levels of prescribed home care hours lies the association of some of the same variables, and others as well, with the extent of agreement among professionals about the home care needs of the elderly. The variables in question are: patient characteristics, information available to care planners, type of service or provider, degree of aggregation of the care plan, and professional role and training.

While no firm conclusions have emerged about which sorts of patients the professionals agree about best, greater disability, greater age, family willingness to maintain the patient at home, and better psychosocial status were associated with enhanced agreement. *Patients about whom professionals agree well should be the patients for whom it should be easier to design effective care plans (reliability being a prerequisite for validity), other things being equal.* Unfortunately, other things are not equal in this case, because the patients professionals agree about relatively weakly tend also to be the patients whose psychosocial status is relatively poor. Hence, the void that might be created by interprofessional disagreement is opened for the patients who would typically have greater difficulty in filling it. Fortunately, this relation is not a strong one.

More familiarity and contact with patients tends to be associated with greater interprofessional agreement. Hospital professionals' coefficients of variation, averaged across patients, were lower than consultants'. This was true as well for average standard deviations, uncontrolled for differences in mean prescribed hours.

Professional agreement varied by type of service and provider. Professionals agreed best about the more technical nursing and medical-therapeutic services, somewhat less well about personal care, and least well about household services. Thus, there is a fortunate matching of relative professional weakness and relative patient-family strength. The latter can be expected to have more informed (and stronger) opinions about need for personal care and household services than for nursing or medical-therapeutic care. Household services in particular appear to be a prime arena for some sort of cooperative planning among patients, families, and professionals. Some degree of patient and family influence is called for, in light of their special knowledge and of professionals' relatively weak agreement. But some professional involvement or institution of ceilings on hours in some relation to objective patient/family/housing characteristics might be desirable as well—in view of the suspected potential attractiveness of many household services (cleaning, cooking, and the like) to many patients and families. Patients' and families' modest requests in these areas should, however, be borne in mind. Unaccustomed to being served in hotels or at home, most older people and their families probably place a higher value on their privacy than they do on seeking unneeded help. To the extent this is true, professional involvement or the institution of ceilings on hours of care may be more necessary symbolically to securing political support for expanding home care than practically to controlling costs of that expansion.

Apparent professional consistency is highest at the most general levels; consistency falls steadily as the components of the care planning process are disaggregated. Among the consultants grouped by role, for example, agreement about total hours of care needed across patients is excellent; agreement about care needed in service or provider subtotals is somewhat worse, and about care in specific services, worse still. When the needs of individual patients—for individual services, prescribed by individual consultants—are examined, very little evidence of consistency is present. This suggests that professional judgments could help set overall patient hours of care, in relation to objective characteristics, and that patients or families might be permitted to allocate that care among specific services and providers. The very discreteness of the disaggregated data, however, hides strong and interesting underlying patterns of association.

Professional role and training seem to have little cohesive influence on inter-professional consistency. Factor analyses uncovered clear patterns of association, but these generally crossed lines of professional role and training. In each category of service, separate clusters of professional agreement can be identified. Few professionals, however, were strongly bonded to others across services. Care planners A, B, C, and D might agree about personal care; A, E, and F about household help; B, E, and G about nursing; and so on. Thus, professionals do not seem to prescribe care in an entirely idiosyncratic manner. Clusters of perceived home care needs exist. The validity of these shared views could be tested.

For the average of the consultants, *intra-rater agreement was excellent.* The consultants on average agreed with themselves about hours of home care needed by the same patients, according to prescriptions written on two different occasions. More experienced consultants were slightly more self-consistent. Professional self-consistency was higher for patients thought to need more home care. Patients about whom professionals had the most trouble agreeing, on the initial care plan, were the same patients for whom intraprofessional agreement was weaker. These were the less disabled patients. Finally, consultants who appeared to make more consistent use of objective patient characteristics in assigning care tended to be more self-consistent. This suggests the possibility of identifying more reliable care planners.

Two other measures were made of reliability. Both Cronbach's alpha and Kendall's W point to important patterns of professional care planning. *Individual care planners agree well about which patients need more help and which need less, by each planner's personal yardstick. Professionals' rankings of patients by care needs tend to agree well. But professionals tend to agree less well about how many hours of home care any particular patient needs* in order to live at home in a safe, adequate, and dignified manner. Thus, professional reliability is excellent in certain respects, but it stops short of perfect consistency.

IMPLICATIONS FOR POLICY AND CARE PLANNING

What are the meanings of the above findings—about the extent of agreement among patients, families, and professionals; about the equity and reasonableness of patient and family views; and about the equity, reasonableness and reliability of professional views—for both the partitioning of influence or control over home care planning, and the prospects of more generous public home care funding?

Partitioning Influence

All three groups—patients, families, and professionals—recommend care in reasonable and equitable ways. Professional reliability, particularly about group needs, is good in many respects. Consistency in home care is far from unbroken, but it is probably better than might have been expected following the general review of professional reliability in Chapter 3. Considering the general obstacles to consistency and the special attributes of long-term care that had been expected to further weaken interprofessional agreement, care planners seem to have acted with surprising congruence.

Partisans of consumers (patients and family) or professionals may seize on selected analyses to support their positions, but no dramatic evidence has really been uncovered for or against dominance of home care planning by any group.

Consequently, whose views of hypothetical home care needs should be used to compare the costs of home and institutional care? In Chapter 7, averages of professional views were employed because, as analyses in Chapters 8 and 9 indicated, professionals wrote home care plans whose prescribed hours appeared equitable, on average, and not unreliable as well. If estimated home care costs were derived from patient or family recommendations, they would be lower still, and home care would appear therefore somewhat more attractive relative to institutional care.

In the absence of strong evidence for or against control of home care services by any of the three groups, and given the apparently defensible positions of all, *it may be possible to devise schemes for home care planning to permit balanced influence by patients, families, and various professionals.* An appropriate balance would be struck by granting precedence to groups' views in ways that draw on the strengths but circumscribe the weaknesses of each. Illustrations of how this approach might be implemented are now offered.

It is fortunate, for example, that professional agreement is clearly worst in an area, household services, where patients and families can be expected to have a good idea what they need. About one-half of paid episodes sought by professionals or patients fell in this area, along with two-fifths of the smaller number of paid episodes sought by families. The latter groups should therefore be permitted wide latitude in determining both total hours of household help required and how they should be allocated among specific services and delivered by specific providers. Because of the supposed inherent attractiveness of some household services to many persons, young and old, public payers might demand that some sort of overall ceiling be placed on spending. Professionals seem somewhat ill-equipped to perform this task because of the wide divergences in their views of needs for household services. One step might be to set ceilings and floors on the number of hours of household help to be allowed any patient. Another would be to validate need for household help in relation to objectively measured functional ability and independence in instrumental activities of daily living. A considerable amount of research would be required to learn the proper relationships: what constitutes too much or too little overall help? Even after such standards were in place, patients and their families might be permitted to distribute the total among particular services. Thus, a measure of patient and family choice could be preserved even in the presence of valid and objective evidence on need.

A preferable way of validating household needs would consider the impact on outcome, not only of various services themselves, but of the process by which they were planned as well. Effects of objectively planned household services might be compared with effects of services selected by patients themselves — perhaps subject to the constraint that these cost no more than the first package. This procedure would measure the consequences for patient well-being of both the services and the planning process.

The desire to plan home care objectively (to plan *for* patients and families rather than *with* them) stems from several motives: to be able to control, or at least predict, cost; to promote equity among patients; to allocate available resources in ways that do the most to enhance patient well-being; and, in some instances, to permit professionals to retain or enlarge their present degree of influence over the home care planning process.

Fears of uncontrollable spending ensuing from patient or family influence over care planning find no support in the present study. Patients and families sought less paid help than professionals typically recommended. Patients, families, and professionals all seemed able to plan care equitably; professionals did a somewhat better job.

In this context, experimentation with the process of care planning and the content of care plans to learn what does the most for which patients would be desirable. We need better knowledge of which method of care planning, involving more or less patient and family choice, best enhances outcomes for various patients. The same is required of the content of care itself. Better capacity to measure outcomes is a prerequisite for both.

As part of any planning process the location of ultimate authority over the cost and content of home care must be fixed. To satisfy legislators and administrators, authority will probably be granted to professionals operating within guidelines. The results of this study indicated, however, that granting to patients or families a share of this authority would, on average, yield savings rather than cost increases. Therefore, in the absence of convincing evidence on the comparative effectiveness of plans prepared by the three groups and in view of the possibility that consumer choice in long-term care enhances outcome, increased patient and family influence over planning for household and probably for personal home care services should be permitted experimentally. Administratively, this could be accomplished through cash payments, vouchers, or cooperative care planning. Because cash payments, such as the Veteran's Administration's Aid and Attendance Allowance, can come to be regarded as general income supplements, vouchers or cooperative care planning should be tried first.

Moving from the question of control over services in a given site (the home) to the question of choice between sites of care (home versus institution), the findings of this study raise an interesting issue: Suppose a more generous home care benefit were legislated by Congress or a state legislature. Eligibility, however, could be restricted to those whose home care would cost only half or three-quarters (as in New York) or no more than (as under Section 2176 waivers) the cost of institutional care. From governments' standpoint, lower or equal cost per person might be the price for expanded eligibility for home care.

In this case, whose view of the needed types, quantities, and providers of home care—and therefore its cost—should be allowed to enter the comparison? Suppose the cost of a professionals' home care plan were slightly greater than the cost of institutional care, but the patient and family together were willing to accept home care costing only half as much as institutional care (and providing only half the hours of care), as the price of remaining at home? Should patients be permitted this choice?

It may well be appropriate to allow choice, especially if professionals tend to overestimate "objective" need for services. There is a danger, however, that this plan could become a vehicle for retaining or dumping patients in home care under conditions that could endanger their health, their safety, or even their lives. Witness much of the state mental hospital deinstitutionalization of recent years.

It seems clearly right to permit patient or family choice if costs of care in the two sites are equal. But it may be wrong to exploit most patients' preference for remaining at home to get them to accept a markedly less generous service package—unless outcome of care turns out to be unaffected or of less concern to patients and families than is site of care.

The easy ways to obtain choice about site of care and a generous service package, if desired, could be to organize paid in-home services more efficiently than is now the case or to secure markedly increased provision of unpaid in-home services. Were this accomplished, lower cost per patient would not have to be gained by sacrificing hours of care. Awaiting these improvements, patients and families might be permitted to choose home care, at the price of accepting slightly reduced levels of services, and measures of objective and subjective outcomes could be closely monitored and compared with outcomes for a control group not allowed such choice.

The costs of home care and nursing home care for the elderly are difficult to compare, given our inability either to measure outcomes of long-term care or to control for the initial characteristics of persons receiving care in the two settings. Not knowing effects, we do not know what services are really required in either setting. Not knowing what services are required, costs cannot be measured with the confidence we would like.

To learn the costs of home and institutional care, this study has obtained estimates of the hypothetical cost of home care for a group of patients in fact about to enter nursing homes. To decide which version of home care costs should appropriately be compared with nursing home costs and to learn which groups should appropriately influence the home care planning process, the reasonableness and reliability of patients', families', and various professionals' views of home care needs have been measured and analyzed. Subsequent work should now aim to learn which estimates of home care service needs are accurate.

Avenues to More Generous Public Funding for Home Care

The thrust of the evidence compiled and analyzed in this study strongly supports more flexible and more generous public funding for noninstitutional long-term care. The reliability and equity of professional views point to professional ability to target public funds appropriately. Professionals free to exercise their trained judgments do not appear likely to simply throw money at problems. Given all the expected barriers to agreement about the home care needs of the elderly, these study findings are particularly encouraging.

Similarly, the modest requests for paid help made by patients, and particularly by their families, suggest citizens who would be reluctant to exploit or abuse new home care benefits. Most citizens are not accustomed to having servants, and they probably value the privacy of their homes more than they do a publicly paid homemaker-home health aide.

Even so, the costs of more generous programs of in-home care to meet the growing long-term care service needs may be greater than Congress is now willing to bear. Three elements suggest themselves for an expanded home care system. The first is some measure of professional or professionally derived boundaries on service use. Congress is likely to retain doubts about the voraciousness of older people and their families; professional limits would be reassuring. The second element is markedly greater support for shared or sheltered housing. By providing clear opportunities for economical provision of noninstitutional services, housing-based approaches merit increased attention. Third, improved federal funding of home care services should be accompanied by efforts to mobilize even greater amounts of unpaid help on behalf of our disabled citizens. Reasons for taking this approach, and explanations of how it might be implemented are as follows:

First, this is not a bland or—hopefully—irresponsible appeal to voluntarism to solve all social ills. Rather, significantly increased public spending on long-term, in-home social services—perhaps to the level of $3 billion to $4 billion annually—is highly desirable. This will be much easier to achieve if Congress is convinced that demand for public resources is finite and containable.

Second, for many areas of noninstitutional, long-term care, time of volunteers—not money—is the more appropriate medium of exchange. Time is more equitably distributed than money across lines of class and race. Time is, or can be, easier to mobilize and coordinate. Its use does not require taxation, legislation, or large administrative overheads.

Third, time when exchanged semiformally and locally does not require lengthy travel for caregivers—as much home care does require today. Help can be exchanged among people who know each other or have shared backgrounds. Prospects for more empathic and compassionate care may be better.

Fourth, mobilization of increased unpaid time on behalf of the disabled elderly will improve the welfare of older citizens without obliging comparable sacrifices elsewhere in the economy or society. There is much spare time in our country—just as there are other slack resources—but time may be easier to put to work in the current political climate. Leisure among the young and lack of purpose among the newly retired elderly should not be problems but rather opportunities.

One mutual aid scheme involving the exchange and banking of time in long-term care could be centered on congregate housing developments or similar concentrations of older citizens. These are usually built without adequate service supports. Residents could be admitted initially across a range of ages and disabilities. When able, they could be encouraged to help care for one another in a variety of ways. Those on waiting lists for apartments could be encouraged to help as well. In exchange, subsequently, residents would receive aid from new and more able helpers. These exchanges are common today. They can probably be increased in number and intensity by a mild effort to back them publicly. People who help others would be guaranteed help in return. If no one volunteered to provide that subsequent help, it would be financed publicly and delivered by paid workers. (This parallels the FHA mortgage insurance arrangements that mobilized funds to build much of today's housing stock.) Time devoted to helping others would be backed hour-for-hour by the full faith and credit of the United States: probably the best form of currency since the silver certificate. In this way, we can build faith in a currency of altruism.

Alternative organizing modes could include any entity that existed over time, such as a religious congregation, labor union, fraternal organization, or neighborhood. Here, to ensure portability of help given—across time or space or organizational boundaries—contributions could be acknowledged with tokens or markers or recorded on a local computer. One person could go shopping for an older neighbor in Boston, receive a token in return, and mail that token to a disabled parient in Ohio, for use in getting the shopping done.

Individuals could retain all markers for hour-for-hour return, or some number of markers could be placed in an insurance pool, from which would be provided unlimited lifetime help if needed. Help from the pool would rely on the gatekeeping of a professional assessment; elsewhere, care could be given in response to privately negotiated marker-exchange. Markers could be placed into circulation gradually today by giving them to people who are disabled and need help. This approach crudely resembles the Townsend Plan of the 1930s. It would prime the pump of the parallel economy of altruism. To a perhaps useful degree, motive of altruism and self-interest would be merged.

People would have spare time to help one another as teenagers, when retired, and occasionally in between. There is free time in our society; arrangements for coupling it with the needs of disabled older citizens should not be beyond our imagination. Today, tremendous burdens are placed on families of those needing long-term care. Families usually feel that they must provide help when needed, even in the face of obligations to children or job. By de-coupling help given from help required by a relative, people can contribute to an insurance-like pool of long-term caring when it is convenient for them to do so.

Citizens would be motivated to help others in part by normal altruistic feelings; in part by removal of the too-common barrier to expression of these instincts—that of appearing foolish or vulnerable to exploitation; in part by the joining of altruistic and self-interested motives; and in part by the educated realization that mutual aid may be the only sensible avenue to a retirement secure from much of today's fear of involuntary nursing home admission. As it becomes almost impossible to save for a retirement secure from fears of dependence on public or family resources, faith in some form of collective security must replace hopes of individual sufficiency.

All home care services for those engaging in mutual aid would be "financed" in combination by retained tokens, merged credits from the insurance pool, family efforts, and public funds. The last would finance care for problems too difficult, unpleasant, or intimate to be suitable for informal exchange.

Those able but unwilling to engage in informal exchanges would be ineligible for aid from the pool. Forced to rely exclusively on limited publicly funded noninstitutional services, help from their own families, and on services they could afford, these persons would probably experience greater-than-average difficulty in living out their lives at home.

Today, burdens on some families for care of disabled relatives can be enormous; on others, negligible. It is difficult to predict where the burdens will fall. It has also been difficult to create a market for traditional private insurance in this arena. Any such market would, in any case, be financially accessible only to a minority of the population. An insurance pool in which time paid the premiums might be far more attractive. Small numbers of individual families would cease to face huge burdens of in-home care; needed jobs could be spread more evenly among citizens with time to help.

In summary, we probably know enough about who needs noninstitutional long-term care—how much and what kinds—to operate a fairly adequate, responsible, and equitable system, without visibly displacing family help. But it will be impossible to legislate a publicly funded system to fill all of the gaps between individuals' needs and families' capacities.

Older people prefer home care and so too should public payors. Only in noninstitutional care are there real possibilities for retaining, enhancing, and building on voluntary efforts. Mutual aid schemes can help mobilize unpaid time. They would reassure Congress about program costs and they would help support families with disabled relatives and disabled persons without families nearby.

This way of seeking more adequate noninstitutional, long-term care is not likely to be implemented immediately. It will require slow development and testing in many different settings. Organizational arrangements need to be more clearly spelled out. In each community, faith in mutual aid would have to be nurtured. Methods of protecting both those who help and those who are helped would have to be established.

The plan sketched here—for increased public funding for home care services in concert with better mobilized voluntary efforts—offers one useful approach to a more adequate and compassionate noninstitutional long-term care system. It would also be a valuable and necessary complement to improved nursing home care. An adequate and compassionate home care system could be created without improving institutional care, but those obliged to live in nursing homes would surely suffer. It is not possible, however, to improve institutional care without greatly enhancing the adequacy of home care programs. Otherwise, better nursing homes would be deluged by applicants unable to live decently at home.

The choice, then, is by no means between more nursing home care and more noninstitutional care, but rather between an acceptable long-term care system and one that is unacceptable. Much more care of all types will be needed in coming decades. Affordable standards of service must be set and met for all citizens in need. The only imaginable alternative is intolerable—a society in which growing numbers of frail or disabled older Americans would live out their lives in very painful circumstances. It is to be hoped that the next few years will be used to design and refine proposals for long-term care reform, to be ready for larger scale demonstration or implementation either in individual states or nationally—when deliberation again succeeds destruction in Washington.

APPENDIXES

APPENDIX A

REVISED PACE FORM

Levinson Policy Institute
Brandeis University

COVER SHEET FOR PACE FORM

PATIENT'S NAME _____ FACILITY _____

PATIENT'S CODE [ ][ ][ ][ ][ ] FLOOR/ROOM # _____

PERSON COMPLETING FORM: _____

PRINCIPAL CAREGIVER (Record here answer to   Phone #
Q5, P15 of PACE Form) _____   _____

ALTERNATIVE CAREGIVER (1) _____   _____

ALTERNATIVE CAREGIVER (2) _____   _____

GENERAL INSTRUCTIONS

1. Unless otherwise specified, all data should be obtained from the most
    reliable source, i.e. patient's chart, physician, nurse, or other
    hospital employee. In Section N, pre-hospital psychosocial informa-
    tion should be sought from the Principal or Alternative Caregiver.

2. Please print or write very clearly with a black or dark blue ball point
    pen.

Levinson Policy Institute
Brandeis University   PACE SCREENING FORM

PATIENT'S CODE ☐☐☐☐☐   FACILITY _____

----

* ANSWERS TO THE FOLLOWING QUESTIONS WILL DETERMINE IF THIS PATIENT WILL BE A FULL OR
  LIMITED PARTICIPANT IN THIS STUDY, OR WILL BE SCREENED OUT.
* Full participation requires that Q1, 2A, 3, 4A, and 5A be answered YES.
* Patients not meeting all criteria for full participation may be considered for
  limited participation.
* Limited participation requires an answer of YES to: Q1, 2A or 2B, 4A or 4B, and 5B.
  Q3 may be answered YES or NO.
* Patients not meeting all criteria for full or limited participation must be screened
  out of the study.
* CIRCLE ONE: FULL PARTICIPANT   LIMITED PARTICIPANT   SCREENED OUT

			Circle One

1. Is it anticipated that this patient will be discharged to a Long Term
   Care Facility for 2 months or more? (In the case of terminal patients,
   circle YES regardless of anticipated length of stay.)   1 YES NO

2.A. PHYSICIAN: In your opinion, would it be medically safe for this
     patient to be a full participant in the study?   2A YES NO

  B. IF NO, do you agree to this patient's inclusion in the study as a
     limited participant?   2B YES NO

2.A. or B. . .Physician signature _____

3. DISCHARGE PLANNER: Would patient be able to understand the nature of
   the study and respond to questions?   3 YES NO

4.A. DISCHARGE PLANNER: Could patient cope with the emotional stress of
     thinking about home care well enough to be a full participant?   4A YES NO

  B. IF NO, could patient be included as a limited participant?   4B YES NO

5.A. FOR FULL PARTICIPANTS: Has the patient signed the consent form?   5A YES NO

  B. FOR LIMITED PARTICIPANTS ONLY: Has the patient's legally authorized
     representative signed the consent form?   5B YES NO

6. SUMMARY OF PACE COMPLETION   COMPLETED BY _____

   COMPLETE   Date of Completion ☐☐☐☐☐☐

                                                          Circle
      Is patient available for consultant visits?   YES   NO

   If NO: Check reason: 1) Patient discharged   ☐
                           2) Patient unable to continue ☐

   INCOMPLETE

   If incomplete, check reason below:

            Patient refused to continue interview   ☐
            Patient unable to understand   ☐
            Patient unable to cope emotionally   ☐
            Patient's condition deteriorated   ☐
            Patient died before PACE completed   ☐
            Patient discharged   ☐
            Other (specify) _____

PACE Screening Form   Patient's Code [| | | |]

A. **Date** of Admission_____ B. Surg. Procedures this hospitalization:

Reason(s) for current hosp. admission: _____

_____   _____

_____   _____

C. Diagnosis(es) (List in approximate   Approximate Date of Onset
                 order of importance)
_____   _____

_____   _____

_____   _____

_____   _____

_____   _____

_____   _____

D. Disabling Conditions*   Approximate Date of Onset
_____   _____

_____   _____

_____   _____

_____   _____

_____   _____

E. (1) SUMMARY OF ALL KNOWN HOSP. ADMISSIONS & DISCHARGES IN PAST 12 MONTHS
       (List most recent 6 only)

Date of Admission	Hospital	Length of Stay	Reason for Admission	Place of Discharge
a)				
b)				
c)				
d)				
e)				
f)				

*Medical, functional, intellectual, or emotional conditions affecting the patient's
ability to perform customary self-care, mobility, and household tasks.

PACE Screening Form   Patient"s Code [ ][ ][ ][ ][ ]

E. (2) <u>SUMMARY OF KNOWN LONG TERM CARE FACILITIES</u>
        (Admissions and discharges in last 2 years)
        (Refer to Q H(1) below, for types of long term care facilities)

Date of Admission	Length of Stay	Type of Facility	Reason for Adm.	Place of Discharge

F. <u>SOCIO.-DEMOGRAPHIC</u>   (Check appropriate boxes)

Birth Date: Mo.   Da.   Yr.   Birth Place: specify state or country
              [ ][ ][ ][ ]   USA _____
                                                    Other _____
Sex: [ ] Male   Height _____   City or Town of Residence Prior to
       [ ] Female   Weight _____   Hospitalization:
                                       _____

Race: Ethnic Origin:
  [ ] Caucasian [ ] American Indian   [ ] Irish   [ ] Jewish
  [ ] Negro   [ ] Oriental   [ ] Italian   [ ] Spanish
  [ ] Other _____   [ ] Anglo-Saxon   [ ] Black American
                                         [ ] Other _____

Religious Preference: None   Languages usually spoken:
  [ ] Catholic   [ ] Protestant   [ ] English
  [ ] Jewish   [ ] Other: _____
  [ ] Other: _____

Marital Status: Education:
  [ ] Single   [ ] Divorced   Years of schooling completed:
  [ ] Married   [ ] Separated   _____ years
  [ ] Widowed
  Duration of Status ___ years   Car in Household: [ ] YES [ ] NO

Usual Living Arrangements:
  [ ] Single family home [ ] Elderly housing   [ ] Rented room(s) in pvt. home
  [ ] 2-3 family home   [ ] Other apartment   [ ] Rooming house
  [ ] Other: _____   [ ] Own   [ ] Rent

Person(s) With Whom Patient Resides: [ ] Alone   [ ] With spouse
                                       [ ] With others: Specify relationship
                                       _____

Usual Occupation: Specify   Employment Status:
_____   [ ] Currently   [ ] Not in Labor
                                             employed   Market
  [ ] Housewife/househusband   [ ] Currently   [ ] Retired
                                             unemployed   [ ] Never employed

PACE Screening Form   Patient's Code ⬚⬚⬚⬚⬚

G. ANTICIPATED DATE OF DISCHARGE   Mo Da Yr
   (Barring placement difficulties)   ⬚⬚⬚

H. (1) ANTICIPATED SITE OF DISCHARGE
       ☐ Rehab. Hospital   ☐ Level 2 SNF
       ☐ Chronic Disease Hospital   ☐ Level 3 ICF
       ☐ Level 1 SNF   ☐ Level 4 Rest Home

   (2) How long is patient expected to remain at site of discharge?
                                    _____ years   _____ months
                               ☐ Check box if indefinite placement

   (3) If less than 6 months, what is next expected place of residence?
       _____

INSTRUCTIONS FOR HOSPITAL COORDINATOR

1. When PACE screening form is completed, if patient is not participating in
   the study, detach cover sheet and forward screening form to Levinson Policy
   Institute.

2. If patient is participating in the study, staple cover sheet and PACE
   screening form to PACE form. PACE form is now ready for completion by
   Discharge Planner.

Patient's Code ☐☐☐☐☐

I.   FUNCTIONING STATUS

Ask the patient the following questions about his/her PRE-HOSPITAL FUNCTIONAL PERFORMANCE. The patient may volunteer all necessary information as to how they accomplished a functional activity eliminating the need for some or all further questions in that category.

Social Worker/Discharge Planner should use her/his best judgement to check appropriate category or categories and supply needed information under ANTICIPATED CAPACITY ON DISCHARGE for each functional status.

> CODES: DK = Doesn't know
>   NA = Not asked

Introduction: "I would like to ask you how you did certain activities of daily living before you came to the hospital. Let's start with walking . . ."

FUNCTION	PRE-HOSPITAL PERFORMANCE	ANTICIPATED CAPACITY ON DISCHARGE
1. WALKING (Indicate to patient a distance of @50 yds. i.e., "down the hall, to the desk and back" "BEFORE YOU CAME TO THE HOSPITAL . . . a. "Were you able to walk 50 yards without help of any kind...such as another person or a cane or brace?" (walks without help)		
b. "Did you use equipment but no other person to help you walk?" (uses equipment, no human help)		
c. "Did another person help you?" (human help only)		
d. "How many persons were needed at one time to help you?" (number of persons helping)		
e. "Did you use both equipment and another person's help?" (human help and equipment)		
f. "Were you unable to walk at all?" (unable to walk)		
g. "What kind of special equipment did you use?" (e.g. prosthesis, crutches, special shoes) (name of equipment)		

Patient's Code [| | | |]

FUNCTION	PRE-HOSPITAL PERFORMANCE	ANTICIPATED CAPACITY ON DISCHARGE
2. STAIRCLIMBING "BEFORE YOU CAME TO THE HOSPITAL...		
a. "Were you able to climb stairs without help of any kind?" (climbs stairs without help)		
b. "Did you use equipment but no other person to help you climb stairs?" (uses equipment, no human help)		
c. "Did another person help you?" (human help only)		
d. "How many persons were needed at one time to help you?" (number of persons helping)		
e. "Did you use both equipment and another person's help?" (human help and equipment)		
f. "Were you unable to climb stairs at all? (unable to climb stairs)		
g. "What kind of special equipment did you use?" (railing, grab bars) (name equipment)		
3. WHEELING (DOES NOT APPLY IF PATIENT CAN WALK) "BEFORE YOU CAME TO THE HOSPITAL...		
a. "Were you able to use a wheelchair without help of any kind?" (such as a power source) (wheels without help)		
b. "Did you use an electric wheelchair without help from another person?" (uses adaptive device, no human help)		
c. "Did you use a non-electric wheelchair without help from another person?" (human help only)		
d. "Were you wheeled by another person?" (is wheeled)		
e. "How many persons were needed at one time to help you?" (number of persons helping)		
f. "Were you unable to use a wheelchair because you were confined to your bed or chair?" (is not wheeled, bedfast, chairfast)		
g. "What kind of special equipment did you use?" (regular, electric wheelchair) (name of equipment)		

Patient's Code [| | | | |]

FUNCTION	PRE-HOSPITAL PERFORMANCE	ANTICIPATED CAPACITY ON DISCHARGE
4. TRANSFERRING TO CHAIR AND BED "BEFORE YOU CAME TO THE HOSPITAL...		
a. "Were you able to transfer from your bed to a chair (or wheelchair, if applicable) and from one chair to another without help of any kind?" (transfers without help)		
b. "Did you use equipment but no other person to help you transfer?" (uses equipment, no human help)		
c. "Did another person help you?" (human help only)		
d. "Were you transferred by another person?" (is transferred)		
e. "How many persons were needed at one time to help or transfer you?" (number of persons helping)		
f. "Were you unable to transfer at all?" (is not transferred, bedfast)		
g. "What kind of special equipment did you use?" (sliding board, lift) (name of equipment)		
5. TRANSFERRING TO TUB OR SHOWER "BEFORE YOU CAME TO THE HOSPITAL...		
a. "Were you able to get in and out of a bathtub or shower stall without help of any kind?" (transfers without help)		
b. "Did you use equipment but no other person to help you transfer?" (uses equipment, no human help)		
c. "Did another person help you?" (human help only)		
d. "Were you transferred by another person?" (is transferred)		
e. "How many persons were needed at one time to help or transfer you?" (number of persons helping)		
f. "Were you unable to get in and out of a tub or shower at all?" (is not transferred, bedfast)		
g. "What kind of special equipment did you use?" (name of equipment)		

Patient's Code [| | | |]

FUNCTION	PRE-HOSPITAL PERFORMANCE	ANTICIPATED CAPACITY ON DISCHARGE
6. BATHING "BEFORE YOU CAME TO THE HOSPITAL...		
a. "Were you able to prepare your bath or sponge bath, then wash and dry yourself without help of any kind?" (does not mean transfer) (bathes without help)		
b. "Did you use equipment but no other person to help you bathe?" (uses equipment, no human help)		
c. "Did another person help you?" (human help only)		
d. "Did you use both equipment and another person's help?" (human help and equipment)		
e. "Were you bathed by another person?" (is bathed)		
f. "How many persons were needed at one time to help or to bathe you?" (number of persons helping)		
g. "What kind of special equipment did you use?" (name of equipment)		
7. TOILET "BEFORE YOU CAME TO THE HOSPITAL...		
a. "Were you able to get on and off the toilet, clean yourself, and adjust your clothing without help of any kind?" (uses toilet without help)		
b. "Did you use equipment but no other person to help?" (uses equipment, no human help)		
c. "Did another person help you?" (human help only)		
d. "How many persons were needed at one time to help?" (number of persons helping)		
e. "Did you use both equipment and another person's help?" (human help and equipment)		
f. "Were you unable to use the toilet at all?" (unable to use toilet)		
g. "What kind of special equipment did you use?" (grab bar, special seat) (name of equipment)		

Patient's Code ☐☐☐☐☐

FUNCTION	PRE-HOSPITAL PERFORMANCE	ANTICIPATED CAPACITY ON DISCHARGE
8. BLADDER FUNCTION "BEFORE YOU CAME TO THE HOSPITAL...		
a. "With respect to bladder control, did you have complete control without any accidents?" (continent)		
b. "Did you have occasional accidents, less than once a week?" (incontinent, less than once a week)		
c. "Did you have accidents once a week or more, but just at night?" (incontinent once a week or more, night only)		
d. "Did you have accidents once a week or more, day and night?" (incontinent, once a week or more, day and night)		

e.   (1) "Did you have an indwelling catheter, ostomy, or other diversion?" If yes, ask name of device and go on to e.(2).
    (2) "Did you care for your device yourself?" If no, ask e.(3).
    (3) "Did you need help in caring for your device?"		

9. BOWEL FUNCTION "BEFORE YOU CAME TO THE HOSPITAL...		
a. "With respect to bowel control, did you have complete control without any accidents?" (continent)		
b. "Did you have occasional accidents, less than once a week?" (incontinent, less than once a week)		
c. "Did you have any accidents once a week or more?" (incontinent, once a week or more)		

d.   (1) "Did you have an ostomy or other diversion?"
        (If yes, ask name of device and ask d.(2).
    (2) "Did you care for your ostomy yourself?" (If no, ask d.(3).
    (3) "Did you need help in caring for your ostomy?"		

Patient's Code [| | | |]

FUNCTION	PRE-HOSPITAL PERFORMANCE	ANTICIPATED CAPACITY ON DISCHARGE
10. DRESSING "BEFORE YOU CAME TO THE HOSPITAL...		
a. "Were you able to dress yourself without help of any kind?" (This includes gathering and arranging your clothing) (dresses without help)		
b. "Did you use equipment but no other person to help you dress?" (uses equipment, no human help)		
c. "Did another person help you?" (human help only)		
d. "Were you dressed by another person?" (is dressed)		
e. "How many persons were needed at one time to help or to dress you?" (number of persons helping)		
f. "Were you unable to get dressed?" (is not dressed)		
g. "What kind of special equipment did you use?" (zipper chain) (name of equipment)		
11. GROOMING "BEFORE YOU CAME TO THE HOSPITAL...		
a. "Were you able to clean your teeth or dentures and do daily grooming such as shaving, (applying makeup) and combing your hair without help of any kind?" (grooms without help)		
b. "Did you use equipment but no other person to help you? (uses equipment, no human help)		
c. "Did another person help you, but no equipment?" (human help only)		
d. "Did you use equipment and another person's help?" (human help and equipment)		
e. "Were you groomed by another person?" (is groomed)		
f. "What kind of special equipment did you use?" (name of equipment)		

Patient's Code ☐☐☐☐☐

FUNCTION	PRE-HOSPITAL PERFORMANCE	ANTICIPATED CAPACITY ON DISCHARGE
12. EATING/FEEDING "BEFORE YOU CAME TO THE HOSPITAL...		
a. "Were you able to eat and drink without help of any kind?" (eat from a dish, tray or table with or without prior preparation such as meat being cut, bread buttered) (feeds self without help)		
b. "Did you use equipment but no other person to help?" (uses equipment, no human help)		
c. "Did another person help you?" (human help only)		
d. "Did you use equipment and another person's help?" (human help and equipment)		
e. "Were you fed by another person?" (If yes, ask: "Were you spoon fed, tube fed, or fed parenterally?")		
(1) (is spoon fed)		
(2) (is tube fed)		
(3) (fed parenterally)		
f. "What kind of special equipment did you use?" (spork, rocking knife) (name of equipment)		
13. MOBILITY LEVEL "BEFORE YOU CAME TO THE HOSPITAL...		
a. "Were you able to go outside without help of any kind?" (goes outside without help)		
b. "Did you use equipment but no other person to help you go outside?" (uses equipment, no human help)		
c. "Did another person help you go outside?" (human help only)		
d. "Were you unable to go outside but able to go out of your own room?" (confined to home)		
e. "How many persons were needed at one time to help you leave your room?" (number of persons helping)		
f. "Were you confined to your own room?" (confined to room)		
g. "What kind of special equipment did you use?" (wheelchair, walker, crutches, cane) (name of equipment)		

Patient's Code [| | | |]

J. INSTRUMENTAL ACTIVITIES OF DAILY LIVING PRIOR TO HOSPITALIZATION

Introduction: Now I'd like to ask you how you did certain household
activities before you came to the hospital.

(Check appropriate box and indicate who provided help, if applicable.)

	Check Category	Helper's Relation to Patient

BEFORE YOU CAME TO THE HOSPITAL did you go
shopping for groceries and clothes. . .
(1) Without help (taking care of all
shopping needs yourself)
(2) Could you have done the shopping though
someone did it for you?
(3) With some help (need someone to go with
you to help on all shopping trips) Who
helped you?
(4) Or were you completely unable to do any
shopping? Who did it?

. . . . did you do your housework. . .
(1) Without help (can clean floors, windows,
refrigerator, etc.)
(2) Could you have done it though someone
did it for you?
(3) With some help (can do light housework,
but need help with heavy work) Who
helped you?
(4) Or were you completely unable to do any
housework? Who did it?

. . . . did you prepare your own meals. . .
(1) Without help (plan and cook full meals
yourself)
(2) Could you have done it though someone
did it for you?
(3) With some help (can prepare some things
but unable to cook full meals yourself)
Who helped you?
(4) Or were you completely unable to prepare
your own meals? Who did it?

. . . . did you do your laundry. . .
(1) Without help (take care of all laundry
yourself)
(2) Could you have done it though someone did
it for you?
(3) With some help (can do small items only)
Who helped you?
(4) Or were you completely unable to do your
own laundry? Who did it?

Patient's Code [| | | |]

BEFORE YOU CAME TO THE HOSPITAL <u>did you take
your medicine on your own</u>. . .
    (1) Without help (in the right doses at
        the right time)
    (2) Could you have done it though someone
        did it for you?
    (3) With some help (able to take medicine
        if someone prepares it for you and/or
        reminds you to take it)
    (4) Or was someone needed to administer as
        couldn't/wouldn't take without help?
        Who administered your medicine?

. . . . <u>did you use public transportation or
drive your own car to get to places further
than walking distance</u>. . .
    (1) Without help (can travel alone on buses,
        taxis, or drive own car)
    (2) Could you have done it though someone did
        it for you?
    (3) With some help (need someone to help
        you or go with you when traveling) Who
        helped you?
    (4) Unable to travel unless emergency
        arrangements were made for specialized
        vehicle like ambulance.

. . . . <u>did you handle your own money</u>. . .
    (1) Without help (write checks, pay bills,
        etc.)
    (2) Could you have done it though someone
        did it for you?
    (3) With some help (day to day, but needs
        help in budgeting, etc.)
    (4) Did someone else do this for you?

DO YOU HAVE A TELEPHONE AT HOME?   Yes   No

. . . . <u>did you use the telephone</u>. . .
    (1) Without help
    (2) Could you have done it though someone
        did it for you?
    (3) With some help (can answer phone or dial
        operator in an emergency, but need a
        special phone or help in getting the
        number or dialing). Who helped you?
    (4) Did someone else do this for you?

Patient's Code ☐☐☐☐

K. ARCHITECTURAL BARRIERS IN PATIENT'S HOME

(Ask Patient)

1. Do you have to climb stairs to get into your home? ☐ Yes ☐ No

2. Do you have to climb stairs inside your home to get to your room or the bathroom? ☐ Yes ☐ No

3. Is there anything else about your home that would make it difficult for you to get around and do the things you did before? (list) ☐ Yes ☐ No

_____

_____

_____

4. (DISCHARGE PLANNER:) List needed architectural modifications or mechanical devices, e.g. ramp, inclinator.

_____

_____

_____

_____

L. PATIENT'S HOUSEHOLD COMPOSITION PRIOR TO HOSPITALIZATION

(List all members of household and be as specific as possible as to when they are at home)

(1) "Who were you living with just before coming to the hospital?" (2) "When were they usually at home?"

Relationship to Patient	When at Home			
	Weekday		Weekend	
	Day	Night	Day	Night
0. Lived Alone				
1. _____	_____	_____	_____	_____
2. _____	_____	_____	_____	_____
3. _____	_____	_____	_____	_____
4. _____	_____	_____	_____	_____
5. _____	_____	_____	_____	_____
6. _____	_____	_____	_____	_____

Patient's Code ☐☐☐☐☐

(3) "Did relatives & friends visit you at home?"

Visiting Family/Neighbors

_____

_____

_____

_____

(4) "How frequently did they visit?"

Frequency of Visits Prior to Hosp.

_____

_____

_____

_____

(5) "Is there one person you feel particularly close to and who you rely on most for help?"

_____
Relationship to Patient

(Record name on PACE cover sheet)

(6) "Where does this person live?"
(Check appropriate box)

☐ same house/apartment

☐ within 10 minutes (walk or drive)

☐ elsewhere in same bldg.

☐ elsewhere

(7) "Does (name person) visit you regularly in the hospital?" ☐ Yes ☐ No

(8) "We'd like to ask (name person) a few questions as part of the study. If he/she is not available, is there someone else who visits you here we could talk with?"

_____
Relationship to Patient

(Record name on PACE cover sheet)

(9) "Is there anyone else?"

_____
Relationship to Patient

(Record name of PACE cover sheet)

M. INFORMAL SUPPORT NETWORK (Assessment by DISCHARGE PLANNER based on knowledge of patient and family network)

(1) Is the network of family and friends able to provide the help needed at discharge?

☐ All help ☐ Some help ☐ No help ☐ Family unsure

(2) Is the network of family and friends willing to provide the help needed at discharge?

☐ All help ☐ Some help ☐ No help ☐ Family unsure

(3) Would the family be willing to maintain the patient at home if supportive outside services were provided?

☐ Yes ☐ No

Patient's Code [| | | | |]

N.   PSYCHOSOCIAL

Ask principal caregiver for evaluation of patient's pre-hospital behavior. Seek
this information by phone if unable to obtain in person. Discharge planner should
indicate current evaluation. If there is no principal caregiver, ask questions of
patient.

1.   RECENT DEATH OF FAMILY MEMBER OR CLOSE FRIEND   [ ] Yes   [ ] No

     IF YES, RELATIONSHIP TO PATIENT   _____

2.   ORIENTATION: Time, Place, and Person – Check one item

          Oriented   [ ]
          Disoriented partially   [ ]
          Disoriented intermittently   [ ]

3.   FOLLOWS INSTRUCTIONS – Check one item
          Follows complex instructions [ ]
          Follows simple instructions   [ ]

4.   BEHAVIOR – Check each item

| | Pre-Hospital | | | Current | | |
	Never	Sometimes	Freq.	Never	Sometimes	Freq.
Talks with others						
Visits with others						
Helps others						
Helps self						
Smiles, laughs						
Apprehensive, Fearful Anxious						
Lethargic						
Withdrawn						
Cries						
Irritable						
Demanding, Angry, Agitated, Hostile						
Restless						
Wandering						
Hallucinates						
Disruptive, Noisy						
Abusive to self						
Abusive to others, assaultive, combative						
Other : specify						

O. IMPAIRMENT ITEMS

Patient's Code [| | | |]

AMPUTATIONS

Date	Extremity Amputated	Prosthesis (if any)

PARALYSIS/PARESIS

Type	Date of Onset	Location (if applicable)

SENSORY IMPAIRMENTS AND COMPENSATION (CURRENT)

Sense	No Impairment	Impairment	Complete Loss	Type of Impairment &/or Comp.
Sight				
Hearing				
Speech				
Touch				

DENTITION

	No Teeth Missing	3 Pairs Opposing Teeth	<3 Pairs Opposing Teeth	All Teeth Missing
Natural Teeth				

Compensation:

DENTURES ☐ Don't fit
         ☐ Needs, but lacks
         ☐ Doesn't use

PARTIAL ☐ Upper ☐ Lower
FULL   ☐ Upper ☐ Lower

P. ACTIVE MOTION OF LIMBS (CURRENT)

Criteria for Evaluation

Good (3) - All muscle groups of the limb complete full range of motion of the joints against moderate or greater resistance. No limitation due to contracture pain, spasticity, diminished sensibility, etc.

Fair (2) - All muscle groups of the limb complete available range of motion against gravity. Any limitation due to contracture, pain, spasticity, etc., still permits ordinary use of the limb.

Poor (1) - Some active motion in the limb or it is used as a helper, includes amputation with functional prosthesis.

Null (0) - No motion and/or usefulness, includes amputation without functional prothesis.

(Circle appropriate numbers according to above criteria.)

LIMBS	Good	Fair	Poor	Null
R Upper	3	2	1	0
L Upper	3	2	1	0
R Lower	3	2	1	0
L Lower	3	2	1	0

Patient's Code ☐☐☐☐☐

Q. ABNORMAL SIGNS
List most recent abnormal results for tests conducted during current
hospitalization, e.g. Vital signs, chest sounds, diagnostic tests, such as
blood, stool, sputum, serous fluids, x-rays, EKG's.

CURRENT			CURRENT		
Date	Sign/Test	Reading/Result	Date	Sign/Test	Reading/Result

Patient's Code ☐☐☐☐☐☐

MEDICATION

List name and dosage of medication and **reason**. Ex. Tetracycline/respiratory infection; aspirin/anticoagulant.

CURRENT MEDICATION	DOSAGE/FREQUENCY/ROUTE OF ADMIN.	PURPOSE	CHECK IF EXPECTED TO CONTINUE AT DISCHARGE

Patient's Code [| | | |]

S. SPECIAL PROCEDURES IN HOSPITAL

(Describe treatments currently being administered and check if they are
likely to be continued at discharge)

Current Procedure	Treatment	Provider's Title	Check If Likely to Continue After Discharge
1. Bowel &/or Bladder Training			
2. Decubitus(i) (Site)(s)			
3. Wound Care (Site)			
4. Eye Care			
5. Irrigation - Bladder	Type & Frequency:		
6. Ostomy Care			
7. Suctioning	Location, Frequency:		
8. Inhalation IPPB			
9. Oxygen RX. Route: _____			
10. Turning	Schedule:		

Patient's Code ☐☐☐☐☐

Current Procedure	Treatment	Provider's Title	Check If Likely to Continue After Discharge
11. Teaching: Foot care _____ Ostomy care _____ Medications _____ Diet _____ Gait Training _____ Prosthetic Training ____ Other _____	Check Instruction Started or Planned:		
12. Range of Motion Exercises	Sites, Types, & Frequency:		
13. Nutrition -Diet	Specify:		
-Food &/or Fluid Supplements	Specify Type & Schedule:		
-Food &/or Fluid Restrictions	Specify Type & Schedule:		
14. Monitoring - (e.g. Vital signs Neurological signs	Specify:		
15. Other	Specify		

Patient's Code _____

T. <u>SPECIAL PERSONALITY, FAMILY OR CULTURAL CHARACTERISTICS INFLUENCING</u>
<u>PATIENT'S NEEDS</u>   (Observations of Discharge Planner)

_____

_____

_____

_____

_____

<u>NOTE TO HOSPITAL COORDINATOR</u>:   Complete Item 6, Summary of PACE completion,
on screening form.

Patient's Code ☐☐☐☐☐

Control Sheet
(To be completed by Hospital Coordinator)

Changes in Patient's Medical Condition that Occur Between Completion of PACE Form and 6th Visit by Outside Consultant.

New Problem   Date of Onset

_____   _____

_____   _____

_____   _____

_____   _____

_____   _____

_____   _____

_____   _____

DESCRIPTION OF PATIENT CHARACTERISTICS

The results of several sets of regression analyses were reported in Chapters 7 and 8. The same sixteen independent variables were used in each regression. They were selected on reasonable grounds; based on theory and selected early analyses of variance, they were expected to be associated with the costs and hours of home care prescribed by professionals and with the extent of agreement about costs and hours. Now follows an explanation of how these variables were defined and coded, along with an indication of why it was thought reasonable to include them.

Age. Calculated from PACE screening form, page 2. Greater age was, other things equal, expected to be associated with need for more help. This variable is not categorized; it is continuous in units of years.

Resides with. Calculated from PACE, page 14. The more people the patient resided with, the greater was expected to be need for home care (because presence of others in household would enable disabled patients to live at home longer than had they been alone) and the greater the proportion of total hours prescribed for unpaid providers. This variable is not categorized; it is continuous in number of persons.

Marital status. Given on PACE screening form, page 3. This variable correlated badly with the number of persons residing with the patients (r = .045). Categorized as 0 = not married (single, widowed, or divorced) and 1 = married.

Anticipated discharge site. Given on PACE screening form, page 4. This is informed opinion of patient's discharge planner. It was expected that patients being discharged to "higher" levels of institutional care would require more home care. Categorized as 1 = rehabilitation hospital or chronic disease hospital; 2 = Medicare SNF (Massachusetts level I); 3 = Medicaid SNF (II); 4 = Medicaid SNF (III). An *inverse* relation thus would be expected to obtain between, for example, anticipated discharge site and cost of institutional care or cost of home care—because "higher" levels of anticipated sites of discharge were assigned lower interval codes.

Indefinite placement. Given on PACE screening form, page 4. This also is informed opinion of actual discharge planner. Patients expected to be placed indefinitely were expected to require more hours of care per week because they were more disabled. Coded as 0 = no; 1 = yes.

Number of medical diagnoses. Calculated from page 2 of PACE screening form. Although little data linking specific diagnoses with more or less costly long-term care have been reported, it was thought that patients with more identified diagnoses might be thought to require more care. This variable is not categorized; it is continuous in number of diagnoses.

Number of disabling conditions. Calculated from page 2 of PACE screening form. Expected to be a subset of above variable, in that some medical diagnoses might not be functionally disabling. Continuous in number of conditions.

Number of known hospital discharges (in past year). Calculated from page 2 of PACE screening form. Thought to be a good predictor of medical instability. Continuous in number of discharges.

Number of long-term care facility discharges (in past two years). Calculated from page 3 of PACE screening form. As above. Continuous in number of discharges.

Number of current medications (in hospital). Calculated from PACE, page 19. Continuous in number of medications.

Percent of nursing services used. Calculated from pages 20 and 21 of PACE. Continuous in number used divided by N = 15 × 100.

Psychosocial percent positive. Calculated from PACE, page 16. Better psychosocial status thought to be associated with need for less care, particularly for continuous supervision. Continuous in items 1 through 5 (sometimes or frequently) plus items 6 through 17 (never) divided by N = 17 × 100.

Anticipated Barthel (ADL). Calculated from pages 5 through 11 of PACE. Thought that higher functional ability would be associated with reduced home care needs. Calculated in accordance with Granger's modifications of the original Barthel index. (These modifications are found at conclusion of this appendix.)

Barthel change. Calculated from pages 5 through 11 of PACE, scored as Granger suggests. Barthel change was thought to be associated with medical instability. Calculated by subtracting prehospital Barthel from anticipated Barthel.

Thus, the greater the value of this variable, the greater the *decline* in Barthel score.

Prehospital independence in instrumental activities of daily living (IADL). Calculated from pages 12 and 13 of PACE form. Independence thought to indicate less need for home care, particularly household help. Continuous in percent positive; total of scores 1 or 2 divided by $N = 8$.

Maintain at home. Recorded on page 15 of PACE. Assessment by patient's discharge planner of whether the patient's informal support network would be willing to maintain the patient at home if supportive outside formal services were provided. Categorized as $0 = $ no; $1 = $ yes.

Frequency distributions, means, medians, and standard deviations for these and other patient characteristics now follow.

FREQUENCY DISTRIBUTIONS

MONTH OF BIRTH

N= 50   MEAN= 7.160   MEDIAN= 6.800   SD= 3.384

VALUE	FREQUENCY	PERCENTAGE	CUMULATIVE
1.000	3	6.00%	6.00%
2.000	2	4.00%	10.00%
3.000	5	10.00%	20.00%
4.000	4	8.00%	28.00%
5.000	3	6.00%	34.00%
6.000	4	8.00%	42.00%
7.000	5	10.00%	52.00%
8.000	3	6.00%	58.00%
9.000	1	2.00%	60.00%
10.000	10	20.00%	80.00%
11.000	7	14.00%	94.00%
12.000	3	6.00%	100.00%

YEAR OF BIRTH

N= 50   MEAN= 53.060   MEDIAN= 84.500   SD= 42.246

VALUE	FREQUENCY	PERCENTAGE	CUMULATIVE
0.000	2	4.00%	4.00%
1.000	2	4.00%	8.00%
3.000	2	4.00%	12.00%
4.000	2	4.00%	16.00%
5.000	3	6.00%	22.00%
6.000	1	2.00%	24.00%
7.000	1	2.00%	26.00%
8.000	2	4.00%	30.00%
9.000	2	4.00%	34.00%
11.000	1	2.00%	36.00%
13.000	1	2.00%	38.00%
15.000	1	2.00%	40.00%
16.000	2	4.00%	44.00%
26.000	1	2.00%	46.00%
83.000	1	2.00%	48.00%
86.000	2	4.00%	52.00%
87.000	1	2.00%	54.00%
88.000	1	2.00%	56.00%
89.000	2	4.00%	60.00%
90.000	2	4.00%	64.00%
91.000	1	2.00%	66.00%
92.000	5	10.00%	76.00%
93.000	5	10.00%	86.00%
94.000	2	4.00%	90.00%
95.000	1	2.00%	92.00%
97.000	1	2.00%	94.00%
98.000	3	6.00%	100.00%

AGE

N= 50   MEAN= 77.920   MEDIAN= 79.500   SD= 9.393

VALUE	FREQUENCY	PERCENTAGE	CUMULATIVE
51.000	1	2.00%	2.00%
61.000	2	4.00%	6.00%
63.000	1	2.00%	8.00%
64.000	1	2.00%	10.00%
65.000	1	2.00%	12.00%
68.000	2	4.00%	16.00%
69.000	2	4.00%	20.00%
70.000	1	2.00%	22.00%
71.000	2	4.00%	26.00%
72.000	2	4.00%	30.00%
73.000	3	6.00%	36.00%
74.000	1	2.00%	38.00%
75.000	1	2.00%	40.00%
76.000	1	2.00%	42.00%
77.000	2	4.00%	46.00%
78.000	1	2.00%	48.00%
79.000	1	2.00%	50.00%
80.000	2	4.00%	54.00%

VALUE	82.000	83.000	84.000	85.000	86.000	87.000	88.000	90.000	95.000
FREQUENCY	1	1	5	5	3	1	2	4	1
PERCENTAGE	2.00%	2.00%	10.00%	10.00%	6.00%	2.00%	4.00%	8.00%	2.00%
CUMULATIVE	56.00%	58.00%	68.00%	78.00%	84.00%	86.00%	90.00%	98.00%	100.00%

RACE

	CAUCASIAN
VALUE	1.000
FREQUENCY	50
PERCENTAGE	100.00%
CUMULATIVE	100.00%

N= 50   MEAN= 1.000   MEDIAN= 0.500   SD= 0.0

SEX

	FEMALE	MALE
VALUE	0.000	1.000
FREQUENCY	38	12
PERCENTAGE	76.00%	24.00%
CUMULATIVE	76.00%	100.00%

N= 50   MEAN= 0.240   MEDIAN= 0.0   SD= 0.427

RESIDES WITH

VALUE	0.000	1.000	2.000	3.000	4.000
FREQUENCY	19	20	8	1	2
PERCENTAGE	38.00%	40.00%	16.00%	2.00%	4.00%
CUMULATIVE	38.00%	78.00%	94.00%	96.00%	100.00%

N= 50   MEAN= 0.940   MEDIAN= 0.300   SD= 0.988

MARITAL STATUS

	SINGLE	MARRIED	DIVORCED	WIDOWED
VALUE	1.000	2.000	4.000	5.000
FREQUENCY	3	16	1	30
PERCENTAGE	6.00%	32.00%	2.00%	60.00%
CUMULATIVE	6.00%	38.00%	40.00%	100.00%

N= 50   MEAN= 3.780   MEDIAN= 4.167   SD= 1.540

ANTIC. DISCH. SITE   N= 50   MEAN= 3.840   MEDIAN= 3.429   SD= 0.946

	REHAB. HOSP	CHRON. DIS.	LEVEL 1 SNF	LEVEL 2 SNF	LEVEL 3 ICF
VALUE	1.000	2.000	3.000	4.000	5.000
FREQUENCY	1	3	12	21	13
PERCENTAGE	2.00%	6.00%	24.00%	42.00%	26.00%
CUMULATIVE	2.00%	8.00%	32.00%	74.00%	100.00%

INDEFINITE PLACEMENT   N= 50   MEAN= 0.680   MEDIAN= 0.265   SD= 0.466

	NO	YES
VALUE	0.000	1.000
FREQUENCY	16	34
PERCENTAGE	32.00%	68.00%
CUMULATIVE	32.00%	100.00%

OF DIAGNOSES   N= 50   MEAN= 4.080   MEDIAN= 3.500   SD= 1.647

VALUE	1.000	2.000	3.000	4.000	5.000	6.000	7.000
FREQUENCY	2	8	9	12	8	6	5
PERCENTAGE	4.00%	16.00%	18.00%	24.00%	16.00%	12.00%	10.00%
CUMULATIVE	4.00%	20.00%	38.00%	62.00%	78.00%	90.00%	100.00%

OF DISABLING CONDITION   N= 50   MEAN= 2.620   MEDIAN= 2.158   SD= 1.310

VALUE	1.000	2.000	3.000	4.000	5.000	6.000	7.000
FREQUENCY	12	10	19	6	1	1	1
PERCENTAGE	24.00%	20.00%	38.00%	12.00%	2.00%	2.00%	2.00%
CUMULATIVE	24.00%	44.00%	82.00%	94.00%	96.00%	98.00%	100.00%

KNOWN HOSPITAL DISCHAR   N= 50   MEAN= 0.920   MEDIAN= 0.071   SD= 1.163

VALUE	0.000	1.000	2.000	3.000	4.000	5.000
FREQUENCY	24	14	7	3	1	1
PERCENTAGE	48.00%	28.00%	14.00%	6.00%	2.00%	2.00%
CUMULATIVE	48.00%	76.00%	90.00%	96.00%	98.00%	100.00%

KNOWN LTC ADMISSIONS

N= 50 MEAN= 0.200 MEDIAN= 0.0 SD= 0.447

VALUE	0.000	1.000	2.000
FREQUENCY	41	8	1
PERCENTAGE	82.00%	16.00%	2.00%
CUMULATIVE	82.00%	98.00%	100.00%

PREHOSPITAL BARTHEL SCOR

N= 50 MEAN= 77.120 MEDIAN= 82.500 SD= 23.577

VALUE	25.000	27.000	32.000	35.000	37.000	47.000	52.000	55.000
FREQUENCY	1	1	1	2	3	1	1	1
PERCENTAGE	2.00%	2.00%	2.00%	4.00%	6.00%	2.00%	2.00%	2.00%
CUMULATIVE	2.00%	4.00%	6.00%	10.00%	16.00%	18.00%	20.00%	22.00%

VALUE	57.000	67.000	69.000	70.000	74.000	75.000	79.000	80.000
FREQUENCY	1	1	1	2	1	2	1	4
PERCENTAGE	2.00%	2.00%	2.00%	4.00%	2.00%	4.00%	2.00%	8.00%
CUMULATIVE	24.00%	26.00%	28.00%	32.00%	34.00%	38.00%	40.00%	48.00%

VALUE	85.000	89.000	90.000	94.000	95.000	99.000	100.000	
FREQUENCY	2	2	4	1	4	1	12	
PERCENTAGE	4.00%	4.00%	8.00%	2.00%	8.00%	2.00%	24.00%	
CUMULATIVE	52.00%	56.00%	64.00%	66.00%	74.00%	76.00%	100.00%	

ANTICIPATED BARTHEL

N= 50 MEAN= 49.840 MEDIAN= 45.750 SD= 21.104

VALUE	5.000	10.000	15.000	17.000	20.000	25.000	30.000	32.000
FREQUENCY	1	1	1	2	1	1	1	3
PERCENTAGE	2.00%	2.00%	2.00%	4.00%	2.00%	2.00%	2.00%	6.00%
CUMULATIVE	2.00%	4.00%	6.00%	10.00%	12.00%	14.00%	16.00%	22.00%

VALUE	35.000	37.000	40.000	42.000	47.000	52.000	55.000	57.000
FREQUENCY	1	3	1	6	4	2	1	4
PERCENTAGE	2.00%	6.00%	2.00%	12.00%	8.00%	4.00%	2.00%	8.00%
CUMULATIVE	24.00%	30.00%	32.00%	44.00%	52.00%	56.00%	58.00%	66.00%

VALUE	60.000	62.000	67.000	69.000	70.000	75.000	80.000	85.000
FREQUENCY	2	2	1	1	3	3	2	2
PERCENTAGE	4.00%	4.00%	2.00%	2.00%	6.00%	6.00%	4.00%	4.00%
CUMULATIVE	70.00%	74.00%	76.00%	78.00%	84.00%	90.00%	94.00%	98.00%

VALUE	99.000
FREQUENCY	1
PERCENTAGE	2.00%
CUMULATIVE	100.00%

PREHOSPITAL IADL   N= 50   MEAN= 40.500   MEDIAN= 27.889   SD= 31.941

VALUE	0.000	13.000	25.000	38.000	50.000	63.000	75.000	88.000
FREQUENCY	8	8	7	9	1	6	4	2
PERCENTAGE	16.00%	16.00%	14.00%	18.00%	2.00%	12.00%	8.00%	4.00%
CUMULATIVE	16.00%	32.00%	46.00%	64.00%	66.00%	78.00%	86.00%	90.00%

VALUE	100.000
FREQUENCY	5
PERCENTAGE	10.00%
CUMULATIVE	100.00%

INFORMAL SUPPORT ABLE   N= 50   MEAN= 2.160   MEDIAN= 1.605   SD= 0.463

	ALL HELP	SOME HELP	NO HELP
VALUE	1.000	2.000	3.000
FREQUENCY	2	38	10
PERCENTAGE	4.00%	76.00%	20.00%
CUMULATIVE	4.00%	80.00%	100.00%

INFORMAL SUPPORT WILLING   N= 50   MEAN= 2.200   MEDIAN= 1.600   SD= 0.529

	ALL HELP	SOME HELP	NO HELP FAMILY	UNSUR
VALUE	1.000	2.000	3.000	4.000
FREQUENCY	1	40	7	2
PERCENTAGE	2.00%	80.00%	14.00%	4.00%
CUMULATIVE	2.00%	82.00%	96.00%	100.00%

MAINTAIN AT HOME   N= 50   MEAN= 0.740   MEDIAN= 0.324   SD= 0.439

	NO	YES
VALUE	0.000	1.000
FREQUENCY	13	37
PERCENTAGE	26.00%	74.00%
CUMULATIVE	26.00%	100.00%

ITEMS 1-6   N= 49   MEAN= 1.408   MEDIAN= 0.654   SD= 1.308   BLANK 1

VALUE	0.000	1.000	2.000	3.000	4.000
FREQUENCY	16	13	8	8	4
PERCENTAGE	32.65%	26.53%	16.33%	16.33%	8.16%
CUMULATIVE	32.65%	59.18%	75.51%	91.84%	100.00%

ITEMS 7-17 N= 48 MEAN= 7.521 MEDIAN= 7.500 SD= 2.291

VALUE	FREQUENCY	PERCENTAGE	CUMULATIVE
2.000	1	2.08%	2.08%
3.000	2	4.17%	6.25%
4.000	1	2.08%	8.33%
5.000	5	10.42%	18.75%
6.000	7	14.58%	33.33%
7.000	8	16.67%	50.00%
8.000	6	12.50%	62.50%
9.000	8	16.67%	79.17%
10.000	5	10.42%	89.58%
11.000	4	8.33%	97.92%
12.000	1	2.08%	100.00%
BLANK	2		

 # OF CURRENT MEDICATIONS N= 50 MEAN= 5.500 MEDIAN= 4.400 SD= 2.975

VALUE	FREQUENCY	PERCENTAGE	CUMULATIVE
0.000	1	2.00%	2.00%
1.000	3	6.00%	8.00%
2.000	3	6.00%	14.00%
3.000	8	16.00%	30.00%
4.000	8	16.00%	46.00%
5.000	5	10.00%	56.00%
6.000	1	2.00%	58.00%
7.000	5	10.00%	68.00%
8.000	8	16.00%	84.00%
9.000	5	10.00%	94.00%
10.000	1	2.00%	96.00%
11.000	1	2.00%	98.00%
14.000	1	2.00%	100.00%

% NURS. SERS. USED N= 50 MEAN= 31.880 MEDIAN= 28.333 SD= 15.116

VALUE	FREQUENCY	PERCENTAGE	CUMULATIVE
0.000	2	4.00%	4.00%
7.000	2	4.00%	8.00%
13.000	4	8.00%	16.00%
20.000	6	12.00%	28.00%
27.000	9	18.00%	46.00%
33.000	9	18.00%	64.00%
38.000	1	2.00%	66.00%
40.000	4	8.00%	74.00%
41.000	1	2.00%	76.00%
47.000	3	6.00%	82.00%
50.000	1	2.00%	84.00%
53.000	6	12.00%	96.00%
60.000	2	4.00%	100.00%

CUR. NUR. SERS. USED   N= 50   MEAN= 4.620   MEDIAN= 3.800   SD= 2.785

VALUE	0.000	1.000	2.000	3.000	4.000	5.000	6.000	7.000	8.000
FREQUENCY	4	2	7	4	10	5	6	3	3
PERCENTAGE	8.00%	4.00%	14.00%	8.00%	20.00%	10.00%	12.00%	6.00%	6.00%
CUMULATIVE	8.00%	12.00%	26.00%	34.00%	54.00%	64.00%	76.00%	82.00%	88.00%

VALUE	9.000	12.000
FREQUENCY	5	1
PERCENTAGE	10.00%	2.00%
CUMULATIVE	98.00%	100.00%

ACTUAL DISCH. SITE   N= 50   MEAN= 4.780   MEDIAN= 3.692   SD= 2.587

	REHAB. HOSP.	CHRON DIS. H	LEVEL 1 SNF	LEVEL 2 NURS	LEVEL 3 ICF	PUBLIC MEDIC	COUNTY HOSPI	VA REHAB.	STILL IN HOS
VALUE	1.000	2.000	3.000	4.000	5.000	6.000	7.000	8.000	9.000
FREQUENCY	1	7	8	13	11	1	1	1	1
PERCENTAGE	2.00%	14.00%	16.00%	26.00%	22.00%	2.00%	2.00%	2.00%	2.00%
CUMULATIVE	2.00%	16.00%	32.00%	58.00%	80.00%	82.00%	84.00%	86.00%	88.00%

	HOME	DIED
VALUE	10.000	11.000
FREQUENCY	3	3
PERCENTAGE	6.00%	6.00%
CUMULATIVE	94.00%	100.00%

CARE IN ACT. DISCH. SITE   N= 50   MEAN= 4.340   MEDIAN= 3.667   SD= 1.818

	REHABILITATI	CHRONIC	LEVEL 1	LEVEL 2	LEVEL 3	N.A.
VALUE	1.000	2.000	3.000	4.000	5.000	8.000
FREQUENCY	2	5	8	15	13	7
PERCENTAGE	4.00%	10.00%	16.00%	30.00%	26.00%	14.00%
CUMULATIVE	4.00%	14.00%	30.00%	60.00%	86.00%	100.00%

PSYCHOSOCIAL

N= 48   MEAN= 52.574   MEDIAN= 50.000   SD= 18.462

VALUE	FREQUENCY	PERCENTAGE	CUMULATIVE
11.765	1	2.08%	2.08%
23.529	3	6.25%	8.33%
29.412	4	8.33%	16.67%
35.294	4	8.33%	25.00%
41.176	3	6.25%	31.25%
47.059	7	14.58%	45.83%
52.941	4	8.33%	54.17%
58.824	8	16.67%	70.83%
64.706	3	6.25%	77.08%
70.588	5	10.42%	87.50%
76.471	2	4.17%	91.67%
82.353	1	2.08%	93.75%
88.235	3	6.25%	100.00%
BLANK	2		

BARTHEL CHANGE

N= 50   MEAN= 27.280   MEDIAN= 26.000   SD= 21.407

VALUE	FREQUENCY	PERCENTAGE	CUMULATIVE
-15.000	1	2.00%	2.00%
-5.000	1	2.00%	4.00%
0.000	6	12.00%	16.00%
5.000	3	6.00%	22.00%
9.000	1	2.00%	24.00%
10.000	2	4.00%	28.00%
15.000	2	4.00%	32.00%
16.000	1	2.00%	34.00%
19.000	1	2.00%	36.00%
20.000	3	6.00%	42.00%
22.000	2	4.00%	46.00%
23.000	1	2.00%	48.00%
25.000	1	2.00%	50.00%
27.000	2	4.00%	54.00%
28.000	2	4.00%	58.00%
29.000	1	2.00%	60.00%
33.000	1	2.00%	62.00%
37.000	1	2.00%	64.00%
38.000	2	4.00%	68.00%
40.000	2	4.0%	72.0%
43.000	4	8.00%	80.00%
47.000	1	2.00%	82.00%
48.000	2	4.00%	86.00%
53.000	2	4.00%	90.00%
58.000	1	2.00%	92.00%
63.000	2	4.00%	96.00%
68.000	1	2.00%	98.00%
83.000	1	2.00%	100.00%

HOSPITAL

N= 50   MEAN= 3.620   MEDIAN= 3.286   SD= 1.247

VALUE	FREQUENCY	PERCENTAGE	CUMULATIVE	Label
1.000	1	2.00%	2.00%	PETER BENT
2.000	12	24.00%	26.00%	NORWOOD
3.000	6	12.00%	38.00%	MERCY
4.000	21	42.00%	80.00%	WORCESTER
5.000	6	12.00%	92.00%	MT. AUBURN N.E. MEMORIA
6.000	4	8.00%	100.00%	

SCREENING RESULTS   N= 50   MEAN= 1.780   MEDIAN= 0.893   SD= 1.566

	IN-FULL	IN-LIMITED	FULL-NO VIS.	LTD.-NO VIS.
VALUE	1.000	2.000	7.000	8.000
FREQUENCY	28	19	1	2
PERCENTAGE	56.00%	38.00%	2.00%	4.00%
CUMULATIVE	56.00%	94.00%	96.00%	100.00%

PARTICIPATION   N= 50   MEAN= 0.580   MEDIAN= 0.138   SD= 0.494

	LIMITED	FULL
VALUE	0.000	1.000
FREQUENCY	21	29
PERCENTAGE	42.00%	58.00%
CUMULATIVE	42.00%	100.00%

OBSERVED   N= 50   MEAN= 0.320   MEDIAN= 0.0   SD= 0.466

	NON-VISIT	VISIT
VALUE	0.000	1.000
FREQUENCY	34	16
PERCENTAGE	68.00%	32.00%
CUMULATIVE	68.00%	100.00%

AGE   N= 50   MEAN= 1.460   MEDIAN= 0.926   SD= 0.498

	51-80	81-95
VALUE	1.000	2.000
FREQUENCY	27	23
PERCENTAGE	54.00%	46.00%
CUMULATIVE	54.00%	100.00%

RESIDES WITH   N= 50   MEAN= 0.620   MEDIAN= 0.194   SD= 0.465

	ALONE	1-4
VALUE	0.000	1.000
FREQUENCY	19	31
PERCENTAGE	38.00%	62.00%
CUMULATIVE	38.00%	100.00%

ANTIC. DISCH. SITE   N= 50   MEAN= 3.300   MEDIAN= 2.286   SD= 1.628

	RE,CH,L1	LEVEL 2 SNF	LEVEL 3 ICF
VALUE	1.000	4.000	5.000
FREQUENCY	16	21	13
PERCENTAGE	32.00%	42.00%	26.00%
CUMULATIVE	32.00%	74.00%	100.00%

OF DIAGNOSES   N= 50   MEAN= 1.380   MEDIAN= 0.806   SD= 0.485

	1-4	5-7
VALUE	1.000	2.000
FREQUENCY	31	19
PERCENTAGE	62.00%	38.00%
CUMULATIVE	62.00%	100.00%

KNOWN HOSPITAL DISCHAR   N= 50   MEAN= 0.520   MEDIAN= 0.038   SD= 0.500

	0	1-5
VALUE	0.000	1.000
FREQUENCY	24	26
PERCENTAGE	48.00%	52.00%
CUMULATIVE	48.00%	100.00%

PRE-HOSPITAL BARTHEL SCO   N= 50   MEAN= 2.000   MEDIAN= 1.500   SD= 0.825

	0-74	75-94	95-100
VALUE	1.000	2.000	3.000
FREQUENCY	17	16	17
PERCENTAGE	34.00%	32.00%	34.00%
CUMULATIVE	34.00%	66.00%	100.00%

ANTICIPATED BARTHEL   N= 50   MEAN= 1.980   MEDIAN= 1.474   SD= 0.787

	0-40	41-60	61-100
VALUE	1.000	2.000	3.000
FREQUENCY	16	19	15
PERCENTAGE	32.00%	38.00%	30.00%
CUMULATIVE	32.00%	70.00%	100.00%

PRE-HOSPITAL IADL   N= 50   MEAN= 1.540   MEDIAN= 1.074   SD= 0.498

	0-25	38-100
VALUE	1.000	2.000
FREQUENCY	23	27
PERCENTAGE	46.00%	54.00%
CUMULATIVE	46.00%	100.00%

PSYCHOSOCIAL   N= 48   MEAN= 1.459   MEDIAN= 0.923   SD= 0.499   BLANK 2

	0-53%	59-100%
VALUE	1.000	2.000
FREQUENCY	26	22
PERCENTAGE	54.17%	45.83%
CUMULATIVE	54.17%	100.00%

 # OF CURRENT MEDICATIONS N= 50 MEAN= 1.540 MEDIAN= 1.074 SD= 0.499

	0-4	5-14
VALUE	1.000	2.000
FREQUENCY	23	27
PERCENTAGE	46.00%	54.00%
CUMULATIVE	46.00%	100.00%

% NURS. SERS. USER N= 50 MEAN= 1.540 MEDIAN= 1.074 SD= 0.493

	0-27%	33-60%
VALUE	1.000	2.000
FREQUENCY	23	27
PERCENTAGE	46.00%	54.00%
CUMULATIVE	46.00%	100.00%

CARE IN ACT. DISCH. SITE N= 43 MEAN= 3.256 MEDIAN= 2.300 SD= 1.699

	RE,CH,LI	LEVEL 2	LEVEL 3	BLANK
VALUE	1.000	4.000	5.000	7
FREQUENCY	15	15	13	
PERCENTAGE	34.88%	34.88%	30.23%	
CUMULATIVE	34.88%	69.77%	100.00%	

BARTHEL CHANGE N= 50 MEAN= 1.500 MEDIAN= 1.500 SD= 0.500

	-15 TO 25	27 TO 83
VALUE	1.000	2.000
FREQUENCY	25	25
PERCENTAGE	50.00%	50.00%
CUMULATIVE	50.00%	100.00%

CONVERSION FROM PACE FORM TO BARTHEL SCORES
(C. Granger — 4/77)

Mobility Level

Goes outside without help
Goes outside with help of equipment
Devices, (no human help)
Goes outside with human help, with or without
    equipment, devices
Confined to facility/home but gets outside room
Confined to room

Walking (for 50 yds)

Walks without help	15
Uses equipment, device (no human help)	15
Human help only	10
Human help and equipment, device	10
Does not walk	0
Number of persons helping	
Name of equipment, device	

Bathing (and transfer tub/shower)

Bathes without help and trs. tub/shower	5
Uses equipment, device (no human help but not independent in trs. tub/shower)	4
Human help only	0
Human help and equipment, device	0
Is bathed	0
Number of persons helping	
Name of equipment, devices	

Dressing

Dresses without help	10
Uses equipment, device (no human help)	10
Human help only	5
Human help and equipment, device	3
Is dressed	0
Is not dressed	0
Number of persons helping	
Name of equipment, devices	

Grooming

Grooms without help	5
Uses adaptive device (no human help)	5

Grooming (cont'd.)

Human help only	0
Human help and adaptive device	0
Is groomed	0
Number of persons helping	
Name of adaptive devices	

Eating/Feeding

Feeds self without help	10
Uses adaptive device (no human help)	5
Human help only	0
Human help and adaptive device	0
Spoon fed	0
Tube fed	0
Fed parenterally	0
Number of persons helping	

Transferring (bed and chair)

Transfers without help	15
Uses equipment, device (no human help)	15
Human help only	7
Human help and equipment, device	7
Is transferred (does not participate)	0
Is not transferred (bedfast)	0
Number of persons helping	
Name equipment, devices	

Wheeling (score *only if not walking*)

Does not wheel − walks	10
Wheels without help (does not walk)	5
Uses adaptive device (no walking or help)	5
Human help and adaptive device	0
Is wheeled (does not participate)	0
Is not wheeled (bedfast or chairfast)	0
Number of persons helping	
Name of adaptive devices	

Stair Climbing

Climbs stairs without help	10
Uses equipment, device (no human help)	10
Human help only	5
Human help and equipment, device	5
Does not climb stairs	0
Numbers of persons helping	
Name of equipment, devices	

Toiletting (and transfers and perineal care)

Uses toilet room without help	10
Uses equipment, device (no human help)	9
Human help only	5
Human help and equipment, device	5
Does not use toilet room	0
Number of persons helping	
Name of equipment, devices	

Bowel Function

Continent	10
Incontinent less than once a week	5
Incontinent once a week or more	0
"Ostomy" or other problem with self-care	10
"Ostomy" or other problem without self-care	5
Type of ostomy (self-care or other) or other problem	

Bladder Function

Continent	10
Incontinent less than once a week	5
Incontinent once/week or more, night only	5
Incontinent once/week or more, night and day	5
Indwelling catheter with self-care	10
Indwelling catheter without self-care	5
"Ostomy" or other problem, self-care	10
"Ostomy" or other problem, no self-care	5
Type of ostomy or catheter care	

PROFESSIONAL CARE PLAN*
FORM AND INSTRUCTIONS

LEVINSON POLICY INSTITUTE
Brandeis University

INSTRUCTIONS FOR PROFESSIONAL CARE PLAN

INTRODUCTION

We are interested in your professional evaluation, from the PACE (and also in some cases from having interviewed the patient or known the patient for some time), of what services this patient would need to return home and be maintained for a *six-month* period following hospital discharge. We seek to learn which types of home care services, and how much of them would be necessary to provide an adequate, safe, and dignified environment for the patient. You should *ignore* the limitations of currently available services and providers. For example, your plan *could* call for meals-on-wheels seven days per week, unlimited sitting/homemaker services, and/or physician home visits monthly. Similarly, the current cost of providing such services should not be taken into account when you select the volume of service and the type of provider. We seek your opinion of what constitutes adequate care at home for each patient, as an alternative to institutional placement. We would like your view of the home care *needs* of each patient, regardless of the types and quantities of services needed to care for the patient at home in a safe, adequate, and dignified manner.

This form is divided into four sets of services: personal care, household, nursing, and other professional care. The format remains virtually identical throughout. Thus, the wording of the questions is consistent. Similarly, use of the codes

---

*To economize on space and avoid repetition, the Professional Care Plan has been abbreviated. What remains is representative of what has been omitted. All services are listed in the appendix to Chapter 4.

is consistent. When appropriate, consideration should be given to anticipated changes in patient status over the six months following discharge. Provision is made on the form to change your selection of services and providers every three months.

For each service we will be asking:

1. Would patient need help?
2. The duration in hours and/or minutes of each episode of service.
3. How many times per week would patient need help? (In some instances, we may be asking for the number of times per month or half-year.)
4. The provider(s) you would recommend to perform a service and how many times a week each provider would perform it.

COMPLETING THE FORM

1. Most services should be prescribed in the following manner.

Starting with Personal Care Services, in answer to Question 3 on the form, CIRCLE *either* (yes) or (no) for each of the 3-month time periods.

Example:

If you feel the patient needs to be checked periodically during months 1-2-3, but not in months 4-5-6, indicate as follows:

	Months 1-2-3		*Months 4-5-6*	
Periodic Checking	(yes)	no	yes	(no)

If a service is *required* for both of the 3-month periods, complete the subsequent questions about that service for each time period. Fill in all boxes.

If a service is *not* required for one of the 3-month periods, CIRCLE the (no.) The boxes for this service, for this time, should be left blank.

If the service is not required at all, CIRCLE (no) under each time period, leave all boxes empty, and proceed to the next service.

2. The second question requires that you estimate how long each activity would take on each occasion. We seek an estimate of the *average* time each task or service would take during the relevant 3-month period(s). Each of the three boxes must be filled, indicating hours and minutes.

Example:

If you estimate that it requires 5 minutes to supervise medication, record

0		0	5

hrs.   mins.

Example:

If you estimate that heavy housework will require 4½ hrs.,

record | 4 | | 3 | 0 |

　　　　　hrs.　 mins.

3. The third question about each service asks that you estimate the number of times each service would be needed. The particular time period will vary from question to question. Usually it will be expressed as times per week, although sometimes as times per month. One exception would be for some of the "other professional services," which will be expressed as visits per six months; that is, over the full six months following discharge.

Example:

To the question how many times per week would the patient need help bathing, the response may read:

Months 1-2-3　　　　　*Months 4-5-6*

| 0 | 7 |　　　　　| 0 | 3 |

indicating a reduction of frequency over the six months time period. As two boxes are provided, any digit less than 10 should be recorded with a zero (0) preceding it.

No option exists for daily services; therefore, all prescriptions must be converted to the time period indicated (weeks, months, half-years).

Example:

If you feel the patient needs to be fed 3 times daily, but the unit is given as times per week, a | 2 | 1 | should be recorded.

Example:

For a patient receiving q.i.d. medications and requiring daily supervision in taking them, | 2 | 8 | should be recorded.

4. The final question requires that you recommend one or several providers to perform each service. We ask that you consider the immediate and/or extended family, neighbors and friends as possible providers. The general ability and willingness of this group to participate as providers is suggested on the PACE form (p. 15). Teaching the patient and/or family should be considered when appropriate.

Referring to the code sheet, list the number(s) of the provider(s) you have selected and the number of times per week you think each should contribute.

Example:

<u>Mo. 1-2-3-</u>   <u>Mo. 4-5-6</u>

P1 | 1 | 1 | | 0 | 1 | wk   P1 | 2 | 1 | | 0 | 2 | wk

P2 | 2 | 1 | | 0 | 4 | wk   P2 | 5 | 1 | | 0 | 5 | wk

P3 | 5 | 1 | | 0 | 2 | wk   P3 | 0 | 0 | | 0 | 0 | wk

The above example indicates that for the first three months an RN (code 11) should bathe the patient once a week (for the purpose of teaching the family). A home health aide (code 21) should do it four times a week, with the family (code 51) bathing the patient on the two remaining occasions. For months 4, 5, and 6, the home health aide (21) would bathe the patient twice a week and the family (51) five times a week. Again, as two boxes are provided, any digit less than 10 should have a zero (0) preceding it.

Please check that the total number of times a service is rendered by the sum of all the providers equals the total number of times a week you have indicated that service to be necessary.

In the example above, bathing would have been prescribed 7 times a week for both 3-month periods.

Form # ____ (LPI only)   PRESCRIBER'S INITIALS _____   CODE [ ]   PATIENT'S CODE [ ]

I. PERSONAL CARE SERVICES

	Months 1-2-3	Months 4-5-6	For Keypunch Only Care Card 1
Caregiving/Supervision...Continuous caregiving/supervision? (This means the patient should never be left alone.) 1) Would patient need continuous caregiving/supervision?	circle one YES NO	circle one YES NO	
(SEE PAGE 9 OF INSTRUCTIONS IF THIS SERVICE IS SELECTED.)			
2) Which providers would you recommend to give this service? How many hours per week per provider? (168 hrs. = 1 week) INSERT PROVIDER CODES	P1 [11-12] [13-15] Wk P2 [21-22] [23-24] Wk P3 [29-30] [31-32] Wk	P1 [16-17] [18-20] Wk P2 [25-26] [27-28] Wk P3 [33-34] [35-36] Wk	11-36
Periodic Checking 3) Would patient need to be checked on periodically?	circle one YES NO	circle one YES NO	
4) How much time would this activity take on each occasion?	Hrs. Mins. [37-39]	Hrs. Mins. [40-42]	
5) How many times a week would he/she need to be checked?	[43-44] Wk	[45-46] Wk	37-70

6) Which provider(s) would you recommend to provide the service? How many times per week per provider?

P1 47-48 / 49-50 Wk   51-52 / 53-54 Wk
P2 55-56 / 57-58 Wk   59-60 / 61-62 Wk
P3 63-64 / 65-66 Wk   67-68 / 69-70 Wk

71-80

Bathing

Months 1-2-3   Months 4-5-6

7) Would patient need help bathing? (That means getting to the bathroom, getting in and out of the tub or shower and washing him/herself, OR giving a spongebath)

circle one   circle one
YES   NO   YES   NO

8) How much time would this activity take on each occasion?

Hrs. Mins.   Hrs. Mins.
71-73   74-76

9) How many times a week would he/she need help to bathe?

Wk 77-78   Wk 79-80

10) Which provider(s) would you recommend to provide the service? How many times per week per provider? (Include patient and/or family teaching, if appropriate)

Card 2
11-34

P1 11-12 / 13-14 Wk   15-16 / 17-18 Wk
P2 19-20 / 21-22 Wk   23-24 / 25-26 Wk
P3 27-28 / 29-30 Wk   31-32 / 33-34 Wk

PRESCRIBER'S INITIALS _____   CODE [ ]   PATIENT'S CODE [ ]

	Months 1-2-3	Months 4-5-6	For Keypunch Only
			Card 2 cont'd
			35-68

PERSONAL CARE SERVICES CONT'D

Dressing

11) Would patient need help dressing? (Getting his/her clothes from drawers and closet, putting on clothes and shoes, and taking them off.)

	Months 1-2-3	Months 4-5-6
	circle one	circle one
	YES NO	YES NO

12) How much time would this activity take on each occasion?

	Months 1-2-3	Months 4-5-6
	Hrs. [ ] Mins. [ ]	Hrs. [ ] Mins. [ ]
	35-37	38-40

13) How many times a week would he/she need help to dress?

	Months 1-2-3	Months 4-5-6
	Wk [ ]	Wk [ ]
	41-42	43-44

14) Which provider(s) would you recommend to provide the service? How many times per week per provider? (Include patient and/or family teaching, if appropriate)

	Months 1-2-3	Months 4-5-6
P1	[ ] Wk [ ]	[ ] Wk [ ]
	45-46 47-48	49-50 51-52
P2	[ ] Wk [ ]	[ ] Wk [ ]
	53-54 55-56	57-58 59-60
P3	[ ] Wk [ ]	[ ] Wk [ ]
	61-62 63-64	65-66 67-68

Toilet

15) Would patient need help with elimination? (Using toilet, bedpan or commode, perineal care, rearranging clothing, emptying bedpan, incontinence care)

	Months 1-2-3	Months 4-5-6
	circle one	circle one
	YES NO	YES NO

16) How much time would this activity take on each occasion?

	Months 1-2-3	Months 4-5-6	For Keypunch Only
	Hrs. [ ] Mins. [ ]	Hrs. [ ] Mins. [ ]	69-78
	69-71	72-74	

Card 3
11-34

35-68

17) How many times a week would he/she need help with elimination?

	Months 1-2-3	Months 4-5-6
	Wk □ 75-76	Wk □ 77-78

18) Which provider(s) would you recommend to provide the service? How many times per week per provider? (Include patient and/or family teaching, if appropriate)

	Months 1-2-3		Months 4-5-6	
P1	11-12	Wk 13-14	15-16	Wk 17-18
P2	19-20	Wk 21-22	23-24	Wk 25-26
P3	27-28	Wk 29-30	31-32	Wk 33-34

Transferring

19) Would patient need help transferring? (That means help moving from bed to chair, from one chair to another or to a wheelchair)

Months 1-2-3	Months 4-5-6
circle one YES NO	circle one YES NO

20) How much time would this activity take on each occasion?

Months 1-2-3	Months 4-5-6
Hrs. □ Mins. □ 35-37	Hrs. □ Mins. □ 38-40

21) How many times a week would he/she need help transferring?

Months 1-2-3	Months 4-5-6
Wk □ 41-42	Wk □ 43-44

22) Which provider(s) would you recommend to provide the service? How many times per week per provider? (Include patient and/or family teaching, if appropriate)

	Months 1-2-3		Months 4-5-6	
P1	45-46	Wk 47-48	49-50	Wk 51-52
P2	53-54	Wk 55-56	57-58	Wk 59-60
P3	61-62	Wk 63-64	65-66	Wk 67-68

PRESCRIBER'S INITIALS _____

CODE [ ]   PATIENT'S CODE [   ]

PERSONAL CARE SERVICES CONT'D

Supervision of Medication

23) Would patient need someone to make sure he/she took the right medicine at the right time?

	Months 1-2-3	Months 4-5-6	For Keypunch Only
	circle one	circle one	Card 3 cont'd
	YES NO	YES NO	

24) How much time would this activity take on each occasion?

Months 1-2-3		Months 4-5-6		
Hrs. [ ] Mins. [ ]	69-71	Hrs. [ ] Mins. [ ]	72-74	69-78

25) How many times a week would he/she need help taking medicine?

Wk [ ] 75-76   Wk [ ] 77-78

26) Which provider(s) would you recommend to provide the service? How many times per week per provider? (Include patient and/or family teaching, if appropriate)

Months 1-2-3		Months 4-5-6		
P1 [ ] 11-12 Wk [ ] 13-14		P1 [ ] 15-16 Wk [ ] 17-18		Card 4
P2 [ ] 19-20 Wk [ ] 21-22		P2 [ ] 23-24 Wk [ ] 25-26		11-34
P3 [ ] 27-28 Wk [ ] 29-30		P3 [ ] 31-32 Wk [ ] 33-34		

Turning in Bed

27) Would patient need help turning in bed?

Months 1-2-3	Months 4-5-6
circle one	circle one
YES NO	YES NO

28) How much time would this activity take on each occasion?

Months 1-2-3		Months 4-5-6		
Hrs. [ ] Mins. [ ]	35-37	Hrs. [ ] Mins. [ ]	38-40	35-68

29) How many times a week would he/she need help turning in bed?

41-42 ☐ Wk

30) Which provider(s) would you recommend to provide the service? How many times per week per provider? (Include patient and/or family teaching, if appropriate)

P1 45-46 ☐   P1 49-50 ☐   43-44 ☐ Wk

P2 53-54 ☐   47-48 ☐ Wk   P2 57-58 ☐   51-52 ☐ Wk

P3 61-62 ☐   55-56 ☐ Wk   59-60 ☐ Wk

63-64 ☐ Wk   P3 65-66 ☐   67-68 ☐ Wk

69-78

Grooming

31) Would patient need help washing his/her face, cleaning teeth, combing hair, and (for men) shaving/(for women) applying makeup?

Months 1-2-3

circle one

YES   NO

Months 4-5-6

circle one

YES   NO

32) How much time would this activity take on each occasion?

69-71 Hrs. ☐ Mins. ☐

72-74 Hrs. ☐ Mins. ☐

33) How many times per week would patient need help with grooming?

75-76 ☐ Wk

77-78 ☐ Wk

34) Which provider(s) would you recommend to give the service? How many times per week per provider? (Include patient and/or family teaching, if appropriate)

P1 11-12 ☐   13-14 ☐ Wk   P1 15-16 ☐   17-18 ☐ Wk

P2 19-20 ☐   21-22 ☐ Wk   P2 23-24 ☐   25-26 ☐ Wk

P3 27-28 ☐   29-30 ☐ Wk   P3 31-32 ☐   33-34 ☐ Wk

Card 5

11-34

ONE PATIENT'S CARE PLANS BY INDIVIDUAL SERVICES, SERVICE SUBTOTALS, AND BY INDIVIDUAL CARE PLANNERS AND MEANS OF GROUPS

A sample print-out of one patient's prescribed hours. The four pages form one table. Services and service subtotals appear in the left-hand margin. Individual prescribers—physicians (MDC), discharge planners (DPC), home health planners (HHC), and the hospital planners—and means of groups head the columns. Hours prescribed by individuals and by means of groups appear in the matrix.

MONTHS: 1-6

BY PATIENT ANALYSIS OF HOURS AND MEAN HOURS
(SERVICE BY PRESCRIBER BY PATIENT)

PATIENT: 4 62 1

SERVICE:	PRESCRIBER: MDC1	MDC2	MDC3	MDC4	MDC5	MEAN MDC	DPC1	DPC2	DPC3	DPC4	DPC5	MEAN DPC
PERSONAL												
CONCARE	63.00	136.79	0.0	68.46	69.79	67.61	119.02	0.0	68.25	109.74	0.0	59.40
PERCH	0.0	0.0	2.92	0.25	0.0	0.63	0.0	2.33	0.08	0.0	73.50	15.18
BATH	1.75	1.50	2.25	1.50	0.58	1.52	2.00	1.75	0.67	5.25	0.75	2.08
DRESS	1.75	2.33	1.88	0.88	1.17	1.60	2.33	2.33	0.58	4.08	2.08	2.28
TOIL	2.92	7.00	2.42	3.50	0.38	3.24	4.42	6.00	2.92	8.75	4.04	5.22
TRANSFER	1.17	2.33	2.50	1.17	0.83	1.60	2.33	4.00	1.17	4.67	2.71	2.97
SUPERMED	0.88	0.0	1.25	0.87	0.0	0.60	1.57	1.52	0.58	0.0	0.08	0.75
TURNSED	2.92	0.87	2.50	1.17	0.58	1.61	2.92	0.87	0.58	1.75	2.92	1.81
GROOM	0.0	0.87	1.17	0.0	0.0	0.41	0.0	2.33	0.75	0.0	1.67	0.95
EATDRINK	0.0	0.0	0.0	0.0	0.0	0.0	0.0	0.0	0.0	0.0	0.0	0.0
SUBTOTAL	74.37	151.70	16.87	77.79	73.33	78.82	134.60	21.14	75.58	134.24	87.75	90.66
% OF TOTAL	74.57	80.15	39.74	67.24	80.10	----	72.38	38.56	69.74	73.96	69.53	----
HOUSE												
SHOPP	2.00	2.00	2.00	0.0	1.00	1.40	3.00	0.21	0.75	1.00	0.33	1.06
MEALPREP	7.88	10.50	4.67	7.75	5.83	7.32	14.00	10.50	7.75	21.00	6.67	11.98
TELEP	0.0	0.0	0.0	0.0	0.0	0.0	0.0	0.0	0.42	0.0	0.0	0.08
TRNSPORT	1.00	2.00	3.00	3.00	1.00	2.00	0.50	4.50	1.96	2.00	0.67	1.93
SOCIAL	7.00	7.00	5.25	14.00	3.25	7.30	7.00	5.50	12.75	8.00	18.50	10.35
LTHOUSE	1.75	3.50	3.00	3.00	1.75	2.60	10.50	2.63	1.00	7.00	2.21	4.67
HVYHOUSE	1.84	1.84	1.38	1.84	0.23	1.43	0.46	1.84	0.46	0.92	0.23	0.78
LAUNDRY	0.92	0.92	1.38	1.38	0.23	0.97	2.99	2.07	1.84	1.84	0.92	1.93
PERSNMGT	0.92	0.0	1.15	0.69	0.23	0.60	0.92	0.92	1.15	0.12	0.15	0.65
SUBTOTAL	23.31	27.76	21.83	31.66	13.52	23.62	39.37	28.17	28.08	41.88	29.69	33.44
% OF TOTAL	23.37	14.67	51.41	27.37	14.77	----	21.17	51.37	25.91	23.07	23.52	----

SERVICE:	PRESCRIBER: HHC1	HHC2	HHC3	HHC4	HHC5	MEAN HHC	MEAN CON	MDH	DPH	FNH	MEAN HOS	MEAN ALL
PERSONAL												
CONCARE	125.50	64.25	48.43	135.58	0.0	74.75	67.25	0.0	71.33	91.08	54.14	65.07
PERCH	0.0	0.0	0.0	0.0	0.0	0.0	5.27	24.50	0.0	0.0	8.17	5.75
BATH	1.50	4.38	3.38	1.50	5.00	3.15	2.25	7.00	1.75	5.25	4.67	2.65
DRESS	1.75	3.50	3.50	7.00	2.33	3.62	2.50	7.00	2.33	1.40	3.53	2.68
TOIL	4.67	3.50	3.50	4.38	3.50	4.03	4.18	14.00	1.75	5.83	7.19	4.69
TRANSFER	2.33	2.33	2.33	0.58	3.50	0.22	2.26	2.63	0.58	1.75	1.65	2.16
SUPERMED	0.0	0.53	1.17	0.0	0.0	0.35	0.57	0.53	0.0	0.58	0.39	0.54
TURNBED	3.50	0.87	2.33	1.46	0.0	1.63	1.68	0.87	0.83	0.70	0.80	1.54
GROCH	0.0	0.0	2.33	1.75	0.0	0.82	0.72	0.0	0.0	0.23	0.03	0.62
EATDRINK	0.0	0.0	0.0	0.0	0.0	0.0	0.0	0.0	0.0	0.0	0.0	0.0
SUBTOTAL	139.25	79.42	66.97	152.25	15.21	90.62	86.70	56.58	78.58	106.83	80.66	85.69
% OF TOTAL	80.08	63.92	60.64	87.11	21.25	----	----	54.34	68.49	72.42	----	----
HOUSE												
SHOPP	1.50	2.00	0.17	1.00	0.25	0.98	1.15	1.50	2.00	2.00	1.83	1.26
MEALPREP	21.00	13.13	15.75	10.50	31.50	18.38	12.56	21.00	14.00	14.00	16.33	13.19
TELEP	0.0	1.00	0.0	0.0	0.0	0.0	0.03	0.0	0.0	0.0	0.0	0.02
TRNSPORT	0.23	1.00	1.00	0.0	0.0	0.45	1.46	1.00	0.75	0.62	0.79	1.35
SOCIAL	0.0	5.00	7.00	0.0	0.0	2.40	6.68	5.00	3.00	0.0	2.67	6.01
LTHOUSE	2.00	10.50	7.00	2.00	14.00	7.10	4.79	3.50	7.00	7.00	5.83	4.96
HVYHOUSE	0.69	1.84	0.46	0.0	1.84	0.97	1.05	0.23	0.46	0.46	0.33	0.95
LAUNDRY	1.38	0.92	0.92	0.46	1.84	1.10	1.33	0.92	0.35	1.38	0.88	1.26
PERSNMGT	0.46	0.92	0.46	0.23	0.92	0.60	0.62	0.92	0.0	0.46	0.46	0.59
SUBTOTAL	27.26	35.31	32.76	14.19	50.35	31.97	29.68	34.07	27.56	25.92	29.18	29.59
% OF TOTAL	15.68	28.42	29.66	8.12	70.36	----	----	32.72	24.02	17.57	----	----

PRESCRIBER:

SERVICE:	MDC1	MDC2	MDC3	MDC4	MDC5	MEAN MDC	DPC1	DPC2	DPC3	DPC4	DPC5	MEAN DPC
NURSE												
DCHELBLA	0.0	1.67	0.0	0.0	0.0	0.33	0.0	0.0	0.0	0.0	0.0	0.0
DECUB	0.0	0.0	0.0	0.0	0.0	0.0	2.92	0.0	0.0	0.0	0.0	0.58
WOUND	0.0	0.0	0.0	0.0	0.0	0.0	0.0	0.0	0.0	0.0	0.0	0.0
EYECARE	0.0	0.0	0.0	0.0	0.0	0.0	0.0	0.0	0.0	0.0	0.0	0.0
BLADIRG	0.0	0.0	0.0	0.0	0.0	0.0	0.0	0.0	0.0	0.0	0.0	0.0
SUCHPT	0.0	0.0	0.0	0.0	0.0	0.0	0.0	0.0	0.0	0.0	0.0	0.0
IKNIFFB	0.0	0.0	0.0	0.0	0.0	0.0	0.0	0.0	0.0	0.0	0.0	0.0
OTONTHER	2.00	0.0	0.0	0.0	0.0	0.0	0.0	0.0	0.0	0.0	0.0	0.0
RCMX	0.0	0.25	0.0	0.0	1.33	0.67	0.83	1.75	0.0	1.75	2.25	0.97
NUTRDIET	0.0	0.0	0.25	0.25	2.63	0.67	0.0	0.63	0.0	0.0	0.05	0.49
MEDADMIN	0.0	0.0	0.0	0.0	0.0	0.0	0.0	0.0	0.0	0.0	0.0	0.0
MONWISIN	0.0	0.0	0.0	0.25	0.29	0.11	0.07	0.58	0.37	0.37	1.08	0.49
FOOTCARE	0.0	0.0	0.0	0.0	0.0	0.0	0.33	0.0	0.25	1.17	0.33	0.42
TCHOTHER	0.0	0.0	0.0	0.0	0.0	0.0	0.03	0.83	0.33	0.0	0.0	0.26
NUROTHER	0.0	0.0	0.0	0.0	0.0	0.0	0.23	0.0	1.75	0.0	0.58	0.51
SUBTOTAL	2.00	1.92	0.25	0.50	4.29	1.79	4.46	3.83	2.71	3.28	4.30	3.72
% OF TOTAL	2.01	1.01	0.59	0.43	4.69	----	2.40	6.99	2.50	1.81	3.41	----
OTH PRO												
PRIMED	0.04	0.02	0.04	0.02	0.12	0.05	0.04	0.12	0.04	0.06	0.04	0.06
SPECMED	0.02	0.05	0.06	0.15	0.06	0.07	0.12	0.06	0.06	0.04	0.08	0.07
DENTIST	0.0	0.0	0.0	0.02	0.0	0.00	0.02	0.02	0.02	0.06	0.02	0.01
PODIAT	0.0	0.0	0.02	0.02	0.0	0.01	0.0	0.0	0.0	0.0	0.0	0.02
PT	0.0	6.90	2.53	5.06	0.23	2.95	7.13	0.0	1.84	1.96	4.03	2.99
OT	0.0	0.92	0.0	0.46	0.0	0.28	0.0	0.0	0.06	0.0	0.0	0.01
PSYCH	0.0	0.0	0.86	0.0	0.0	0.17	0.23	1.50	0.0	0.0	0.31	0.41
SUBTOTAL	0.06	7.90	3.51	5.74	0.40	3.52	7.54	1.69	2.01	2.11	4.47	3.56
% OF TOTAL	0.06	4.17	8.27	4.96	0.44	----	4.05	3.08	1.86	1.16	3.54	----
TOTAL	99.74	189.28	42.46	115.69	91.55	107.75	185.96	54.83	108.33	161.51	126.20	131.38

PRESCRIBER:

SERVICE:	HHC1	HHC2	HHC3	HHC4	HHC5	MEAN HHC	MEAN CON	MDH	DPH	FNH	MEAN HOS	MEAN ALL
NURSE												
BONELBLA	0.25	0.0	0.0	2.00	0.0	0.45	0.26	0.0	0.0	0.0	0.0	0.22
DECUB	0.0	0.0	0.0	0.0	0.0	0.0	0.19	0.0	0.0	0.0	0.0	0.16
WOUND	0.0	0.0	0.0	0.0	0.0	0.0	0.0	0.0	0.0	0.0	0.0	0.0
EYECARE	0.0	0.0	0.0	0.0	0.0	0.0	0.0	0.0	0.0	0.0	0.0	0.0
BLADIRG	0.0	0.0	0.0	0.0	0.0	0.0	0.0	0.0	0.0	0.0	0.0	0.0
SUCHPT	0.0	0.0	0.0	0.0	0.0	0.0	0.0	0.0	0.0	0.0	0.0	0.0
INHIPFB	0.0	0.0	0.0	0.0	0.0	0.0	0.0	0.0	0.0	0.0	0.0	0.0
OTOXTHER	0.88	0.0	0.0	0.0	0.0	0.47	0.71	0.0	0.0	2.63	0.88	0.73
ROMX	0.13	1.50	1.75	0.0	0.0	0.42	0.53	0.50	0.0	0.87	0.46	0.52
NUTRDIET	0.0	0.25	0.58	1.75	0.0	0.47	0.16	0.0	0.0	0.0	0.0	0.13
MEDADMIN	0.50	0.0	0.75	1.50	0.0	0.65	0.42	0.0	0.0	0.0	0.0	0.42
MONVISIN	0.0	0.50	1.25	0.0	0.0	0.48	0.30	0.0	0.75	0.50	0.42	0.31
FOOTCARE	0.0	1.17	0.0	1.00	0.0	0.20	0.15	0.0	0.0	1.17	0.39	0.17
TCROTHER	0.0	0.0	0.0	0.0	0.0	0.0	0.0	0.0	0.75	0.0	0.25	0.0
NUROTHER	2.63	1.54	1.00	1.00	0.73	1.33	0.63	0.0	5.25	2.03	2.43	0.93
SUBTOTAL	4.38	4.96	5.33	7.25	0.73	4.53	3.35	0.50	6.75	7.20	4.82	3.59
% OF TOTAL	2.52	3.99	4.83	4.15	1.02	----	----	0.48	5.88	4.88	----	----
OTH PRO												
PRIMED	0.12	0.02	0.12	0.12	0.06	0.08	0.06	0.04	0.12	0.06	0.07	0.06
SPECMED	0.0	0.06	0.06	0.06	0.04	0.04	0.06	0.04	0.0	0.02	0.02	0.05
DENTIST	0.0	0.0	0.02	0.0	0.0	0.00	0.01	0.0	0.0	0.0	0.0	0.01
PCDIAT	0.0	0.0	0.12	0.0	0.0	0.02	0.02	0.0	0.0	0.02	0.01	0.01
PT	2.30	4.49	3.68	0.92	5.18	3.31	3.08	12.89	1.73	7.48	7.36	3.80
OT	0.12	0.0	0.69	0.0	0.0	0.16	0.15	0.0	0.0	0.0	0.0	0.12
PSYCH	0.46	0.0	0.69	0.0	0.0	0.23	0.27	0.0	0.0	0.0	0.0	0.22
SUBTOTAL	2.99	4.56	5.37	1.09	5.27	3.86	3.65	12.97	1.84	7.58	7.46	4.28
% OF TOTAL	1.72	3.67	4.86	0.63	7.37	----	----	12.45	1.61	5.14	----	----
TOTAL	173.88	124.25	110.43	174.78	71.57	130.98	123.37	104.12	114.73	147.52	122.12	123.16

HOURS OF CARE BY SERVICE AND PROVIDER CATEGORIES

Hours of Care Prescribed by the Average of Professionals: Agreement and Distribution by Service: A) Personal Care.

| Service | Hours of Care | | | Percentage of Total | Percentage of Subtotal |
	Mean	Standard Deviation[a]	Coefficient of Variation[a]		
Continuous care	63.2	46.4	100.5%	50.6%	73.8%
Periodic checking	2.0	5.5	268.8	1.6	2.3
Bathing	2.8	1.8	70.3	2.2	3.3
Dressing	3.0	1.8	80.9	2.4	3.5
Toilet	4.9	3.2	86.5	3.9	5.7
Transferring	2.7	1.9	113.6	2.2	3.2
Supervision of medications	1.4	1.2	121.6	1.1	1.6
Turning in bed	1.3	1.4	184.7	1.0	1.5
Grooming	2.0	1.4	120.2	1.6	2.3
Eating–Drinking	2.4	1.9	181.5	1.9	2.8
Subtotal personal care	85.6	45.8	67.6%	68.6%	100.0%

a. Coefficient of variation = individual patient's standard deviation across care planners, divided by mean across care planners, averaged over fifty patients.

Hours of Care Prescribed by the Average of Professionals:
Agreement and Distribution of Service: B) Household.

| Service | Hours of Care | | | | |
	Mean	Standard Deviation	Coefficient of Variation	Percentage of Total	Percentage of Subtotal
Shopping	1.7	0.9	52.1%	1.4%	5.7%
Meal preparation	13.8	7.6	56.5	11.1	46.5
Telephone	0.1	0.2	278.8	0.1	0.3
Transportation	1.6	1.6	107.5	1.3	5.4
Socialization	3.7	4.0	104.3	3.0	12.5
Light housework	5.1	3.7	72.7	4.1	17.2
Heavy housework	1.2	0.9	74.5	1.0	4.0
Laundry	1.8	1.2	64.3	1.4	6.1
Management of personal affairs	0.7	0.6	90.0	0.5	2.4
Subtotal Household	29.7	12.3	41.2%	23.8%	100.0%

Hours of Care Prescribed by the Average of Professionals:
Agreement and Distribution by Service: C) Nursing.

| Service[a] | Hours of Care | | | | |
	Mean	Standard Deviation	Coefficient of Variation	Percentage of Total	Percentage of Subtotal
Bowel and bladder care	1.3	1.7	212.1%	1.0%	17.6%
Decubitus care	0.6	0.9	266.6	0.5	8.1
Range-of-motion exercises	0.9	1.3	192.3	·0.7	12.2
Nutrition–Diet	0.9	1.5	209.7	0.7	12.2
Administration of medications	0.8	1.1	187.4	0.8	10.8
Monitoring vital signs	0.7	0.7	115.4	6.6	9.5
Other nursing	2.2	NA	NA	1.8	29.7
Subtotal nursing	7.4	5.7	87.5%	5.9%	100.0%

a. Selected nursing services only.

Hours of Care Prescribed by the Average of Professionals: Agreement and Distribution by Service: D) Medical–Therapeutic.

	Hours of Care				
Service	Mean	Standard Deviation	Coefficient of Variation	Percentage of Total	Percentage of Subtotal
Primary medical care	0.08	0.05	68.5%	0.1%	3.8%
Specialist medical care	0.02	0.03	225.3	a	1.0
Dentist	0.01	0.01	230.3	a	0.5
Podiatrist	0.01	0.02	183.9	a	0.5
Physical therapy	1.4	1.4	142.6	1.0	66.7
Occupational therapy	0.3	0.5	214.8	0.2	14.3
Psychotherapy	0.2	0.4	211.2	0.2	9.5
Subtotal Medical–therapeutic	2.1	1.8	100.3%	1.7%	100.0%

a. Less than 0.05 percent.

Hours of Care Prescribed by the Average of Professionals: Agreement and Distribution by Selected Providers.

	Hours of Care			
Provider	Mean	Standard Deviation	Coefficient of Variation	Percentage of Total
Registered nurse	2.1	4.7	185.2%	1.7%
LPN	3.3	8.1	343.7	2.6
Homemaker	5.9	10.9	225.9	4.7
Personal care attendant	32.0	42.4	162.2	25.6
Social worker	0.2	0.4	232.9	0.2
Sitting service	7.5	16.3	270.1	6.0
Companion	0.6	2.4	415.3	0.5
Resident family	33.7	26.6	152.6	27.0
Resident friend	0.1	0.5	403.9	0.1
Nonresident family	5.1	6.6	152.7	4.1
Nonresident friend	1.3	2.0	199.8	1.0
Total	124.8	48.8	41.7%	95.2%

**Hours of Care Prescribed by the Average of Professionals:
Agreement and Distribution by Provider Subtotals.**

Provider Subtotals	Mean Hours	Coefficient of Variation in Hours	Percentage of Total
Medical	0.1	75.1%	0.1%
Nursing	5.4	189.6	4.3
Care	66.1	69.6	52.9
Support	9.2	193.7	7.4
Therapy	1.9	119.8	1.5
Miscellaneous	1.6	158.3	1.3
Unpaid–Resident	33.9	157.1	27.2
–Nonresident	6.8	119.8	5.4
–total	40.7	82.8	32.6
Paid	84.2	56.8	67.4
Skilled	7.1	142.0	5.7
Unskilled	117.8	44.9	94.3
Total	124.8	41.7%	100.0%

MEAN HOURS BY CARE PLANNER
Service Subtotals and Total

Care Planner[b]	Mean Hours[a] Prescribed For:				
	Personal Care	Household	Nursing	Medical–Therapeutic	Total
MDC-1	97	34	4.8	2.5	138
-2	126	24	3.9	1.7	156
-3	35	26	9.6	3.6	74
-4	104	22	8.0	3.7	138
-5	110	18	4.1	1.2	134
$\bar{X}$ MDC	95	25	5.5	2.5	128
DPC-1	95	33	8.6	1.8	138
-2	31	30	5.8	1.3	69
-3	70	24	3.3	1.0	98
-4	116	29	9.5	1.1	155
-5	92	25	10.6	2.3	130
$\bar{X}$ DPC	81	28	7.6	1.5	118
HHC-1	86	28	7.1	1.9	123
-2	105	35	12.7	4.2	157
-3	51	35	11.7	2.7	101
-4	122	17	4.4	0.6	144
-5	24	50	2.9	1.3	79
$\bar{X}$ HHC	78	33	7.8	2.1	121
$\bar{X}$ CON	84	29	7.0	2.0	122
MD–H	102	39	7.7	2.9	152
DP–H	101	34	10.0	2.3	148
FN–H	90	37	9.9	2.4	139
$\bar{X}$ HOSP	98	37	9.2	2.5	146
Total	87	30	7.4	2.1	125

a. Across fifty patients.
b. MDC = physician consultant;
   DPC = discharge planner consultant;
   HHC = home health consultant;
   CON = Consultant;
   MDH = hospital physician;
   DPH = discharge planner;
   FNH = floor nurse.

BIBLIOGRAPHY

Aging Program, National Association of Counties Research Foundation. "A Report on Services to the Elderly: Security." Washington, D.C.: National Association of Counties Research Foundation, 1977.

Allardt, Erik. "On the Relationship Between Objective and Subjective Predicaments." Research Report no. 16. Helsinki: Research Group for Comparative Sociology, University of Helsinki, 1977.

American Foundation for the Blind. *Washington Report*, December 1977.

American Public Welfare Association. "Report on Long Term Care." Washington, D.C.: American Public Welfare Association, November 1978.

Anderson, Nancy N.; Sharon K. Patten; and Jay N. Greenberg. "A Comparison of In-home and Nursing Home Care for Older Persons in Minnesota." U.S. Administration on Aging Project no. 90-A-682. Minneapolis: H.H. Humprey Institute, University of Minnesota, June 1980.

Annas, George J. "Homebirth: Autonomy vs. Safety." *Hastings Center Report* 8, no. 4 (August 1978).

Applied Management Sciences. "Evaluation of Personal Care Organizations and Other In-Home Alternatives to Nursing Home Care for the Elderly and Long-term Disabled." Final Report and Executive Summary (Revised), Contract HEW-OS-74-294. Silver Spring, Maryland: AMS, 1 May 1976.

Arluke, Arnold, and John Peterson. "Old Age as Illness: Notes on Accidental Medicalization." Paper delivered at the annual meeting of the Society for Applied Anthropology, San Diego, California, April 5-9, 1977.

Bachrach, Leona L. "Deinstitutionalization: An Analytical Review and Sociological Perspective." National Institute of Mental Health, ser. D, no. 4, DHEW Pub. no. (ADM) 76-351. Washington, D.C.: Government Printing Office, 1976.

Barney, Jane Lockwood. "Community Presence as a Key to Quality of Life in Nursing Homes." *American Journal of Public Health* 64, no. 3 (March 1974): 265–68.

_____. "The Prerogative of Choice in Long-term Care." *The Gerontologist* 17, no. 4 (August, 1977): 309–14.

Bassuk, Ellen L., and Samuel Gerson. "Deinstitutionalization and Mental Health Services." *Scientific American* 238, no. 2 (February 1978): 46–53.

Battelle Human Affairs Research Centers. "Evaluation of the Outcomes of Nursing Home Care." NTIS PB 266-301. Prepared for the National Center for Health Services Research, Seattle: Battelle, October 1976.

Bay Area Consortium. *Final Report of the Homemaker-Chore Study*. Berkeley: University of California School of Social Welfare, September, 1977.

Beatrice, Dennis F. "Case Management: A Policy Option for Long-term Care." In James J. Callahan, Jr. and Stanley S. Wallack, eds., *Reforming the Long-term Care System*, ch. 6. Lexington, Mass.: D.C. Heath, 1981.

Beckman, Alan C.; Linda S. Noelker; and Debra David. "PEER REVIEW: Overt and Covert Factors in the Decision to Institutionalize." Cleveland: Benjamin Rose Institute, 1977. Paper presented at the 1977 meeting of the Gerontological Society.

Belknap, Ivan, and John G. Steinle. *The Community and Its Hospitals*. Syracuse, N.Y.: Syracuse University Press, 1963.

Bell, William G. *Community Care for the Elderly: An Alternative to Institutionalization*. Tallahassee: Program in Social Policy and the Aging, Florida State University, June 1971.

Benedict, Robert. "The Family and Long Term Care Alternatives." Address to the 1978 Groves Conference on Marriage and the Family, Washington, D.C., April 28, 1978.

Benton, Bill; Tracey Field; and Rhona Millar. "State and Area Agency on Aging Intervention in Title XX." Working Paper 0990–24. Washington, D.C.: The Urban Institute, December 1977.

Bentsen, Lloyd. United States Senate Bill 2591. 94th Congress.

Berg, Robert L.; Francis E. Browning; John G. Hill; and Walter Wenkert. "Assessing the Health Care Needs of the Aged." *Health Services Research* 5, no. 1 (Spring 1970): 36–59.

Bigot, Arthur. "Protective Services for Older People: A Reanalysis of a Controversial Demonstration Project." Paper presented at the 31st Scientific Meeting of the Gerontological Society, Dallas, 17 November 1978.

Binstock, Robert H. "Interest Group Liberalism and the Politics of Aging." *The Gerontologist* 12, no. 3 (Autumn 1972): 265–80.

Block, L. "Hospital and Other Institutional Facilities and Services." 1939, *Vital Statistics*, Special Reports 13, nos. 1–57. Washington, D.C.: U.S. Bureau of the Census, 1942.

Bradshaw, Jonathan. "The Concept of Social Need." *New Society* 30 (March 1972): 640–44.

Branch, Laurence G., and Floyd J. Fowler, Jr. *The Health Care Needs of the Elderly and Chronically Disabled in Massachusetts*. Boston: Survey Research Program of the University of Massachusetts, March 1975.

Branch, Laurence G. *Understanding the Health and Social Service Needs of People Over Age 65*. Boston: Survey Research Program of the University of Massachusetts, 1977.

Brody, Elaine M. "The Aging and the Family." *Annals* of the American Academy of Political and Social Sciences. *Planning for the Elderly* 438 (July 1978): 13–26.

Brody, Stanley J. "Health Care for Older Americans: The Alternatives Issue." Testimony before the U.S. Senate Special Committee on Aging, 17 May 1977.

Brook, Robert H., and Francis A. Appel. "Quality of Care Assessment: Choosing a Method for Peer Review." *New England Journal of Medicine* 228, no. 25 (21 June 1973): 1323–29.

Burton, Richard M.; William W. Damon; and David C. Dellinger. "Estimating the Impact of Health Services in a Community." *Behavioral Science* 21 (1976): 478–89.

Butler, Patricia R. "Financing Non-institutional Long-term Care Services for the Elderly and Chronically Ill: Alternatives to Nursing Homes." *Clearinghouse Review* 13, no. 5 (September 1979): 335–76.

Callahan, James J., Jr. "The Channeling Demonstration: Summary Statement of Issues, Environment, Intervention, and Outcome." Waltham, Mass.: Levinson Policy Institute, Brandeis University, March 1981.

_____. "Single Agency Option for Long-term Care." In James J. Callahan, Jr. and Stanley S. Wallack, eds., *Reforming the Long-term Care System*, ch. 9. Lexington, Mass.: D.C. Heath, 1981.

Campbell, Donald T., and Julian C. Stanley. *Experimental and Quasi-Experimental Designs for Research*. Chicago: Rand McNally, 1966.

Carlson, Rick J. *The End of Medicine*. New York: Wiley, 1975.

Casscells, Ward; Arno Schoenberger; and Thomas B. Graboys. "Interpretation by Physicians of Clinical Laboratory Results." *New England Journal of Medicine* 299, no. 18 (2 November 1978): 999–1001.

Cochrane, A.L. *Effectiveness and Efficiency*. London: Nuffield Provincial Hospital Trust, 1972.

Cohn, Victor. "Science Comes to Medicine – Slowly." *Technology Review*, December 1974, pp. 8–9.

Commonwealth of Massachusetts. *Report of the Long-term Task Force*. Boston: Office of State Health Planning, August 1977. (Mimeo.)

Comptroller General of the United States. "Federal Fire Safety Requirements Do Not Insure Life Safety in Nursing Home Fires." Report to The Congress, MWD–76–136. Washington, D.C.: General Accounting Office, 3 June 1976.

_____. "Home Health–The Need for a National Policy to Better Provide for the Elderly." Report to the Congress, HRD–78–19. Washington, D.C.: General Accounting Office, 30 December 1977.

_____. "History of the Rising Costs of the Medicare and Medicaid Programs and Attempts to Control these Costs: 1966-1975." Washington, D.C.: General Accounting Office, 11 February 1976.

_____. Letter to Rep. Edward I. Koch. MWO–76–30, B–164031 (3), 17 September 1975.

Congressional Budget Office. *Long-Term Care: Actuarial Cost Estimates.* Washington, D.C.: Government Printing Office, August 1977.

_____. *Long-Term Care for the Elderly and Disabled.* Washington, D.C.: Government Printing Office, February 1977.

Connelly, Kathleen; Philip K. Cohen; and Diana Chapman Walsh. "Periodic Medical Review: Assessing the Quality and Appropriateness of Care in Skilled Nursing Facilities." *New England Journal of Medicine* 296, no. 15 (14 April 1977): 878–80.

Corwin, E.H.L. *The American Hospital.* New York: Commonwealth Fund, 1946.

"Cost Analysis: Home Health Care as an Alternative to Institutional Care." Kalamazoo, Michigan: Homemakers Upjohn, October 1975.

Costello, J.P., and G.M. Tanaka. "Mortality and Morbidity in Long-term Institutional Care of the Aged." *Journal of the American Geriatric Society* 9 (1961): 959 ff.

Council on Wage and Price Stability. *The Complex Puzzle of Rising Health Care Costs.* Washington, D.C.: Executive Office of the President, December 1976.

Craig, John. "Cost Issues in Home Health Care." In Marie Callender and Judy La Vor, *Home Health Development, Problems, and Potential.* Washington, D.C.: Disability and Long-term Care Study, Office of the Assistant Secretary for Planning and Evaluation, Department of Health, Education and Welfare, April 1975.

Cronbach, Lee J. "Test 'Reliability': Its Meaning and Determination." *Psychometrika* 12, no. 1 (March, 1947): 1–16.

Davis, Carolyne K. "Medicaid Action Transmittal on Title XX, Social Security Act: Decisions on Reducing Bias Towards Institutional Care." Transmittal no. 82–8. Washington, D.C.: Health Care Financing Administration, May 1982.

Davis, Marcella Z. "The Organizational-Interactional Structure of Patient Participation in Continuity of Care: A Framework for Staff Intervention." Paper presented at the 30th Annual Scientific Meeting of the Gerontological Society, San Francisco, November 1977.

Davis, Michael M. *Clinics, Hospitals, and Health Centers.* New York: Harpers, 1927.

Delany, Carol A., and Kathleen F. Davies. *Nursing Home Ombudsman Report: The Pennsylvania Experience.* Harrisburg: Pennsylvania Advocates for Better Care, January 1979.

Demlo, Linda K.; Paul M. Campbell; and Sarah Spaght Brown. "Reliability of Information Abstracted from Patients' Medical Records." *Medical Care* 16, no. 12 (December 1978): 995–1005.

Department of Health, Education and Welfare. "Control Medicaid Cost Increases for Expensive Institutional Long Term Care." Memorandum for July 14, 1978 Briefing, Major Initiative: Long-term Care/Community Services, app. 6.

_____. "Critical Review of Research on Long-term Care Alternatives Sponsored by the Dept. of HEW." Washington, D.C.: Office of the Assistant Secretary for Planning and Evaluation, DHEW, June 1977.

_____. "Home Health Care: Report on the Regional Public Hearings." Washington, D.C.: DHEW, 29 October 1975.

Diamond, Larry M., and David E. Berman. "The Social/Health Maintenance Organization: A Single Entry, Prepaid, Long-term Care Delivery System." In James J. Callahan, Jr. and Stanley S. Wallack, eds., *Reforming the Long-term Care System*, ch. 8. Lexington, Mass.: D.C. Heath, 1981.

Dibner, Andrew S. Personal communication, 12 February 1979.

Doherty, Neville; J. Segal; and Barbara Hicks. "Alternatives to Institutionalization for the Aged." *Aged Care and Services Review* 1, no. 1 (1978): 1-16.

Duke University Center for the Study of Aging and Human Development. *Multidimensional Functional Assessment: The OARS Methodology*. Durham, N.C.: Duke University Center for the Study of Aging and Human Development. 1978.

Dunlop, Burton D. "Expanded Home-based Care for the Elderly: Solution or Pipe Dream?" *American Journal of Public Health* 70, no. 5 (May 1980): 514-19.

Dunn, Carl V., and David W. Conrath. "Primary Care: Clinical Judgment and Reliability." *New York State Journal of Medicine* 77, no. 4 (April 1977): 748-54.

Dupuis, Francois. "France: Restoring Dignity to Death." *Washington Post*, 23 May 1974.

Ennis, Bruce J., and Thomas R. Litwack. "Psychiatry and the Presumption of Expertise: Flipping Coins in the Courtroom." *California Law Review* 62 (1974): 693-752.

Etzioni, Amitai; Alfred J. Kahn; and Sheila B. Kamerman. "Public Management of Health and Home Care for the Aged and Disabled." Position Paper. New York: Center for Policy Research, January 1975.

Federal Council on the Aging. *Annual Report to the President-1976*. Washington, D.C.: Government Printing Office, 1977.

Ferrari, Nelida A. "Freedom of Choice." *Social Work* 8, no. 4 (October 1963): 104-06.

Foley, Senator Daniel J. Senate Bill 575, Massachusetts State Senate, 1975.

Foley, William J., and Donald P. Schneider. "A Comparison of the Level of Care Predictions of Six Long-term Care Patient Assessment Systems." *American Journal of Public Health* 70, no. 11 (November 1980): 1152-61.

Friedman, Susan Rosenfeld; Leonard Kaye; and Sharon Farago. "Maximizing the Quality of Homecare Services for the Elderly." Paper presented at the 30th Scientific Meeting of the Gerontological Society, San Francisco, 21 November 1977.

Gans, Herbert. *The Urban Villagers*. New York: The Free Press, 1962.

Garen, Wendy; Monica Lindeman; Leslie Lareau; and Leonard Herman. "Alternatives to Institutionalization: An Annotated Research Bibliography on Housing and Service for the Aged." Urbana-Champaign, Illinois: Housing Research and Development. University of Illinois, July 1976.

Gerson, Elihu M., and Anselm L. Straus. "Time for Living: Problems in Chronic Illness Care." *Social Policy* 6, no. 3 (November-December 1975).

Gibson, Robert M., and Charles R. Fisher. "National Health Expenditures, Fiscal Year 1977." *Social Security Bulletin* 41, no. 7 (July 1978): 1-18.

Gibson, Robert M., and Daniel R. Waldo. "National Health Expenditures, 1980." *Health Care Financing Review* 3, no. 1 (September 1981): 1-54.

Glazer, Nathan. "The Attack on the Professions." *Commentary* 66, no. 5 (November 1978): 34–41.

Granger, Carl V.; Gary L. Albrecht; and Byron B. Hamilton. "Outcomes of Comprehensive Medical Evaluation: Measurement with the Barthel Index and the PULSES Profile." Providence, R.I.: Brown University School of Medicine, 1978.

Granger, Carl V.; Marilyn Kaplan; Richard H. Fortinsky; and Donna A. Dryer. "Long-Term care: Evaluation and Proposed Model for Delivery of Services to Chronically Ill People in the Metropolitan Providence Area." Providence, R.I.: Metropolitan Nursing and Health Services Association, 31 March 1978.

Greenberg, Jay. "The Determinants of Bias in Observational Studies: A Simulation Study and a Long-Term Care Example." Ph.D. dissertation, Harvard School of Public Health, Boston, 1978.

Guttman, David. "Seekers, Takers, and Users – The Elderly as Decision Makers." Paper presented at the 30th Scientific Meeting of the Gerontological Society, San Francisco, November 1977.

Hamburg, David A., and Sarah Spaght Brown. "The Science Base and Social Context of Health Maintenance: An Overview." *Science* 200, no. 4344 (26 May 1978): 847–49.

Health Care Financing Administration. *Long-term Care: Backgrounds and Future Directions.* HCFA Pub. no. 81–20047. Washington, D.C.: HCFA, January 1981.

_____. "New Directions for Skilled Nursing and Intermediate Care Facilities." Notice of Public Meetings. n.d.

_____. *Research and Statistics Note* no. 2, June 1978.

_____. "Long Term Care Quality Assurance." Memorandum, 24 June 1978. (Draft.)

_____. "Memorandum for July 14, 1978 Briefing, Major Initiative: Long-term Care/Community Services," app. 9. Washington, D.C.: HCFA, 1978.

Health Policy Group, Commonwealth of Massachusetts. "Health Care Expenditures in Massachusetts: 1978 Update." White Paper. Boston: Office of State Health Planning, Massachusetts Department of Public Health, June 9, 1978. (Multilith.)

Holahan, John, and Bruce Stuart. "The Extent and Cost of Unnecessary and Inappropriate Utilization." In *Controlling Medicaid Utilization Patterns* vol. 2, ch. 2. Washington, D.C.: Urban Institute, 1977.

Holmberg, R. Hopkins, and Nancy N. Anderson. "Implications of Ownership for Nursing Home Care." Paper presented to the Medical Care Section, American Public Health Association, Miami Beach, 23 October 1967.

Hospital Care Commission. *Hospital Care in the United States.* New York: Commonwealth Fund, 1947.

Hudson, Robert B. "The 'Graying' of the Federal Budget and Its Consequences for Old-age Policy." *The Gerontologist* 18, no. 5, pt. 1 (October 1978): 428–40.

Illich, Ivan. *Medical Nemesis.* New York: Pantheon, 1976.

Institute for Gerontology, University of Michigan. "Pennsylvania Nursing Home Relocation Program, June 1973–June 1975, Part I: Program Activities." Report prepared for the Pennsylvania Department of Public Welfare. Ann Arbor: Institute for Gerontology, October 1975.

Institute of Medicine. *The Elderly and Functional Dependency: A Policy Statement.* Washington, D.C.: National Academy of Sciences, 1977.

Isaacs, Bernard; Maureen Livingstone; and Yvonne Neville. *Survival of the Unfittest: A Study of Geriatric Patients in Glasgow.* London: Routledge and Kegan Paul, 1972.

Jones, Ellen W.; Barbara J. McNitt; and Eleanor M. McKnight. *Patient Classification for Long-term Care: User's Manual.* DHEW Pub. no. HRA 74–3107. Washington, D.C.: Bureau of Health Services Research and Evaluation, December, 1973.

Jones, Priscilla Pitt, and Kenneth J. Jones. "Costs of Ideal Services to the Developmentally Disabled Under Varying Levels of Adequacy." Waltham, Mass.: Heller School, Brandeis University, 1 July 1976.

Kane, Robert L.; Lou Ann Jorgensen; Barbara Teteberg; and Jean Kuwahara. "Is Good Nursing-Home Care Feasible?" *Journal of the American Medical Association* 235, no. 5 (2 February 1976).

Kane, Robert L., and Rosalie A. Kane. "Care of the Aged: Old Problems in Need of New Solutions." *Science* 200, no. 4344 (26 May 1978): 913–19.

Karnes, Liz. "Alternatives to Institutionalization for the Aged: An Overview and Bibliography." Monticello, Illinois: Council of Planning Librarians Exchange Bibliography no. 877, September 1975.

Kasl, Stanislav V. "Physical and Mental Health Effects of Involuntary Relocation and Institutionalization on the Elderly—A Review." *American Journal of Public Health* 62, no. 3 (March 1972): 377–84.

Kasschau, Patricia Lee, and Vern L. Bengston. "The New American Dilemma: Decision-makers View Aging and Social Policy." Los Angeles: University of Southern California, Andrus Gerontology Center, August, 1977.

Kastenbaum, Robert, and Sandra E. Candy. "The 4% Fallacy: A Methodological and Empirical Critique of Extended Care Facility Population Statistics." *International Journal of Aging and Human Development* 4, no. 1 (1973): 15–21.

Katz, Sidney; Amasa B. Ford; Thomas D. Downs; Mary Adams; and Dorothy I. Rusby. "Effects of Continued Care: A Study of Chronic Illness in the Home." DHEW Pub. no. (HSM) 73–3010. Washington, D.C.: National Center for Health Services Research and Development, December 1972.

Katz, Sidney; Laura Halstead; and Mary Wierenga. "A Medical Perspective of Team Care." In Sylvia Sherwood, ed. *Long-term Care: A Handbook for Researchers, Planners, and Providers,* pp. 213–52. New York: Spectrum, 1975.

Keith, Pat M. "A Preliminary Investigation of the Role of the Public Health Nurse in Evaluation of Services for the Aged." *American Journal of Public Health* 66, no. 4 (April 1976): 379–81.

Kent, Donald P. "Aging-Fact or Fancy." *The Gerontologist* 5, no. 2 (June 1955): 51–56.

Kessner, David M. "Quality Assessment and Assurance: Early Signs of Cognitive Dissonance." *New England Journal of Medicine* 298, no. 7 (16 February 1978): 381–86.

Kihss, Peter. "Nursing Home Audits Find Overpayments." *New York Times*, 20 March 1978.

_____. "Point System of Reclassifying Nursing-Home Patients Is Under Attack." *New York Times*, 20 December 1977.

Kinoy, Susan K. "Discussion of Problems Concerning the Selection of Home Attendants by Patients or Their Families." Testimony before the United States Senate Special Committee on Aging, Washington, D.C., 16 May 1977.

Kline, Janet. Letter to the author from Legislative Analyst, Education and Public Welfare Division, Congressional Research Service, Library of Congress, 5 March 1976.

Koch, Representative Edward. United States House of Representatives Bill 10422, 94th Congress.

Koran, Lorrin M. "The Reliability of Clinical Methods, Data, and Judgments." *New England Journal of Medicine* 293, no. 13 (20 October 1975): 695–701.

Laurie, William F. "Employing the Duke OARS Methodology in Cost Comparisons: Home Services and Institutionalization." In *Multidimensional Functional Assessment: The OARS Methodology*, 2nd ed., pp. 110–20. Durham, N.C.: Center for the Study of Aging and Human Development of Duke University, 1978.

LaVor, Judith. "Long-Term Care: A Challenge to Service System." rev. ed., app. A. Washington, D.C.: Office of the Assistant Secretary for Planning and Evaluation, DHEW, April 1977. (Photo-offset.)

LaVor, Judith, and Marie Callender. "Home Health Cost Effectiveness: What Are We Measuring?" *Medical Care* 14, no. 10 (October 1976): 866–72.

Lawson, Ian R. "The Antithesis Between Fiscal and Clinical Systems in Geriatric Care." In Edward J. Hinman, ed., *Advanced Medical Systems: The Third Century*, pp. 93–101. Miami: Medical Books, 1977.

Lawton, M. Powell. "Social and Structual Aspects of Prosthetic Environment for Older People." Paper presented at the Third Annual Institute On Man's Adjustment to a Complex Environment, V. A. Hospital, Brocksville, Ohio, 1963.

Lee, R.I., and L.W. Jones. *The Fundamentals of Good Medical Care*. Chicago: University of Chicago Press, 1933.

Lenzer, Anthony, and Avedis Donabedian. "Needed ... Research in Home Care." *Nursing Outlook* 10, no. 10 (October 1967): 42–45.

Lerner, Monroe. "When, Why and Where People Die." In Orville G. Brim; Howard E. Freeman; Sol Levine; and Norman A. Scotch, eds.; *The Dying Patient*, pp. 5–29. New York: Russell Sage Foundation, 1970.

Levey, Samuel, and Bernard A. Stotsky. *Nursing Homes in Massachusetts*. Boston: Massachusetts Health Research Institute, Inc., March 1968. (Mimeo.)

Levey, Samuel, and S.M. Lubow. "Survey of Nursing Home Licensing Agencies." *Nursing Homes* (May 1968): 27–30.

Levinson Gerontological Policy Institute. "Alternatives to Nursing Home Care: A Proposal." Special Committee on Aging, United States Senate. Washington, D.C.: Government Printing Office, October 1971.

Liberman, M.A. "Relationship of Mortality Rates to Entrance to a Home for the Aged." *Geriatrics* 16 (October 1961): 515–19.

Liebman, Lance. "The Definition of Disability in Social Security and Supplemental Security Income: Drawing the Bounds of Social Welfare Estates." *Harvard Law Review* 89, no. 5 (March 1976): 833–67.

Linden v. King, Civil Action no. 79–862–T (D. Mass., 2 May 1979).

Linn, Margaret W.; Lee Gurel; and Bernard S. Linn. "Patient Outcome as a Measure of Quality of Nursing Home Care." *American Journal of Public Health* 67, no. 4 (April 1977): pp. 337–44.

Lister, John. "Training for What?—Winter of Discontent." *New England Journal of Medicine* 300, no. 12 (22 March 1979): 656–58.

Lombardi, Senator Tarkey. Senate Bill 6739, New York State Senate, 1977.

McCaffree, Kenneth M.; Sharon Winn; and Carl A. Bennett. "Final Report of Cost Data Reporting System for Nursing Home Care." Seattle: Battelle Human Affairs Research Centers, 1 October 1976.

Maddox, George L. "Community and Home Care: United States and United Kingdom." In A.N. Exton-Smith and J. Grimley Evans, eds., *Care of the Elderly: Meeting the Challenge of Dependency*, pp. 147–60. New York: Grune and Stratton, 1977.

_____. "Families as Context and Resource in Chronic Illness." In Sylvia Sherwood, ed., *Long-term Care: A Handbook for Researchers, Planners, and Providers*, pp. 317–48. Holliswood, N.Y.: Spectrum, 1975.

Mahoney, Florence I., and Dorothea W. Barthel. "Functional Evaluation: The Barthel Index." *Maryland State Medical Journal* 14, no. 2 (February 1965): 61–65.

Massachusetts Department of Public Health. *Health Data Annual 1974*. Boston: Mass. Department of Public Health, 30 October 1974.

_____. *Health Data Annual 1976*. Boston: Mass. Department of Public Health, 12 May 1977.

McAuliffe, William E. "Measuring the Quality of Medical Care: Process Versus Outcome." *Milbank Memorial Fund Quarterly, Health and Society* 57, no. 1 (Winter 1979): 118–52.

McKinlay, John B., and Sonja M. "The Questionable Contribution of Medical Measures to the Decline of Mortality in the United States in the Twentieth Century." *Milbank Memorial Fund Quarterly, Health and Society* 55, no. 3 (Summer 1977): 405–28.

Master, Robert J.; Marie Feltin; John Jainchill; Roger Mark; William N. Kavesh; Mitchell T. Rabkin; Barbara Turner; Sarah Bachrach; and Sara Lennox. "A Continuum of Care for the Inner City: An Assessment of Its Benefits for Boston's Elderly and High-risk Populations." *New England Journal of Medicine* 302, no. 26 (26 June 1980): 1434–40.

Mechanic, David. "Approaches to Controlling the Costs of Medical Care: Short-range and Long-range Alternatives." *New England Journal of Medicine* 298, no. 5, (2 February 1978): 249–54.

_____. "The Growth of Medical Technology and Bureaucracy: Implications for Medical Care." *Milbank Memorial Fund Quarterly, Health and Society* 55, no. 1 (Winter 1977): 61–78.

Mendelson, Mary Adelaide. *Tender Loving Greed*. New York: Knopf, 1974.

Mitchell, Janet B. "Patient Outcomes in Alternative Long-term Care Settings." *Medical Care* 16, no. 6 (June 1978): 439–52.

Moroney, Robert. *The Family and the State: Considerations for Social Policy.* London: Longman, 1976.

Moroney, Robert M., and Norman R. Kurtz. "The Evolution of Long-term Care Institutions. In Sylvia Sherwood, ed., *Long-term Care: A Handbook for Researchers, Planners, and Providers*, pp. 81–124. Holliswood, New York: Spectrum, 1975.

Morris, Robert. "Family Responsibility: Implications of Recent Demographic and Service Trends for a Natural Helping System." Working Paper. Waltham, Mass.: Levinson Policy Institute, Brandeis University, November 1977.

Moss, Frank E., and Val J. Halamandaris. *Too Old, Too Sick, Too Bad.* Germantown, Md.: Aspen, 1977.

Mueller, Candace, and Eileen Wolff. "Home Based Services." Title XX CASP Plans, Technical Note No. 10. Washington, D.C.: Office of Assistant Secretary for Planning and Evaluation, DHEW, February 20, 1976.

Myers, Robert J. *Medicare.* Homewood, Illinois: Irwin, 1970.

Nagi, Saad. "Congruency in Medical and Self-Assessment of Disability." *Industrial Medicine* 38, no. 3 (March 1969): 27–36.

National Center for Health Statistics. "Acute Conditions: Incidence and Associated Disability, United States, July 1975–June 1976." *Vital and Health Statistics*, ser. 10, no. 120. Washington, D.C.: Government Printing Office, January 1978.

National Center for Health Statistics. Advance Data from Vital and Health Statistics, no. 29. 17 May 1978.

_____ . "Characteristics, Social Contacts, and Activities of Nursing Home Residents, United States 1973–1974." National Nursing Home Survey, *Vital and Health Statistics*, ser. 13, no. 27 (May 1977). Washington, D.C.: Government Printing Office.

_____ . "Health Characteristics of Persons with Chronic Activity Limitation, United States, 1974." *Vital and Health Statistics*, ser. 10, no. 112. Washington, D.C.: Government Printing Office, October 1976.

_____ . "Home Care for Persons Fifty-Five and Over." United States, July 1966–June 1968. *Vital and Health Statistics*, ser. 10, no. 73. Washington, D.C.: Government Printing Office, 1972.

_____ . "Limitation of Activity and Mobility Due to Chronic Conditions, United States–1972." *Vital and Health Statistics*, ser. 10, no. 96. Washington, D.C.: Government Printing Office, November 1974.

_____ . "Marital Status and Living Arrangements Before Admissions to Nursing and Personal Care Homes, United States, May–June 1964." *Vital and Health Statistics*, ser. 12, no. 12. Washington, D.C.: Government Printing Office, May 1969.

_____ . "Some Trends and Comparisons of United States Life-Table Data: 1900–1971." *U.S. Decennial Life Tables for 1969–71*, vol. 1, no. 4. Washington, D.C.: Government Printing Office, May 1973.

National Center for Social Statistics. "Medicaid Statistics, December 1976." NCSS Report B-1. Washington, D.C.: NCSS, April 1977.

National Conference on Social Welfare. "The Future of Long Term Care in the United States." The Report of the Task Force. Washington, D.C.: National Conference on Social Welfare, February 1977.

Neugarten, Bernice. "Commentary." In A. N. Exton–Smith and J. Grimley, eds., *Care of the Elderly: Meeting the Challenges of Dependency*, pp. 102–04. New York: Grune and Stratton, 1977.

Neuhauser, Duncan. "The Really Effective Health Delivery System." *Health Care Management Review* 1, no. 1 (Winter 1976): 25–32.

Newfield, Jack. "The Last Unspeakable Nursing Home." *Village Voice*, 18 September 1978.

New York State Moreland Act Commission. *Political Influence and Political Accounting: One Foot in the Door.* New York: Moreland Act Commission, February 1976.

_____. *Regulating Nursing Home Care: The Paper Tigers.* New York: Moreland Act Commission, October 1975.

_____. *Reimbursing Operating Costs*, report 5. New York: Moreland Act Commission, March 1976.

_____. *Assessment and Placement: Anything Goes*, report 6. New York: Moreland Act Commission, March 1976.

Nielsen, Margaret. "Home Aide Service and the Aged: A Controlled Study," pt. 1. Cleveland: Benjamin Rose Institute, August 1970.

Nielsen, Margaret; Margaret Blenkner; Martin Bloom; Thomas Downs; and Helen Beggs. "Older Persons After Hospitalization: A Controlled Study of Home Health and Services." *American Journal of Public Health* 62, no. 8 (August 1972): 1094–1101.

Partridge, Anthony, and William B. Eldridge. "The Second Circuit Sentencing Study: A Report to the Judges of the Second Circuit." New York: Federal Judiciary Center, August 1974.

Perrin, Ellen C., and Helen C. Goodman. "Telephone Management of Acute Pediatric Illnesses." *New England Journal of Medicine* 298, no. 3 (19 January 1978): 130–35.

Pfeiffer, Eric, ed. *Multidimensional Functional Assessment: The OARS Methodology.* Durham, N.C.: Duke University Center for the Study of Aging and Human Development, 1975.

Pike, Representative Otis. United States House of Representatives Bill 4869, 94th Congress.

Plant, Janet. "Various Approaches Proposed to Assess Quality in Long-term Care." *Hospitals* 51, no. 17 (1 September 1977): 93–98.

Pollak, William. "Utilization of Alternative Care Settings by the Elderly: Normative Estimates and Current Patterns." Working Paper 963–12. Washington, D.C.: Urban Institute, 13 March 1973.

Powell, M. Lawton. "The Functional Assessment of Elderly People." *Journal of the American Geriatric Society* 19, no. 6 (December 1971): 465–81.

The President's Commission on Mental Retardation. *The Mentally Retarded Citizen and the Law.* New York: The Free Press, 1976.

Quality of Life Committee. *Draft Report.* Washington, D.C.: Veterans Administration, 15 July 1977.

Raab, Selwyn. "Investigation of Private Home Care Programs Urged," *New York Times*, 13 December 1977.

Roberts, Pearl R. "Human Warehouses: A Boarding Home Study." *American Journal of Public Health* 64, no. 3 (March 1974): 277–82.

Robinson, Nancy; Eugene Shinn; Esther Adams; and Florence Moore. "Cost of Homemaker-Home Health Aide and Alternative Forms of Service: A Survey of the Literature." New York: National Council for Homemaker-Home Health Aide Services, Inc., 1974.

Rosen, George. "The Hospital: Historical Sociology of a Community Institution." In Eliot Freidson, ed., *The Hospital in Modern Society*, pp. 1–36. New York: Free Press, 1963.

Rosenfeld, Alan S., and Milton F. Bornstein. "Quality of Life and Care in Long Term Care Institutions: An Empirical Study." Worcester, Mass.: Commission on Elder Affairs, 1978.

Rosser, Rachel M. "The Reliability and Application of Clinical Judgment in Evaluating the Use of Hospital Beds." *Medical Care* 14, no. 1 (January 1976): 39–48.

Rothman, David. *The Discovery of the Asylum*. Boston: Little, Brown, 1971.

Rozeboom, William W. *Foundations of the Theory of Prediction*. Homewood, Ill.: Dorsey, 1966.

Sager, Alan; Sylvia Pendleton; Celia Lees-Low; Deborah Dennis; and Victor Hoffman. *Living at Home: The Role of Public and Informal Supports in Sustaining Disabled Older Americans*. Waltham, Mass.: Levinson Policy Institute, Brandeis University, March 1982.

Schulz, Richard, and Barbara Hartman Hanusa. "Long-Term Effects of Control and Predictability Enhancing Interventions: Findings and Ethical Issues." Pittsburgh: Carnegie-Mellon University Department of Psychology, 1977.

Schuman, John E., and Harold N. Willard. "Role of the Acute Hospital Team in Planning Discharge of the Chronically Ill." *Geriatrics* 31, no. 2 (February 1976): 63–67.

Seidl, Fredrick W.; Kevin Mahoney; and Carol D. Austin. "Providing and Evaluating Home Care: Issues of Targetting." Paper presented at the Gerontological Society's 31st Scientific Meeting, Dallas, 20 November 1978.

Select Committee on Aging, U.S. House of Representatives. "Elderly Crime Victims: Personal Accounts of Fears and Attacks." Hearing, Los Angeles, 18 September 1976. Washington, D.C.: Government Printing Office, 1976.

_____. "New York Home Care Abuse." Hearing, New York, 6 February 1978. Washington, D.C.: Government Printing Office, 1978.

Shanas, Ethel. "The Family as a Social Support System in Old Age." Paper presented at the 30th Annual Meeting of the Gerontological Society, San Francisco, November 1977.

Shapiro, Alan R. "The Evaluation of Clinical Prediction." *New England Journal of Medicine* 296, no. 26 (30 June 1977): 1509–14.

Sheldon v. Tucker, 364 U.S. 479, 488 (1960).

Shenkin, Budd N. "Stalking the Irrational." Review Essay, *Journal of Health Politics, Policy, and Law* 1, no. 3 (Fall 1976): 355–71.

Siegel, Barry, and Judith Lasker. "Deinstitutionalizing Elderly Patients: A Program of Resocialization." *The Gerontologist* 18, no. 3 (June 1978): 293–300.

Siegel, Sidney. *Nonparametric Statistics for the Behavioral Sciences*. New York: McGraw-Hill, 1956.

Slater, Philip. *The Pursuit of Loneliness*. Boston: Beacon, 1970.

Smyer, Michael E. "Differential Usage and Differential Effects of Services for Impaired Elderly." *Advances in Research* (Duke University Center for the Study of Aging and Human Development) 1, no. 4 (Winter 1977).

Sneed, Eleanor. Administration on Aging. Washington, D.C. Personal communication.

Social Security Administration. *Compendium of National Health Expenditures.* Washington, D.C.: Government Printing Office, 1973.

State Communities Aid Association. "Report of the Arden House Institute on Continuity of Long Term Care." New York: State Communities Aid Association, 1978.

Somers, Anne R., and Florence M. Moore. "Homemaker Services – Essential Option for the Elderly." *Public Health Reports* 91, no. 4 (July–August 1976): 354–59.

Special Committee on Aging. U.S. Senate, *Developments in Aging: 1977*, pt. 1, Report no. 95–771. Washington, D.C.: Government Printing Office, 1978.

Stein, Maurice R. *The Eclipse of Community.* Princeton, N.J.: Princeton University Press, 1960.

Speir, H.B. "Characteristics of Nursing Homes and Related Facilities: Report of a 1961 Nationwide Inventory." U.S. Public Health Service Pub. no. 930–F–S. Washington, D.C.: Government Printing Office, 1963.

Subcommittee on Federal Spending Practices, Efficiency, and Open Government, U.S. Senate Committee on Government Operations. "Problems Associated with Home Health Agencies and Medicare Program in Florida." Washington, D.C.: Government Printing Office, August 1976.

Subcommittee on Health and Long-Term Care, Select Committee on Aging. "New Prespectives in Health Care for Older Americans." Washington, D.C.: Government Printing Office, January 1976.

Subcommittee on Long-Term Home Care, U.S. Senate Special Committee on Aging. "The Continuing Chronicle of Nursing Home Fires." Washington, D.C.: Government Printing Office, 1975.

Sussman, Marvin B. "Family Life of Old People." In Robert Binstock and Ethel Shanas, eds., pp. 218–43. *Handbook of Aging and the Social Sciences.* New York: Van Nostrand, 1975.

Townsend, Claire. *Old Age: The Last Segregation.* New York: Grossman, 1971.

Trager, Brahna. "Home Health Services in the United States: A Report to the Special Committee on Aging." Washington, D.C.: Government Printing Office, April 1972.

_____. "In Place of Policy: Public Adventures in Long-term Care." Paper presented at the American Public Health Association's Annual Meeting, Los Angeles, November 1981.

Treas, Judith. "Family Support Systems for the Aged: Some Social and Demographic Considerations." *The Gerontologist* 17, no. 6 (December 1977): 486–91.

"25 Years for Health." Cleveland: Cleveland Press, 16 May 1941.

U.S. Administration on Aging, Office of Human Development Services. *Statistical Notes from the National Clearinghouse on Aging*, no. 2. August 1978.

U.S. Bureau of the Census. "Demographic Aspects of Aging and the Older Population in the United States." *Current Population Reports.* Special Studies P-23, no. 59. Washington, D.C.: Government Printing Office, January 1978.

_____. *Historical Statistics of the United States, Colonial Times to 1970*, pt. 1. Washington, D.C.: Government Printing Office, September 1975.

_____. "Households and Families by Type: March 1977 (Advance Report)." *Current Population Reports*, ser. P-20, no. 313. Washington, D.C.: Government Printing Office, September 1977.

_____. *"Persons by Family Characteristics."* Subject Reports, Final Report PC (2)-4B, U.S. Census of Population: 1960. Washington, D.C.: Government Printing Office, 1964.

_____. "Projections of the Population of the United States: 1977 to 2050." *Current Population Reports*, ser. P-25, no. 704. Washington, D.C.: Government Printing Office, July 1977.

_____. "1976 Survey of Institutionalized Persons: A Study of Persons Receiving Long-term Care." *Current Population Reports*, ser. P-23, no. 69. Washington, D.C.: Government Printing Office, June 1978.

U.S. Congress. "Proprietary Home Health Care." Joint Hearing before Subcommittee on Long-term Care of U.S. Senate Special Committee on Aging and Subcommittee on Health and Long-term Care of Select Committee on Aging of U.S. House of Representatives (28 October 1975). Washington, D.C.: Government Printing Office, 1976.

Vladeck, Bruce C. "Some Issues in the Economics and Financing of Long-term Care." Paper prepared for the Institute on Continuity of Long-term Care, Arden House, New York, December 18-20, 1977.

_____. *Unloving Care.* New York: Basic, 1980.

Walker, Francis A. *Statistical Atlas of the United States Based on the Results of the Ninth Census 1870 with Contributions from Many Eminent Men of Science and Several Departments of the Government.* Julius Bien, Lith. 1874.

Wan, Thomas T.H.; William G. Weissert; and Barbara B. Livieratos. "Determinants of Outcomes of Care in Two Geriatric Service Modalities: An Experimental Study." Paper presented at the 31st Annual Scientific Meeting of the Germtological Society, Dallas, 16-20 November 1978.

Weber, Max. "Bureaucracy and Political Leadership." In *Economy and Society: An Outline of Interpretive Sociology*, app. 2. Guenther Roth and Claus Wittich, eds., New York: Bedminster Press, 1968.

Weiler, Phillip; Eugene Shinn; Steven B. Clauser; Joyce Tufts and Hadley Hall; Rick T. Zawadski; Anne Klapfish; and J. Alan Baker. "Comments on the Weissert Report." *Home Health Care Services Quarterly* 1, no. 3 (Fall 1980): 97-121.

Weissert, William; Thomas Wan; and Barbara Livieratos. "Effects and Costs of Day Care and Homemaker Services for the Chronically Ill: A Randomized Experiment." DHEW Pub. no. PHS-79-3250. Hyattsville, Maryland: National Center for Health Services Research, August 1979.

Wenkert, Walter; John G. Hill; and Robert L. Berg. "Concepts and Methodology in Planning Patient Care Services." *Medical Care* 7, no. 4 (July–August 1969): 327-31.

Wershow, Harold J. "The Four Percent Fallacy: Some Further Evidence and Policy Implications." *The Gerontologist* 16, no. 1, pt. 1 (1976): 52–55.

Wilensky, Harold L., and Charles N. Lebeaux. *Industrial Society and Social Welfare.* New York: Free Press, 1965.

Willemain, Thomas R. "Beyond the GAO Cleveland Study: Client Selection for Home Care Services." *Home Health Care Services Quarterly* 1, no. 3 (Fall 1980): 65–83.

Williams, T. Franklin; John G. Hill; Matthew E. Fairbank; and Kenneth G. Knox. "Appropriate Placement of the Chronically Ill and Aged." *Journal of the American Medical Association* 226, no. 11 (10 December 1973): 1332–35.

Witte, Edwin. *The Development of the Social Security Act.* Madison: University of Wisconsin Press, 1963.

Wolff, Eileen; Barbara E. Bird; and Patricia L. Sullivan. *Technical Notes: Summaries and Characteristics of States' Title XX Social Services Plans for Fiscal Year 1977.* Washington, D.C.: DHEW, Office of the Secretary, 1977.

INDEX

ABOUT THE AUTHOR

Alan Sager has served as research director of the Levinson Policy Institute at Brandeis University's Heller School since 1976. Since 1979, he has also been assistant professor of Urban and Health Planning at the Heller School. Dr. Sager holds a Ph.D. from the Department of Urban Studies and Planning at M.I.T. He sits on the boards of the Health Planning Council for Greater Boston, the Massachusetts Health Data Consortium, and the Massachusetts Easter Seals Society. His other research and policy interests include the problem of assuring equal access to acute health care services. He is currently writing a book entitled *The Closure of Hospitals That Serve the Poor.*